EXERCISES IN FREEDOM

1968—1981

Polnische Konzeptkunst

Polish Conceptualism

Herausgeber | Editor

Staatliche Kunstsammlungen Dresden

Kupferstich-Kabinett

Björn Egging

KERBER ART

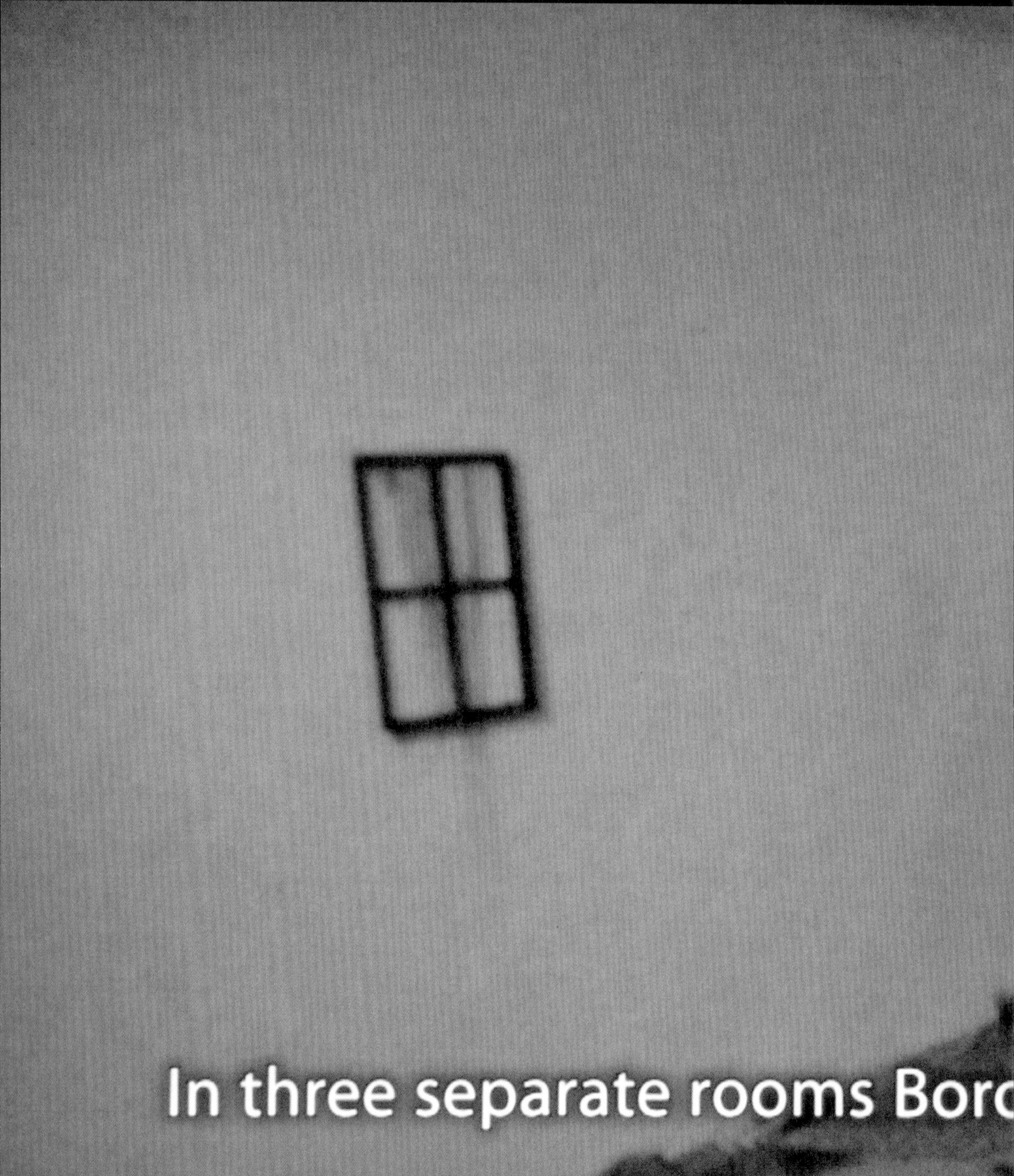

Agnieszka Polska, *Sensitization to Colour*, 2009, Film HD, 5:02 min.
Courtesy ŻAK | BRANICKA, Berlin

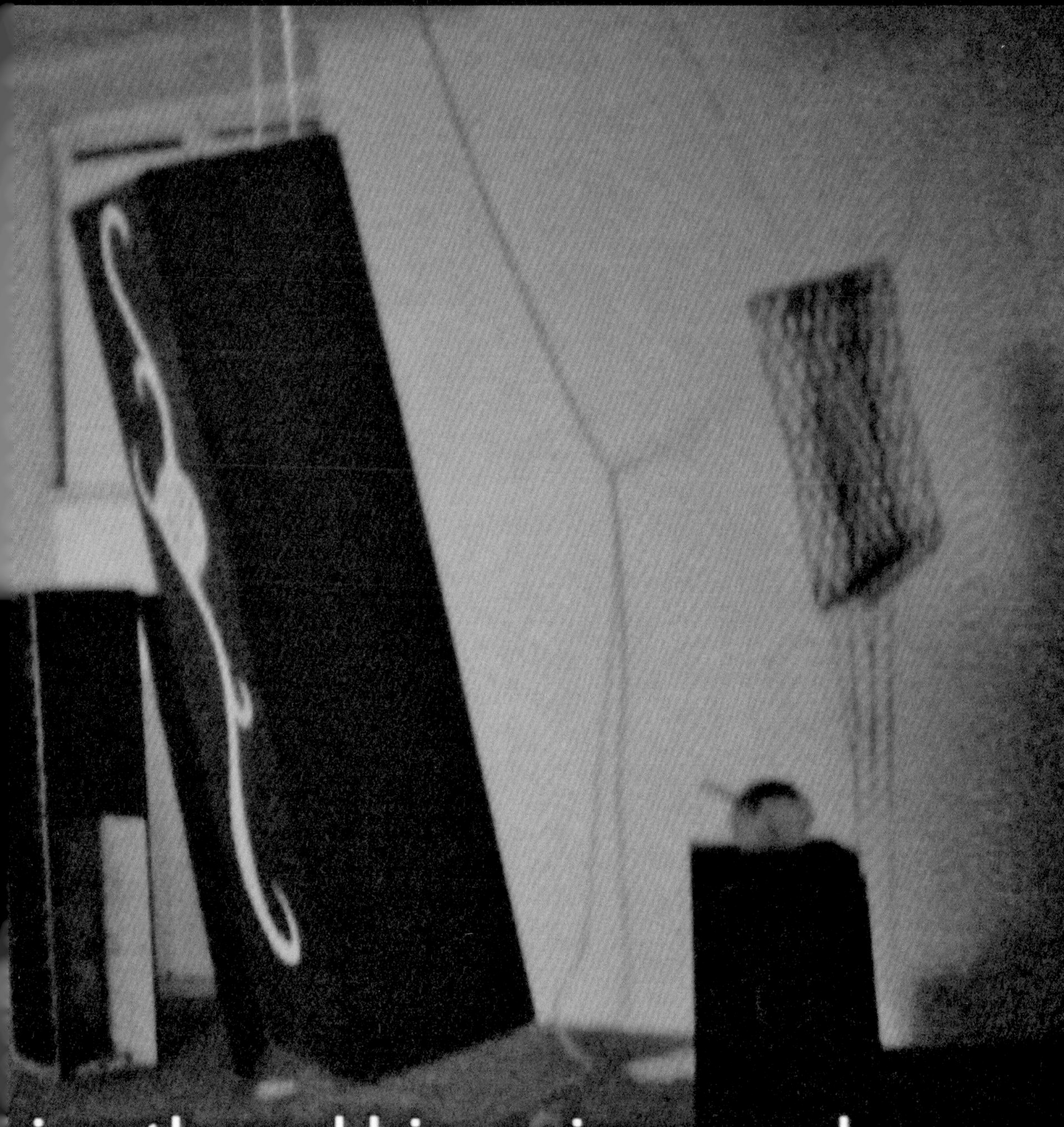
ki gathered his various works:

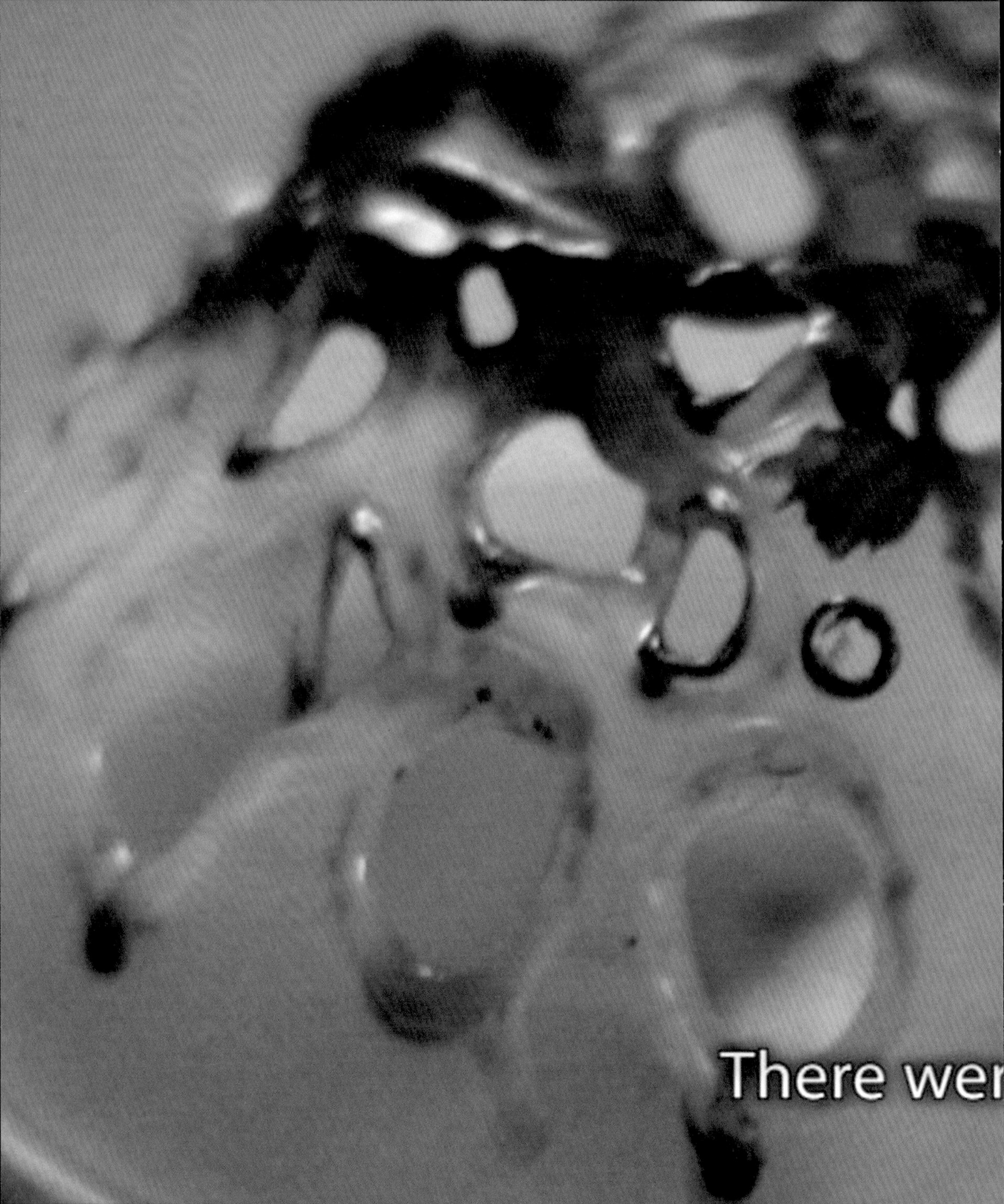

Agnieszka Polska, *Sensitization to Colour*, 2009, Film HD, 5:02 min.
Courtesy ŻAK | BRANICKA, Berlin

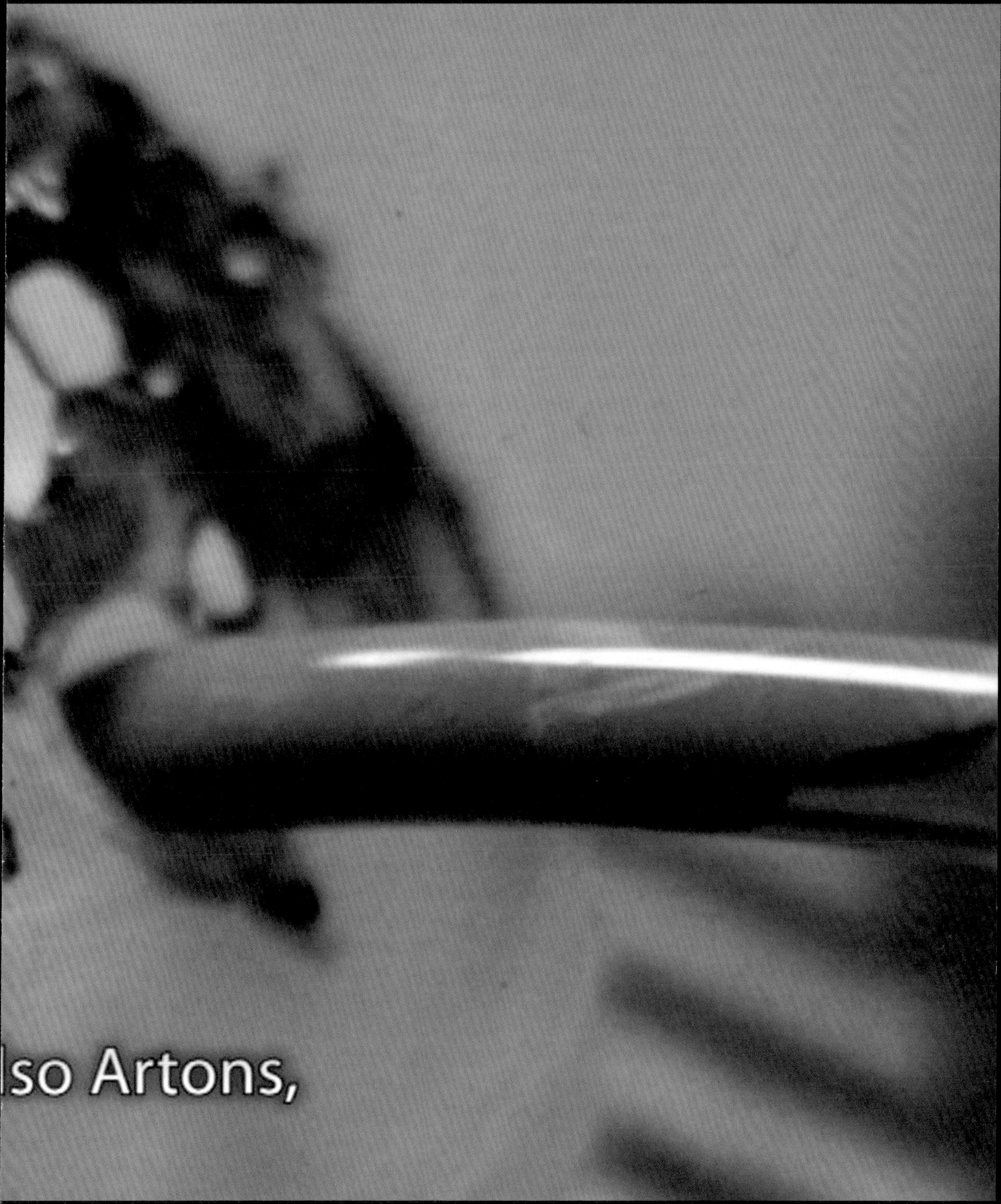

lso Artons,

PREFACE

It seems particularly important today to understand and celebrate art as a contribution to the attainment and exercise of freedom.

Diversity and openness characterized Polish art of the 1960s and 1970s, the free unfolding of which was barely hindered by the state, in contrast to most of Poland's socialist neighbors. In debate with its own modernist tradition and in contact with artistic movements in the West, an individual and well-connected conceptual art scene developed on an international level, although it still remains nearly unknown today in Germany.

Exercises in Freedom introduces the stages and protagonists of this scene, with a focus on the period from the end of the 1960s until 1981, when martial law was declared in order to break up the democracy movement that emerged from the trade unions' Solidarność. The spectrum of conceptual works stretches from positions that critiqued institutions and society to works that analyzed words and images.

This anniversary year, 50 years after the landmark year of 1968, which also yielded social protests in Poland, and 100 years after the founding of the Second Polish Republic, offers us a special opportunity to make a contribution to the self-chosen task of the Staatlichen Kunstsammlungen Dresden—namely, to take a look at Eastern European artistic movements and artists. Through its proximity to Poland, Dresden seems predestined for this undertaking. At the Kupferstich-Kabinett, we can make a connection to Werner Schmidt's exhibition from 1980 about contemporary Polish art. And in the context of conceptual art, we can point to Timm Rautert's series of works, *Bildanalytische Photographie 1968–74*, an exhibition that was presented in 2016. Another objective of the exhibition was to make use of the nearly inexhaustible Archiv der Avantgarden (AdA), which the collector Egidio Marzona generously donated to the SKD. The involvement of the AdA goes beyond complementing the materials with historical documents, letters, manifestos, and photographs. The principle of the network, which was so central for the Polish art scene, and likewise primarily determined the archive, has been associatively incorporated by Ruldolf Fischer and Marcelo Rezende into its own exhibition section.

Without the unstinting support of numerous institutions, private collections, artists and colleagues, *Exercises in Freedom* could not have been realized. A heatfelt thanks goes to all of the lenders, especially the Muzeum Sztuki in Łódź and its director Jarosław Suchan. Among the most important

VORWORT

Gerade heute ist es wichtig, den Beitrag der Kunst bei der Erlangung und Ausübung von Freiheit zu begreifen und zu feiern.

Die polnische Kunst der 1960er- und 1970er-Jahre prägt eine Vielfalt und Offenheit der Positionen, deren freie Entfaltung im Unterschied zu den meisten sozialistischen Nachbarländern kaum vom Staat behindert wurde. In Auseinandersetzung mit der eigenen modernistischen Tradition und im Kontakt mit künstlerischen Strömungen im Westen entwickelte sich in Polen eine eigenständige und gut vernetzte Szene konzeptueller Kunst auf internationalem Niveau, die in Deutschland bis heute aber nahezu unbekannt geblieben ist.

Unsere Ausstellung *Exercises in Freedom* stellt deshalb Etappen und Protagonist*innen dieser Kunstrichtung vor. Der Fokus liegt auf der Zeit vom Ende der 1960er-Jahre bis 1981, als das Kriegsrecht mit dem Ziel ausgerufen wurde, die Demokratiebewegung um die Gewerkschaft Solidarność zu zerschlagen. Das Spektrum der Arbeiten reicht von institutions- und gesellschaftskritischen Positionen bis hin zu bild- und sprachanalytischen.

50 Jahre nach dem Epochenjahr 1968, als es auch in Polen zu gesellschaftlichen Protesten kam, und 100 Jahre nach der Gründung der Zweiten Polnischen Republik bietet uns das Jubiläumsjahr eine besondere Gelegenheit, einen Beitrag zur selbstgestellten Aufgabe der Staatlichen Kunstsammlungen Dresden zu leisten, künstlerische Positionen aus Osteuropa in den Blick zu nehmen. Durch die Nähe zu Polen ist Dresden dazu prädestiniert; im Kupferstich-Kabinett können wir auf Werner Schmidts Ausstellung *Polnische Kunst aus drei Jahrzehnten* von 1980 anknüpfen. Im Hinblick auf konzeptuelle Kunst verweisen wir auf die Ausstellung zu Timm Rauterts Werkreihe *Bildanalytische Photographie 1968–74*, die wir 2016 präsentierten. Ein weiteres Anliegen ist die Nutzbarmachung des geradezu unerschöpflichen Archivs der Avantgarden (AdA), das der Kunstsammler Egidio Marzona den SKD großzügig überlassen hat. Die Einbeziehung des AdA geht über die Ergänzung des Materials mit historischen Dokumenten, Briefen, Manifesten und Fotografien hinaus; das für die polnische Kunstszene so zentrale Prinzip der Vernetzung, das auch das Archiv wesentlich bestimmt, ist von Rudolf Fischer und Marcelo Rezende in einem eigenen Ausstellungskapitel assoziativ weiterentwickelt worden.

Ohne die freigiebige Unterstützung zahlreicher Institutionen, Privatsammlungen, Künstler*innen und Kolleg*innen hätten die *Exercises in Freedom* nicht realisiert werden können. Im Namen des

loans is Roman Opałkas's first picture of his radical number progression, created in 1965. The artists Jarosław Kozłowski, Ewa Partum, and Ryszard Waśko have generously enriched the exhibition with their own works. On the occasion of this project Jarosław Kozłowski even realised the annual edition for the Friends of the Staatliche Kunstsammlungen Dresden, MUSEIS SAXONICIS USUI, this year. My thanks also go to Agnieszka Polska, current recipient of the Berlin Nationalgalerie's prize, who kindly contributed an important video work. I thank Paweł Polit for his enlightening essay. We are especially obliged to Monika Branicka, Asia Zak Persons and Egidio Marzona, who contributed decisively to the realization of the project. Finally, I would like to offer heartfelt thanks to the whole team at the Kupferstich-Kabinett and all the involved colleagues at the SKD for their unfailing engagement, especially the guiding spirit of the exhibition Björn Egging, and the equally level-headed and energetic assistant curator Katrin Kruppa.

Stephanie Buck
Director Kupferstich-Kabinett

Kupferstich-Kabinetts bedanke ich mich herzlich bei allen öffentlichen und privaten Leihgebern. Ein besonderer Dank gebührt dem Muzeum Sztuki in Łódź und seinem Direktor Jarosław Suchan. Unter den zentralen Leihgaben ist Roman Opałkas erstes, 1965 entstandenes Bild seiner radikalen Zahlenprogression. Die Künstler*innen Jarosław Kozłowski, Ewa Partum und Ryszard Waśko haben die Ausstellung großzügig mit eigenen Werken bereichert. Jarosław Kozłowski hat anlässlich des Projektes sogar die diesjährige Jahresgabe für MUSEIS SAXONICIS USUI – die Freunde der Staatlichen Kunstsammlungen Dresden e. V. geschaffen. Mein Dank gilt auch Agnieszka Polska, aktuelle Trägerin des Preises der Nationalgalerie in Berlin, die eine bedeutende Videoarbeit beigesteuert hat, sowie dem Kollegen Paweł Polit aus Łódź für seinen erhellenden Essay. Besonders verpflichtet sind wir Monika Branicka, Asia Zak Persons und Egidio Marzona, die maßgeblich zur Realisierung des Projekts beigetragen haben. Abschließend danke ich herzlichst dem gesamten Team des Kupferstich-Kabinetts und allen beteiligten Kolleg*innen der SKD für ihr unermüdliches Engagement, allen voran dem Spiritus Rector der Ausstellung, Björn Egging, und der ebenso besonnenen wie tatkräftigen Assistenzkuratorin Katrin Kruppa.

Stephanie Buck
Direktorin Kupferstich-Kabinett

EXERCISES IN FREEDOM. ON AUTONOMY IN POLISH CONCEPTUAL ART

Björn Egging

The central origin myth of Polish conceptual art was founded on March 6, 1968 with the so-called *VIII. Syncretic Show* in the OdNOWA Gallery in Poznań. At this event, Włodzimierz Borowski submitted the definition of art that was currently accepted in Poland to a radical revision.[1] Borowski had long prepared for this step. Since the middle of the 1950s, the artist had been critically engaged with the tendencies that reigned in Poland following the end of socialist realism, especially with the Post-Impressionist Colorism and Informalism. With his citational aesthetic, Borowski's pictures were intended as ironic commentary on state-approved painting (ill. p. 22); his *Artons*, created from the end of the 1950s, are likewise consciously "unartistic" objects, referring to Marcel Duchamp's readymades in their found-object, assembled materiality (ill. 2, p. 38). Borowski sharpened this critique of modernism's autonomy concept even more in an art action in Poznań, where he—with the help of the public—used a drill to maltreat self-portraits hanging in corners until the light from hidden lamps shone out of their drilled eyes. The whole action may have been primarily a critique of mediocre Colorism, which enjoyed a special esteem at the Academy of Fine Arts in Poznań at the time, but in the performance, Borowski made use of artistic means that left most of the viewers at a loss. Through this "blinding" of his portrait, he put the visionary abilities of his own artistry into question to some extent; in fact, the actual artwork was an ephemeral performance and today exists only as prepared texts and documenting photographs, at most. The objects in the space—including crumpled newspapers and strangely painted wooden boxes with threads—seemed kitschy or ironic, and in no way worthy of being exhibited.[2] In this way, Borowski's *VIII Syncretic Show* presents itself on the same level as international conceptual art; artists and objects disappear behind idea and process, and the artwork appropriates extra-artistic contexts.

Unsurprisingly, we can diagnose a similar attitude in many artists who are counted among Poland's conceptual art scene, for instance, Jarosław Kozłowski with his image- and language-analytic works. Here, the artist also recedes behind his artifacts; the character of these artifacts as art is only perceptible upon second look; externally, they are only insignificantly distinguishable from the linguistic permutations and logistical detours of the models of the philosophy of language. His *Exercises in Freedom* (*Ćwiczenia Ze Swobody*, p. 107) are primarily self-referential color fields, which refuse authorship, originality, and pictorial representation. The disappearance

ÜBUNGEN ZUR FREIHEIT. ZUR AUTONOMIE IN DER POLNISCHEN KONZEPTKUNST

Björn Egging

Der zentrale Entstehungsmythos der polnischen Konzeptkunst begründet sich am 6. März 1968 mit der sogenannten *VIII. Synkretistischen Schau* in der Galerie OdNOWA in Poznań. Hier unterzieht Włodzimierz Borowski den damals in Polen gültigen Kunstbegriff einer radikalen Revision.[1] Diesen Schritt hat Borowski lange vorbereitet. Schon seit der Mitte der 1950er-Jahre setzt sich der Künstler kritisch mit den in Polen nach dem Ende des Sozialistischen Realismus vorherrschenden Richtungen auseinander, vor allem mit dem postimpressionistischen Kolorismus und dem Informel. Borowskis Bilder sind in ihrer zitathaften Ästhetik ironische Kommentare zur staatlich anerkannten Malerei (Abb. S. 22), seine seit Ende der 1950er-Jahre entstandenen *Artons* (Abb. 2, S. 38) sind ebenfalls bewusst „unkünstlerische" Objekte und beziehen sich in ihrer aus gefundenen Gegenständen montierten Materialität auf Marcel Duchamps Readymades. Diese Kritik am Autonomiebegriff der Moderne spitzt Borowski in der Kunstaktion in Poznań noch zu, als er unter Mithilfe des Publikums seine in den Raumecken aufgehängten Selbstporträts mit der Bohrmaschine traktiert, bis aus den aufgebohrten Augen das bunte Licht versteckter Lampen kommt. Die gesamte Aktion ist zwar vordergründig eine Kritik am mediokren Kolorismus, der zu dieser Zeit an der Kunsthochschule in Poznań eine besondere Wertschätzung genießt, Borowski bedient sich hierzu allerdings künstlerischer Mittel, die die meisten damaligen Zuschauer ratlos machen. Durch die „Blendung" seines Porträts stellt er gewissermaßen die visionären Fähigkeiten des eigenen Künstlertums infrage, während das eigentliche Kunstwerk aus der ephemeren Performance besteht und allenfalls noch aus vorbereitenden Texten und dokumentierenden Fotografien. Die Objekte im Raum – u. a. zerknüllte Zeitungen und eigentümlich bemalte Holzkisten mit Fäden – wirken kitschig oder ironisch und auf keinen Fall ausstellungswürdig.[2] Damit zeigt sich Borowskis *VIII. Synkretistische Schau* auf der Höhe der internationalen Konzeptkunst: Künstler*innen und Objekte verschwinden zugunsten von Idee und Prozess, und die Kunst eignet sich außerkünstlerische Kontexte an.

Eine vergleichbare Haltung gegenüber ihrer eigenen Rolle und der des Werkes lässt sich ohne Überraschung bei vielen Künstlerinnen und Künstlern, die der konzeptuellen Kunst in Polen zu zurechnen sind, diagnostizieren, etwa bei Jarosław Kozłowski und seinen bild- und sprachanalytischen Arbeiten. Auch hier tritt der Künstler hinter seine Artefakte zurück, deren Kunstcharakter

of artist and work is even more pronounced in the conflation of art and life that is present in the socially critical work of KwieKulik (Zofia Kulik and Przemysław Kwiek), Ewa Partum and Krzysztof Wodiczko, whose performances and photo series operate in the public sphere. For this reason, it is even more remarkable that, as is emphasized in the Polish sources and secondary literature, the Eastern European, meaning, also Polish, neo-avant-garde held onto the Modernist notion of autonomy: "It is important to keep in mind that the overwhelming majority of the central European neo-avant-garde artists, including those who produced Conceptual art, continued to work within the Modernist value system, grounded in the idea of the autonomy of art and its disengagement from Socialist Realism and detachment from politics [...]."[3] From the perspective of Western conceptual art, this adherence to the formative Modernist ideals of the New York art critic Clement Greenberg seems not only outdated but also contradictory, given that a whole generation of artists who came of age around 1960 had already vanquished the genius cult and translated art into a "life practice."[4] At this point, it is important to remind ourselves that the concept of the autonomous artist has to be seen historically, as the result of secularization and emancipation processes of the bourgeois era following the Enlightenment and the French Revolution. The end of traditional patronage relationships with the court and church liberated the artist. However, avant-garde movements at the beginning of the 20th century were already predisposed to anti-bourgeois gestures, sometimes going as far as having explicitly revolutionary, or socially reformatory, programs such as with Russian Constructivism and the Bauhaus. Fundamentally, Socialist Realism was also part of the tradition of this anti-bourgeois reform movement. The dogma of the state art doctrine quickly alienated many Polish artists and made them aware of the need of protecting their freedom. For the Polish avant-garde, then, the claim to independence is primarily based in the fear of state control.

It is true that as a result of the so-called Khrushchev Thaw of 1956, and the associated disappearance of Socialist Realism, artists in Poland had more creative freedom than artists in other Eastern European countries, as long as they did not voice statements overly critical of the system. However, they were still bound to the state in a dependent relationship, which consisted of internships, stipends, contracts, and exhibition opportunities. Additionally, the activities of artists were distrustfully observed by the Polish security service. Only a largely independent, anti-institutional network, free from state reach, could create the necessary free space, since there only a few public institutions, such as the Muzeum Sztuki in Łódź, that were sympathetic to progressive art trends.[5] The fact that the art scene around 1970 was not only concentrated in Warsaw but that other cities like Łódź, Wrocław and Poznań also had important centers in exchange with each other fostered a special feature of the Polish situation: the multitude of largely independently operating galleries. Although the Foksal Gallery in Warsaw, well-known outside of Poland, was financed by the state, it was an open exhibition site for contemporary artistic trends and artists, including those from the West. The already-mentioned OdNOWA Gallery in Poznań, founded in 1964, hosted happenings, performances, and installations. Further influential galleries were created by the art theorist Jerzy Ludwiński's Pod Moną Lisą in Wrocław, Krzysztofory in Krakau and

sich erst auf den zweiten Blick erschließt, da sich die linguistischen Permutationen und logischen Ableitungen von sprachphilosophischen Modellen äußerlich nur unwesentlich unterscheiden. Seine *Exercises in Freedom* (*Ćwiczenia Ze Swobody,* S. 107) sind zunächst selbstreferenzielle Farbfelder, die Autorschaft, Originalität und bildliche Repräsentation verweigern. Noch stärker ausgeprägt ist das Verschwinden von Künstler und Werk in der Zusammenführung von Kunst und Leben, welche sich in den gesellschaftskritischen Arbeiten von KwieKulik, Ewa Partum oder Krzysztof Wodiczko zeigt, die mit ihren Performances und Fotoserien im öffentlichen Raum agieren. Umso bemerkenswerter ist es, wie sehr zugleich in der polnischen Quellen- und Sekundärliteratur betont wird, dass die osteuropäische und damit auch polnische Neo-Avantgarde an der Vorstellung von modernistischer Autonomie festhielt: „It is important to keep in mind that the overwhelming majority of the central European neo-avant-garde artists, including those who produced conceptual art, continued to work within the Modernist value system, grounded in the idea of the autonomy of art and its disengagement from Socialist Realism and detachment from politics [...]."[3] Aus der Perspektive westlicher Konzeptkunst wirkt das Festhalten an den prägenden modernistischen Idealen des New Yorker Kunstkritikers Clement Greenberg unzeitgemäß, sogar widersprüchlich, da schließlich eine ganze Künstlergeneration um 1960 angetreten war, den Geniekult zu überwinden und die Kunst in „Lebenspraxis" zu überführen.[4] An dieser Stelle sei daran erinnert, dass der autonome Künstler historisch betrachtet ein Ergebnis der Säkularisierungs- und Emanzipationsprozesse im bürgerlichen Zeitalter seit der Aufklärung und der Französischen Revolution war. Das Ende der traditionellen Dienstverhältnisse mit Fürstenhof und Kirche hatte den Künstler in die Freiheit entlassen. Aber schon die Strömungen der Avantgarde am Anfang des 20. Jahrhunderts zeichneten sich durch einen antibürgerlichen Gestus aus, bisweilen sogar wie im Fall von russischem Konstruktivismus und Bauhaus durch ein explizit revolutionäres bzw. gesellschaftsreformerisches Programm. Grundsätzlich war auch der Sozialistische Realismus zunächst in der Tradition dieser antibürgerlichen Reformbewegungen angetreten. Das Dogma der staatlichen Kunstdoktrin verprellte rasch viele polnische Künstler*innen und sensibilisierte sie für die Wahrung ihrer Freiheit. Der Anspruch auf Unabhängigkeit begründet sich für die polnische Neo-Avantgarde also primär aus der Furcht vor staatlicher Bevormundung.

Zwar hatten Künstler*innen in Polen in der Folge der sogenannten Tauwetterperiode 1956 und des damit verbundenen Abschieds vom Sozialistischen Realismus mehr gestalterische Freiheiten als in anderen osteuropäischen Staaten, solange sie sich nicht allzu systemkritisch äußerten. Sie waren dennoch eingebunden in ein Abhängigkeitsverhältnis zum Staat, bestehend aus Ausbildungsplätzen, Stipendien, Aufträgen und Ausstellungsmöglichkeiten. Zusätzlich wurden die Aktivitäten der Künstler*innen vom polnischen Sicherheitsdienst argwöhnisch beobachtet. Nur ein vom staatlichen Zugriff weitestgehend unabhängiges anti-institutionelles Netzwerk konnte die notwendigen Freiräume schaffen, denn nur wenige öffentliche Einrichtungen wie das Muzeum Sztuki in Łódź sympathisierten mit der progressiven Kunstströmung.[5] Die Tatsache, dass sich die Kunstszene um 1970 nicht nur auf Warschau konzentrierte, sondern auch in anderen Städten wie Łódź, Wrocław und Poznań wichtige Zentren hatte, die miteinander im Austausch standen,

the EL Gallery in Elbąg. Many artists ran their own galleries (Galerie Autorskie); Ewa Partum had the Adres Gallery in Łódź, Barbara Kozłowska had the Babel Gallery in Wrocław, and Natalia LL, together with Zbigniew Dłubak and Andrzej Lachowicz, ran the PERMAFO Gallery in the same city. In addition to galleries, the network was constituted by pleinairs, conferences, and art festivals. It was at the legendary art symposium *Wrocław '70* that it first became noticeable how widely the conceptual approaches had disseminated in the contemporary Polish art scene. Of the many diverse initiatives of Polish artists to come into contact with the international art scene, one of the most extensive and successful was the *NET* project, started by Kozłowski and the art historian Andrzej Kostołowski, in 1971. More than 350 artists from all over the world were invited to an artistic dialogue. The Akumulatory 2 Gallery in Poznań, which arose out of the project, showed more than 100 exhibitions between 1972 and 1980. Finally, the exhibition *Construction in Process* (*Konstrukcja w procesie*), conceived and realized by Ryszard Waśko in 1981, underlined the desire of Polish artists to get to know foreign perspectives. Opened just weeks before the declaration of martial law in 1981, the exhibition included an invitation to contemporary international art scene to visit Łódź. The network sketched here, along with distributable media like catalogues, unofficial journals, artists' books, and mail art, enabled a largely unhindered exchange between artists, critics, theorists, and the public, which mainly consisted of students. The platforms offered the contemporary actors the freedom to inform themselves, without constraint, about the newest developments and to be able to exhibit these new trends without restrictions on content and administrative hurdles.

Progressive artists in the East, like those in the West, were concerned with having artistic freedom of thought and the largest scope of action possible. In socialism, the state ideology was the adversary of this freedom; in capitalism, ca. 1968, it was the so-called establishment, which consisted of the art market, collectors, and "the culture industry." Whereas in the West, artists either politicized using agitation, attempted to leverage the commodity character of art, or continued to place their trust in the authority of the autonomous artwork (which alone had the potential of what Theodor W. Adorno has formulated as "it should be different"[6]), Polish Conceptual artists referred to the autonomy concept of classical Modernism. It was a protected realm, which enabled self-determination and incorruptibility for the work and the producer and guaranteed the status of the artist through his self-merit—although at the price of social involvement. In other Eastern European countries, an artist's decision to exist outside of the socialist collective was often considered to be "asocial behavior" and meant complete isolation, but in Poland, the state granted artists a certain openness within their network as long as they followed the rules.[7] Jarosław Kozłowski continues to use this strategy of free thought and political restraint even today: "What always mattered to me is the autonomy of art; it allows me to speak critically about various aspects of politics, not necessarily connected to any ideology that I more or less sympathize with."[8] The artist who too clearly proclaimed the social aspects of her art made herself suspect, which is why many critical artists imbedded their conceptual statements in a subjective system of reference, through which the works refer back to themselves. Kozłowski's *Imagination Zone* (ill. 1, p. 16) could be read as the

begünstigte ein besonderes Merkmal der polnischen Situation: die Vielzahl von nahezu frei agierenden Galerien. Obwohl die über Polen hinaus berühmte Galerie Foksal in Warschau staatlich finanziert wurde, war sie ein offener Ausstellungsort für aktuelle Positionen, auch für die aus dem Westen. Die bereits erwähnte Galerie OdNOWA in Poznań, 1964 gegründet, zeigte Happenings, Performances und Installationen. Weitere einflussreiche Galerien waren außerdem Pod Moną Lisą des Kunsttheoretikers Jerzy Ludwiński in Wrocław, Krzysztofory in Krakau und die Galerie EL in Elbląg. Viele Künstler*innen betrieben Autorengalerien (Galerie Autorskie): Ewa Partum die Galerie Adres in Łódź, Barbara Kozłowska die Galerie Babel in Wrocław und ebenfalls dort Natalia LL gemeinsam mit Zbigniew Dłubak und Andrzej Lachowicz die Galerie PERMAFO. Zum künstlerischen Netzwerk gehörten neben den Galerien Pleinairs, Tagungen und Kunstfestivals. Auf dem legendären Kunstsymposion Wrocław '70 wurde die starke Verbreitung konzeptueller Ansätze in der polnischen Gegenwartskunst erstmals sichtbar. Von den vielfältigen Initiativen polnischer Künstler*innen, mit der internationalen Kunstszene in Verbindung zu treten, war das 1971 gemeinsam von Kozłowski und dem Kunsthistoriker Andrzej Kostołowski gestartete Projekt NET eines der umfänglichsten und erfolgreichsten. Mehr als 350 Künstler*innen in aller Welt wurden zum künstlerischen Dialog eingeladen. Die daraus hervorgegangene Galerie Akumulatory 2 in Poznań zeigte von 1972 bis 1980 mehr als 100 Ausstellungen. Schließlich unterstrich die wenige Wochen vor Ausrufung des Kriegsrechts im Herbst 1981 von Ryszard Waśko konzipierte und realisierte Ausstellung *Construction in Process* (*Konstrukcja w procesie*) mit der Einladung der aktuellen internationalen Kunstszene nach Łódź das Bedürfnis, ausländische Positionen kennenzulernen. Das hier skizzenhaft dargestellte Netzwerk, zu dem auch distributive Medien wie Kataloge, inoffizielle Zeitschriften, Künstlerbücher und Mail-Art zählten, ermöglichte den weitgehend ungehinderten Austausch zwischen Künstler*innen, Kritiker*innen, Theoretiker*innen und dem Publikum, das sich in erster Linie aus Studierenden rekrutierte. Die Plattformen boten den damaligen Akteuren die Freiheit, sich unbehelligt über die neuesten Entwicklungen zu informieren und diese ohne inhaltliche Vorgaben und administrative Hürden ausstellen zu können.

Den progressiven Künstler*innen im Osten wie im Westen ging es um künstlerische Gedankenfreiheit und möglichst große Handlungsspielräume. Im Sozialismus war die staatliche Ideologie der Gegner dieser Freiheit, im Kapitalismus war es um 1968 das sogenannte Establishment, bestehend aus Kunsthandel, Sammlern und „Kulturindustrie". Während man im Westen entweder mit agitatorischen Mitteln offen politisierte, mit künstlerischen Konzepten den Warencharakter der Kunst auszuhebeln versuchte oder stattdessen nach wie vor der Autorität des autonomen Kunstwerks vertraute (das allein das Potenzial des „Es soll anders sein" habe, wie es Theodor W. Adorno formuliert hatte[6]), beriefen sich die polnischen Konzeptkünstler*innen, um frei arbeiten zu können, auf den Autonomiebegriff der Klassischen Moderne. Er war der Schutzraum, der Werk und Produzent Selbstbestimmung und Unbestechlichkeit ermöglichte und den Status des Künstlers in seiner Selbstbegründetheit garantierte, allerdings zum Preis des Verzichts auf gesellschaftliches Mittun. Während in anderen osteuropäischen Ländern die Entscheidung eines Künstlers für

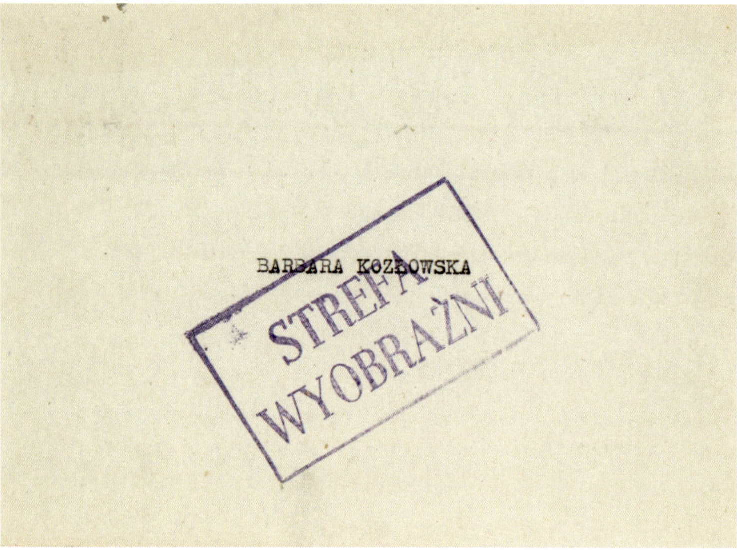

Abb. | ill. 1 Jarosław Kozłowski
Aus der Serie | from the series
Correspondences V, 1971
Schreibmaschine, Stempel auf Postkarte | typescript, stamp on postcard, 11,4 × 15,7 cm
Staatliche Kunstsammlungen Dresden, Archiv der Avantgarden – Egidio Marzona

private poetry of a dreamer; in their experimental artistic arrangements, Ewa Partum, Krzysztof Wodiczko and Józef Robakowski seemed to exclusively plumb their own dispositions and consciously forwent provocative political gestures, a strategy that resulted in works that were otherwise free of daily agitation and thereby made them stronger: "The only way to make political art was to exclude politics."[9] In reality, the public understood the critical dimension of the art, of course, since the retreat into autonomy was a "weapon of the anti-authoritarian resistance"[10] in itself and served as an "exercise in freedom" from ideological immunization.

Even the *VIII Syncretic Show* by Włodzimierz Borowski was interpreted politically, as the protest of the artist against the political crisis of Poland's Communist rulers, which found its most brutal expression in the agitation against the Jewish population 1967/68.[11] Indeed, audible screams and marching music played during the performance, permitting such a reading of the whole setting and especially the auto-aggressive behavior of the artist. More decisive in this context, however, is that Borowski found an artistic free space within a protective network of like-minded people, where he could develop and realize his ideas. His position of artistic autonomy contributed to the fact that *VIII Syncretic Show*, in all of its intended complexity, has remained mysterious to this day. It has become a legend of Polish conceptual art, which Agnieszka Polska congenially tried to explain in her video from 2009, *Sensitization to Colour* (ill. pp. 2–5, 124–125) but in her attempt, she only manages to underline the complexity of this great artwork.

eine Existenz außerhalb des sozialistischen Kollektivs häufig als „asoziales Verhalten" galt und die komplette Isolation bedeutete, gewährte der Staat den polnischen Künstler*innen unter Einhaltung der „Spielregeln" innerhalb ihres Netzwerkes eine gewisse Öffentlichkeit.[7] Diese Strategie aus gedanklicher Freiheit und politischer Zurückhaltung verfolgt Jarosław Kozłowski bis heute: „What always mattered to me is the autonomy of art; it allows me to speak critically about various aspects of politics, not necessarily connected to any ideology that I more or less sympathize with."[8] Wer den gesellschaftlichen Aspekt seiner Kunst zu deutlich proklamierte, machte sich verdächtig, weshalb viele kritische Künstler*innen ihren konzeptuellen Ansatz in ein subjektives Bezugssystem einbetteten, durch das die Arbeiten auf sie selbst zurückverwiesen. Kozłowskis *Imaginationszone* (Abb. 1, S. 16) war im Zweifelsfall die private Poesie eines Träumers, Ewa Partum, Krzysztof Wodiczko oder auch Józef Robakowski loteten in ihren künstlerischen Versuchsanordnungen scheinbar ausschließlich ihre eigene Verfasstheit aus und verzichteten bewusst auf den provokanten Gestus des Politischen, was die Arbeiten im Übrigen frei von tagesaktueller Agitation macht und dadurch qualitativ stärkt: „The only way to make political art was to exclude politics."[9] In Wirklichkeit verstand das Publikum natürlich die kritische Dimension der Kunst, denn allein schon der Rückzug in die Autonomie war eine „Waffe des antiautoritären Widerstands"[10] und diente als „Übung zur Freiheit" der ideologischen Immunisierung.

Auch die *VIII. Synkretistische Schau* von Włodzimierz Borowski wurde politisch interpretiert, als Protest des Künstlers gegen die politische Krise der kommunistischen Machthaber in Polen, die in der Hetze gegen die jüdische Bevölkerung 1967/68 ihren brutalsten Ausdruck fand.[11] Sicherlich lassen die während der Performance zu hörenden Schreie und die Marschmusik, das gesamte Setting und insbesondere das autoaggressive Verhalten des Künstlers eine solche Lesart zu. Entscheidender in diesem Kontext ist allerdings, dass Borowski nicht zuletzt im schützenden Netzwerk Gleichgesinnter den künstlerischen Freiraum vorfand, seine Ideen zu entwickeln und zu realisieren. Sein Standpunkt der künstlerischen Autonomie trug dazu bei, dass die *VIII. Synkretistische Schau* in ihrer beabsichtigten Komplexität bis heute rätselhaft geblieben ist und zur Legende der polnischen Konzeptkunst wurde, die Agnieszka Polska in ihrem Video *Sensitization to Colour* von 2009 (Abb. S. 2–5, 124–125) auf kongeniale Weise freizulegen versucht, womit sie doch nur die Vielschichtigkeit eines großen Kunstwerks unterstreicht.

Notes:

1 See Piotr Piotrowski, "Künstler und Geschichte: Über die Grenzen der polnischen Gegenwartskunst," in *Der Riss im Raum. Positionen der Kunst seit 1945 in Deutschland, Polen, der Slowakei und Tschechien*, exh. cat. Martin-Gropius-Bau, Berlin/Zacheta Narodowa Galeria Sztuki, Warschau / Galerie hlavního města Prahy, Prague 1994/95, ed. Matthias Flügge with Jiri Svestka (Leipzig 1994), 58–64.

2 Luiza Nader, "The Meaning of Autonomy. Conceptual Art in 1960s and 1970s in Poland," in *The Procedures in 1970s Art (Procedery sztuki lat 70)*, exh. cat. Profile Foundation, ed. Bożena Czubak (Warsaw 2016), 125–139, here 129f.

3 Piotr Piotrowski, *In the Shadow of Yalta. Art and the Avant-garde in Eastern Europe, 1945–1989* (London 2009): 322. See further: Łukasz Ronduda, *Polish Art of the 70s* (Warsaw 2009), 8–15; Nader 2016.

4 Peter Bürger, *Theorie der Avantgarde* (Frankfurt a. M. 1974), 63ff.

5 See Martin Patrick, "Contexts for Experimental Art: Notes on Polish 'Author's' Galleries and Open-Air Festivals 1960s–1980s," in *Centropa. A Journal of Central European Architecture and Related Arts*, Vol. 3, Nr. 2 (New York 2003), 141–156.

6 Theodor W. Adorno, "Engagement," in Charles Harrison and Paul Wood (eds.), *Kunsttheorie im 20. Jahrhundert* (Ostfildern-Ruit 2003), 937–940, here 940.

7 Nader 2016, 136.

8 Jarosław Kozłowski, cited in: "'Even today you need permission for using your imagination.' Jarosław Kozłowski in conversation with Bożena Czubak," in Bożena Czubak (ed.), *Jarosław Kozłowski. Neither East nor West, neither North nor South* (Warsaw 2017), 10–25, here 10.

9 Józef Robakowski cited in: Fabio Cavallucci, "Political Arts Excuses Politics," in *Józef Robakowski, Nearer-Farther*, exh. cat. Base Milano (Milan 2017), 5.

10 Piotrowski 1994, 63.

11 Nader 2016, 130.

Anmerkungen:

1 Vgl. dazu Piotr Piotrowski, „Künstler und Geschichte: Über die Grenzen der polnischen Gegenwartskunst", in: *Der Riss im Raum. Positionen der Kunst seit 1945 in Deutschland, Polen, der Slowakei und Tschechien*, Ausst.-Kat. Martin-Gropius-Bau, Berlin/Zacheta Narodowa Galeria Sztuki, Warschau / Galerie hlavního města Prahy, Prag 1994/95, hrsg. von Matthias Flügge in Zusammenarbeit mit Jiri Svestka, Leipzig 1994, S. 58–64.

2 Luiza Nader, „The meaning of Autonomy. Conceptual Art in 1960s and 1970s in Poland", in: *The Procedures in 1970s Art (Procedery sztuki lat 70.)*, Ausst.-Kat. Profile Foundation, hrsg. von Bożena Czubak, Warschau 2016, S. 125–139, hier S. 129f.

3 Piotr Piotrowski, *In the Shadow of Yalta. Art and the Avant-garde in Eastern Europe, 1945–1989*, London 2009, S. 322. Siehe weiterhin: Łukasz Ronduda, Polish Art of the 70s, Warschau 2009, S. 8–15; Nader 2016.

4 Peter Bürger, *Theorie der Avantgarde*, Frankfurt a. M. 1974, S. 63ff.

5 Siehe Martin Patrick, „Contexts for Experimental Art: Notes on Polish ‚Author's' Galleries and Open-Air Festivals 1960s–1980s", in: *Centropa. A journal of central european architecture and related arts*, Bd. 3, Nr. 2, New York 2003, S. 141–156.

6 Theodor W. Adorno, „Engagement", in: Charles Harrison und Paul Wood (Hrsg.), *Kunsttheorie im 20. Jahrhundert*, Ostfildern-Ruit 2003, S. 937–940, hier S. 940.

7 Nader 2016, S. 136.

8 Jarosław Kozłowski zit. nach: „Even today you need permission for using your imagination". Jarosław Kozłowski in conversation with Bożena Czubak, in: Bożena Czubak (Hg.), *Jarosław Kozłowski. Neither East nor West, neither North nor South*, Warschau 2017, S. 10–25, hier S. 10.

9 Józef Robakowski zit. nach: Fabio Cavallucci, „Political arts excluses politics", in: *Józef Robakowski, Nearer-Farther*, Ausst.-Kat. Base Milano, Mailand 2017, S. 5.

10 Piotrowski 1994, S. 63.

11 Nader 2016, S. 130.

ABSCHIED VON DER MALEREI

FAREWELL TO PAINTING

Włodzimierz Borowski

Roman Opałka

Edward Krasiński

Andrzej Dłużniewski

Jerzy Rosołowicz

Zdzisław Jurkiewicz

Not only in the Western art world were the 1960s a time of radical upheaval. In Poland, too, a younger generation of artists began to question the dominant role of painting. While neo-constructivist and abstract positions had emerged alongside representational tendencies in the years up to 1960, during the thaw after Stalin's death and the renunciation of socialist realism, what still prevailed was the traditional idea of the authoritative status of the aesthetic work produced by the creative hand of the artist. Young artists responded to this model of modernity with the legacy of Marcel Duchamps, who with his ready-mades had initiated a departure from the concepts of authorship, and of the original as well as from figurative representation. As a result, the work of art lost its objecthood and could appear as a performance, process or even as written instructions or the photographic documentation of an idea.

Włodzimierz Borowski commented ironically on contemporary painting even in his early pictures; in his performance pieces he challenged the narrow concept of art at the time with a "syncretic" variety of media. At the same time, Jerzy Rosołowicz advocated for a new beginning in art and proposed "neutral action" as an artistic principle, free from conventions, fashions and ideologies. Edward Krasiński expanded sculpture and painting by using blue tape to reduce scultpure to markings in space and extend pictures into their surroundings. Both the performance art of Andrzej Dłużniewski, in which he painted pictures, cut and sold them according to rigid schema as well as the photoseries of Zdzisław Jurkiewicz on processual image production in bathrooms are critical departures from panel painting. Finally, Roman Opałka gave painting a conceptual dimension. His work *OPAŁKA 1965/1 – ∞*, begun in 1965, with its counting from 1 to infinity, is self-referential, as it represents nothing but the work and lifetime of the artist.

B. E.

Nicht nur in der westlichen Kunstwelt waren die 1960er-Jahre eine Zeit des radikalen Aufbruchs. Auch in Polen machte sich eine jüngere Generation von Künstler*innen daran, die dominante Rolle der Malerei infrage zu stellen. Zwar hatten sich in den Jahren der Tauwetterperiode nach Stalins Tod und der Abkehr vom Sozialistischen Realismus bis 1960 neben gegenständlichen Richtungen auch neo-konstruktivistische und abstrakte Positionen entwickelt, vorherrschend geblieben war jedoch die traditionelle Vorstellung von der Autorität des durch schöpferische Künstlerhand erzeugten ästhetischen Werkes. Diesem Modell der Moderne setzten die Künstler*innen das Erbe Marcel Duchamps entgegen, der mit dem Readymade den Abschied von Autor, Original und bildlicher Darstellung eingeleitet hatte. In der Konsequenz verlor das Kunstwerk seinen Objektcharakter und konnte als Performance, als Prozess oder auch nur als schriftliche Anleitung oder fotografische Dokumentation einer Idee in Erscheinung treten.

Włodzimierz Borowski hatte bereits in seinen frühen Bildern die zeitgenössische Malerei ironisch kommentiert; in seinen Aktionen forderte er den engen Kunstbegriff seiner Zeit mit der „synkretistischen" Vielfalt der Mittel heraus. Zeitgleich setzte sich Jerzy Rosołowicz für einen Neuanfang in der Kunst ein und schlug dafür die „Neutrale Handlung" als künstlerisches Prinzip vor, frei von Konventionen, Moden und Ideologien. Edward Krasiński erweiterte Bildhauerei und Malerei durch die Verwendung eines blauen Klebebandes, mit dem er die Skulptur auf eine Markierung im Raum reduzierte und die Bilder in die Umgebung fortsetzte. Sowohl die Aktion von Andrzej Dłużniewski, in der er Bilder nach festem Schema malte, zerschnitt und verkaufte, als auch die Fotoserie von Zdzisław Jurkiewicz zur prozesshaften Bilderzeugung im Badezimmer sind kritische Abschiede vom Tafelbild. Roman Opałka schließlich gab der Malerei eine konzeptuelle Dimension. Sein 1965 begonnenes Werk *OPAŁKA 1965/1 – ∞* mit der fortlaufenden Zählung von 1 bis unendlich ist selbstreferenziell, da es nichts weiter abbildet als die Arbeits- und Lebenszeit des Künstlers.

B. E.

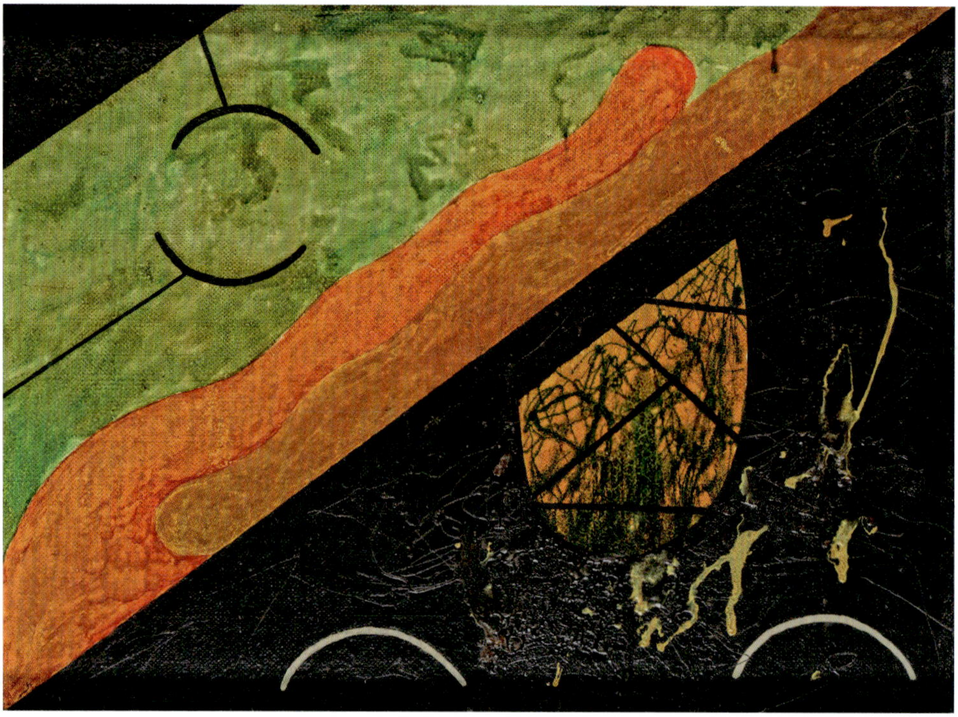

Włodzimierz Borowski

Włodzimierz Borowski
Groteska / Groteske / Grotesque, 1956
Acryl auf Holz | acrylic on wood
72 × 88 cm
Privatsammlung | Private collection, Berlin

Fotografie im Rahmen der *VIII. Synkretistischen Schau* von Włodzimierz Borowski, 1968 |
photograph in context of the *VIII Syncretic Show* by Włodzimierz Borowski 1968
Staatliche Kunstsammlungen Dresden,
Archiv der Avantgarden – Egidio Marzona

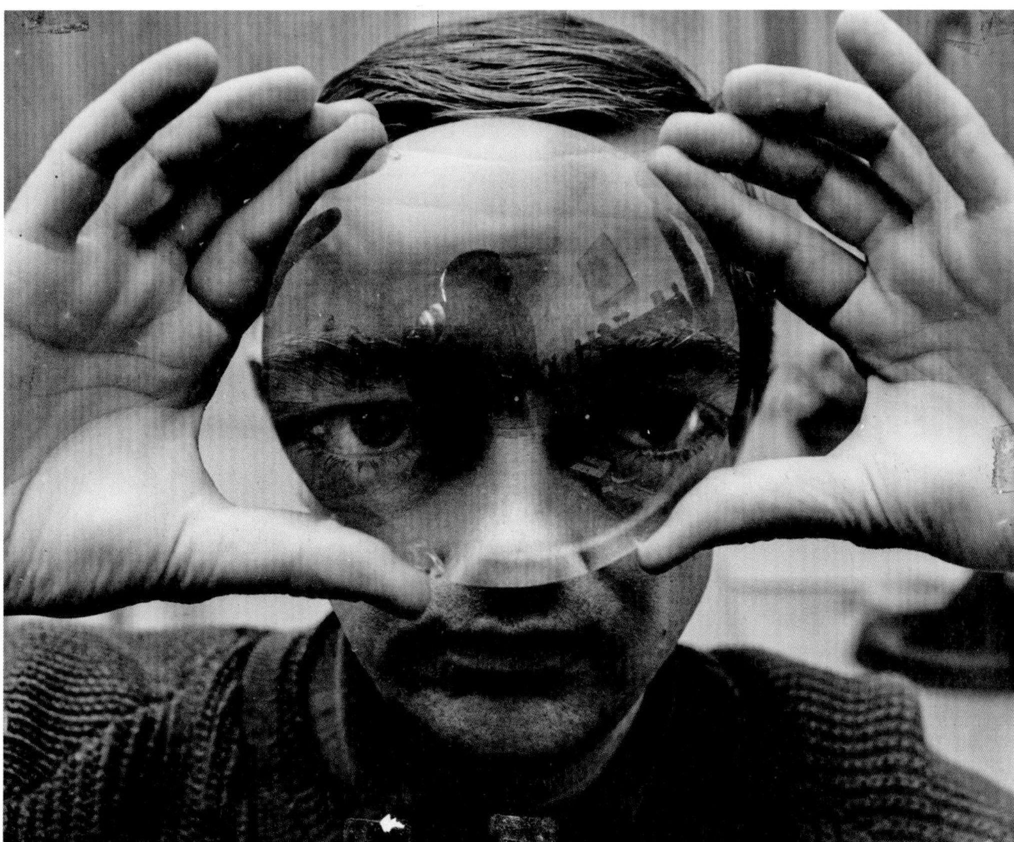

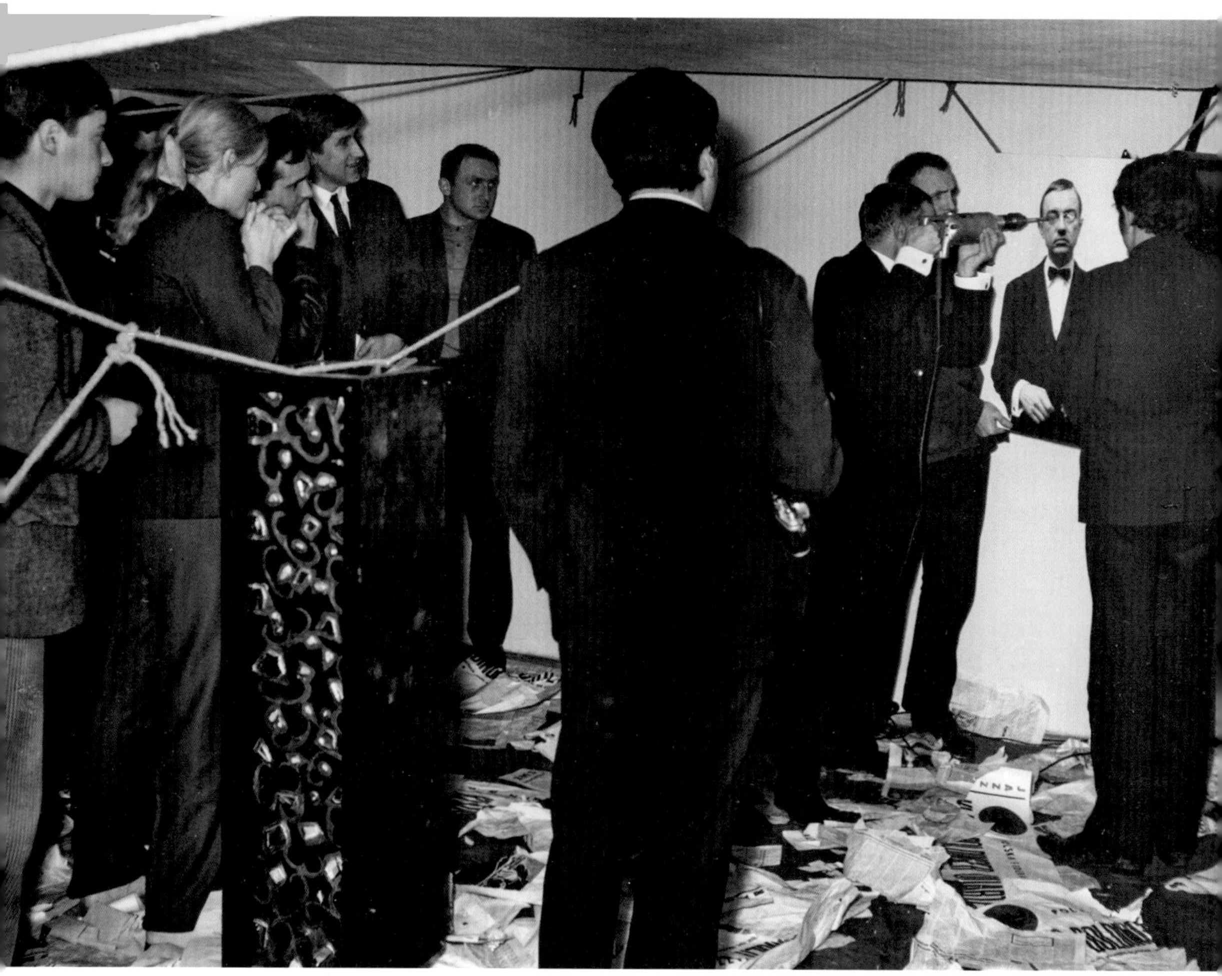

Włodzimierz Borowski

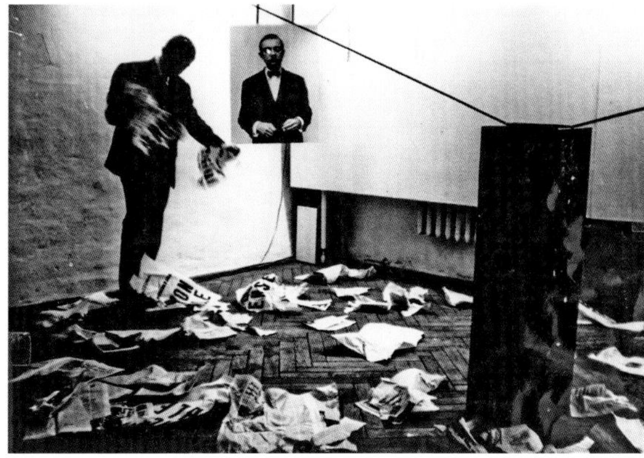

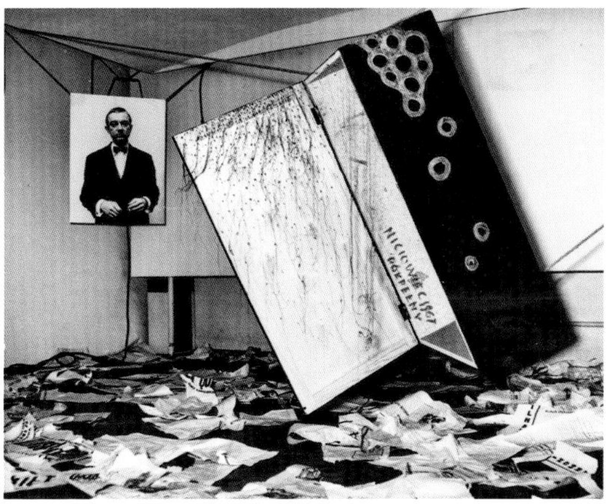

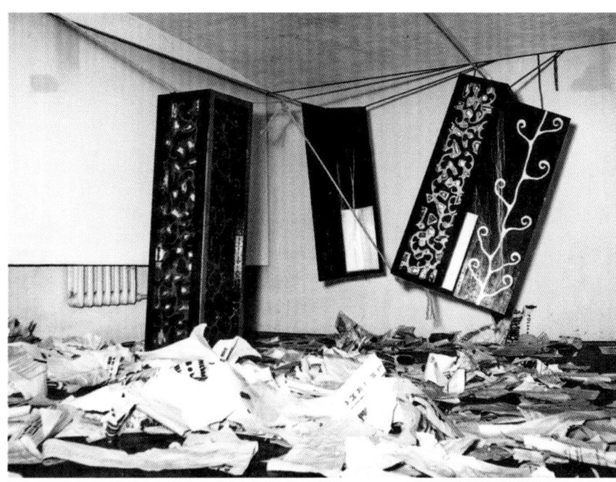

Włodzimierz Borowski
VIII Pokazu Synkretycznego – Uczulanie na kolor |
VIII. Synkretistische Schau – Farbsensibilisierung |
VIII Syncretic Show – Sensitization to Colour
Galeria odNOWA, Poznań, März | March 1968
Fotografien von | photographs by Jerzy Nowakowski
Staatliche Kunstsammlungen Dresden,
Archiv der Avantgarden – Egidio Marzona

Włodzimierz Borowski

Włodzimierz Borowski, Jan Świdziński, Krzysztof Wodiczko
Action in Space, 1972
Fotografien, Text | photographs, text
20 × 100 cm
Staatliche Kunstsammlungen Dresden, Archiv der Avantgarden – Egidio Marzona

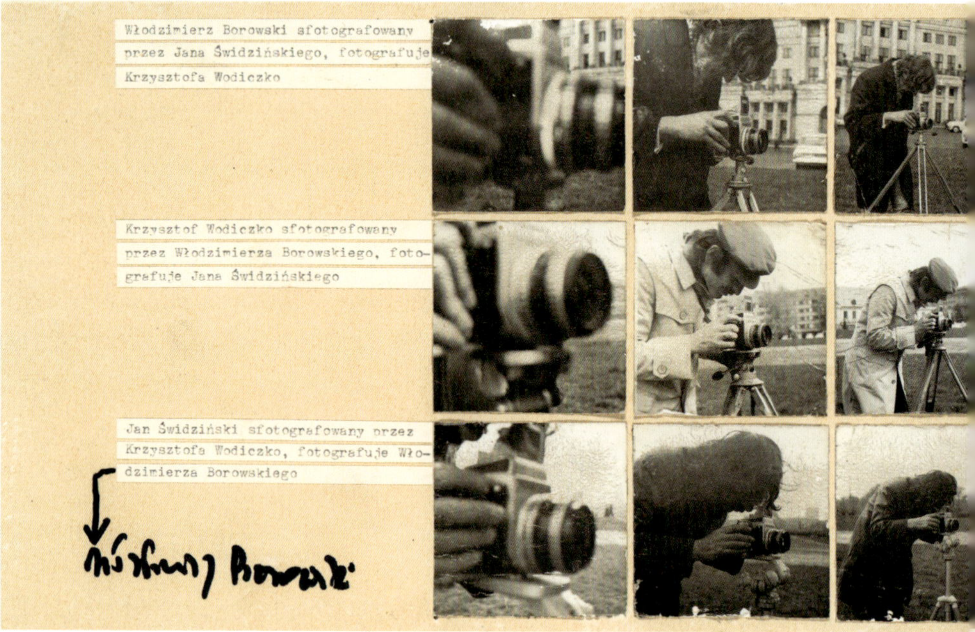

Action in Space, 1972
On 21 April 1972 in Warsaw, Włodzimierz Borowski, Jan Świdziński and Krzysztof Wodiczko, each equipped with a photo camera, stood as close as possible to each other, forming an equilateral triangle. Then all three took pictures: Borowski photographed Wodiczko, Wodiczko photographed Świdziński, and Świdziński photographed Borowski. Then they formed a triangle again, a larger one, superscribed on the previous one, and took pictures of each other again. Then they formed a triangle superscribed on the previous one and photographed each other for the third time. Proceeding in this way, they formed six more triangles, each larger than the one before, continuing to photograph each other. Having positioned themselves for the ninth time, Borowski no longer distinguished Wodizcko's figure in his lens, Wodiczko no longer distinguished Świdziński's, and Świdziński no longer distinguished Borowski's. Due to the increased distance, all three had blended with the surroundings.

Am 21. April 1972 statteten sich Włodzimierz Borowski, Jan Świdziński und Krzysztof Wodiczko in Warschau mit Fotoapparaten aus und stellten sich in möglichst geringer Entfernung voneinander in Form eines gleichseitigen Dreiecks auf. Anschließend haben sie gleichzeitig fotografiert: Włodzimierz Borowski fotografierte Krzysztof Wodiczko, und dieser fotografierte Jan Świdziński, Świdziński hingegen fotografierte Włodzimierz Borowski. Danach bildeten sie wieder ein Dreieck, diesmal ein größeres, das auf dem vorherigen basierte, und fotografierten sich erneut. Dann bildeten sie noch ein Dreieck auf dem vorherigen und fotografierten sich zum dritten Mal. Dieser Vorgehensweise folgend, stellten sie sich noch sechsmal in jeweils größeren Dreiecken auf und fotografierten sich gegenseitig. Als sie sich zum neunten Mal aufstellten, konnte Włodzimierz Borowski auf der Mattscheibe seines Apparates Krzysztof Wodiczkos Gestalt nicht mehr erkennen, Krzysztof Wodiczko sah Jan Świdziński nicht mehr, und Świdziński konnte Włodzimierz Borowski nicht mehr sehen. Durch die zunehmende Entfernung sind alle drei mit der Umgebung eins geworden.

Włodzimierz Borowski wurde von Jan Świdziński fotografiert, während er Krzysztof Wodiczko fotografierte.
Krzysztof Wodiczko wurde von Włodzimierz Borowski fotografiert, während er Jan Świdziński fotografierte.
Jan Świdziński wurde von Krzysztof Wodiczko fotografiert, während er Włodzimierz Borowski fotografierte.

Włodzimierz Borowski photographed by Jan Świdziński, photographing Krzysztof Wodiczko.
Krzysztof Wodiczko photographed by Włodzimierz Borowski, photographing Jan Świdziński.
Jan Świdziński photographed by Krzysztof Wodiczko, photographing Włodzimierz Borowski.

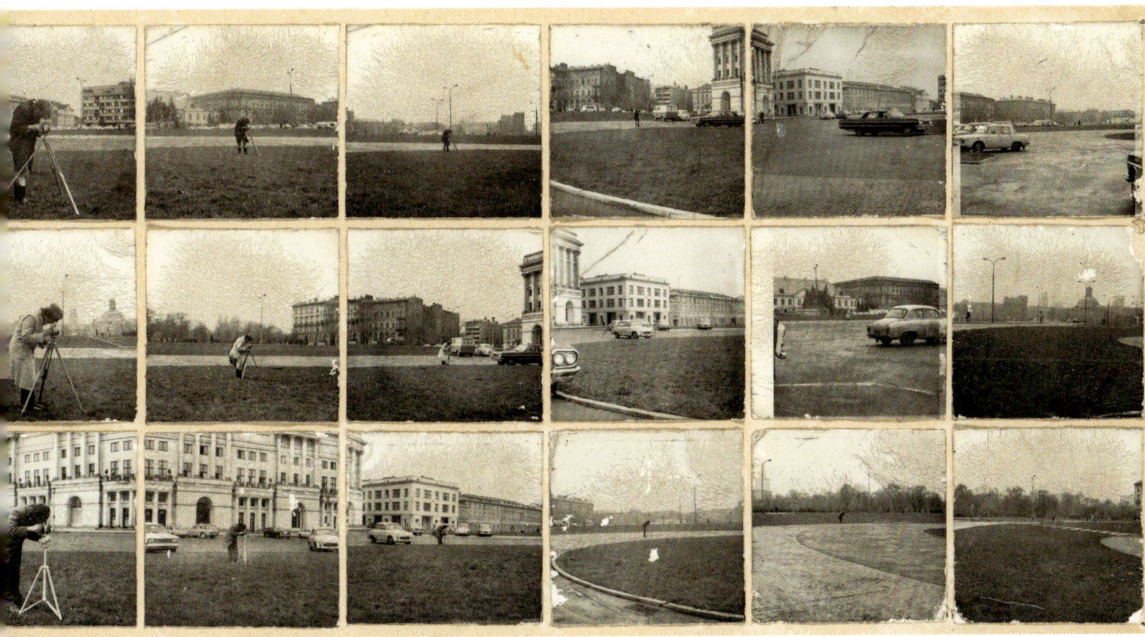

W dniu 21 kwietnia 1972 r. w Warszawie Włodzimierz Borowski, Jan Świdziński i Krzysztof Wodiczko, zaopatrzeni w aparaty fotograficzne, ustawili się w możliwie najmniejszej odległości od siebie i utworzyli trójkąt równoboczny.
Następnie, wszyscy trzej jednocześnie wykonali zdjęcia, Władzimierz Borowski sfotografował Krzysztofa Wodiczkę, ten Jana Świdzińskiego, a ten Włodzimierza Borowskiego. Poczem utworzyli znów trójkąt, większy, opisany na poprzednim i powtórnie się sfotografowali. Następnie ustawili się w trójkąt opisany na poprzednim i po raz trzeci się sfotografowali.
Działając w ten sposób ustawili się jeszcze siedem razy, na coraz to większych trójkątach, fotografując się wzajemnie. Ustawiwszy się po raz dziewiąty Włodzimierz Borowski, na matówce swego aparatu, przestał rozróżniać postać Krzysztofa Wodiczki, Krzysztof Wodiczko postać Jana Świdzińskiego, a Jan Świdziński Włodzimierza Borowskiego.
Na skutek zwiększającej się odległości wszyscy trzej wtopili się w otoczenie.

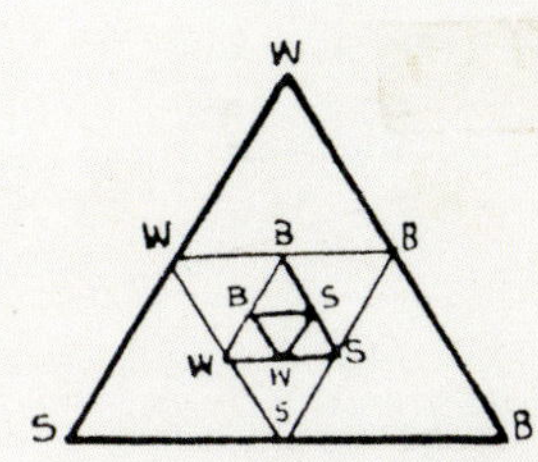

Roman Opałka
Carte de voyage, OPAŁKA 1965/1-∞,
detail 3151760-3154150
Tusche auf Papier | ink on paper
32,9 × 24 cm
Privatsammlung | Private collection, Berlin

Roman Opałka

Roman Opałka
OPAŁKA 1965/1-∞, detail 1-35327
Tempera auf Leinwand | tempera on canvas
195 × 135 cm
Muzeum Sztuki w Łodzi

Edward Krasiński
Interwencja XIII / Intervention XIII, 1977
Acryl, Klebeband auf Faserplatte |
acryl, Scotch Tape on fiberboard
100 × 70 cm
Muzeum Sztuki w Łodzi

Edward Krasiński

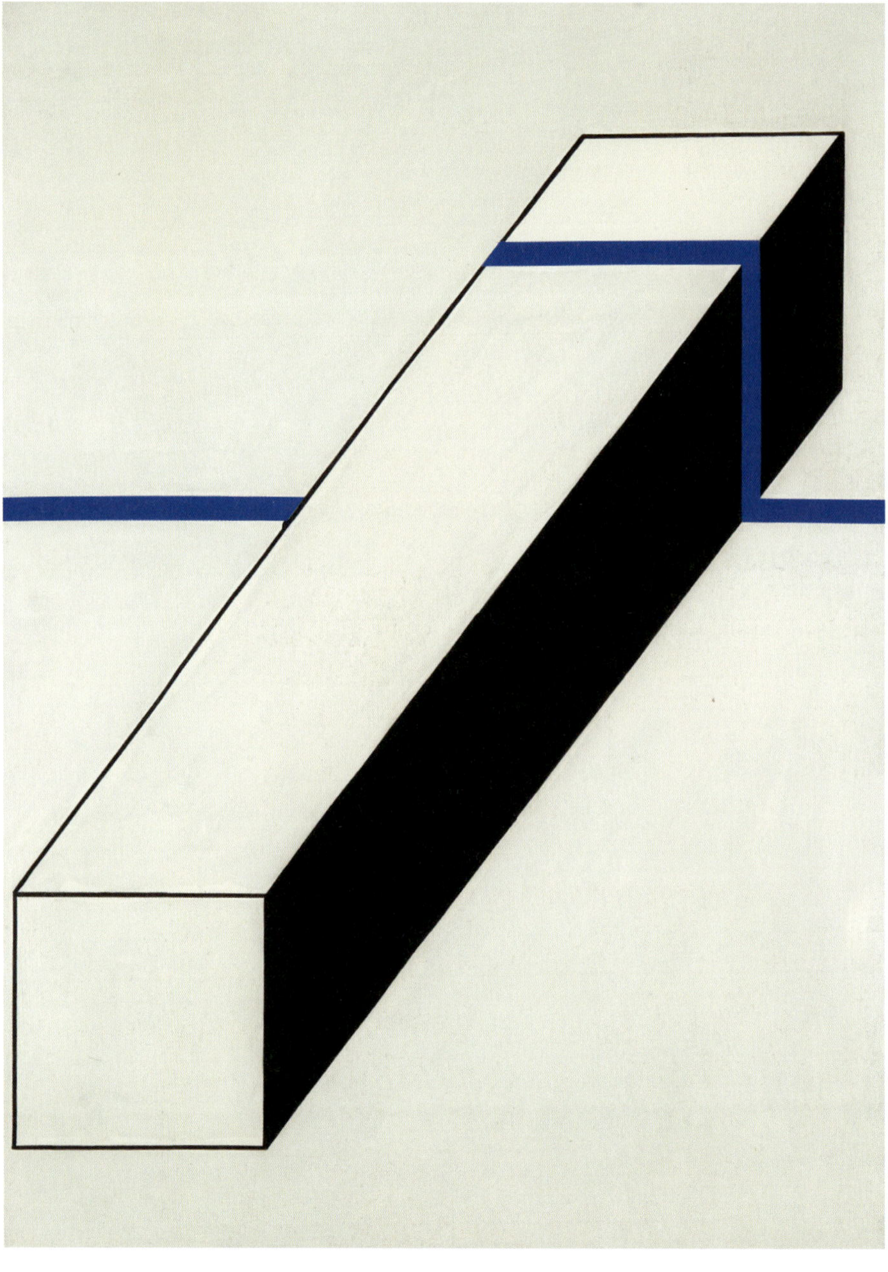

Jerzy Rosołowicz

Jerzy Rosołowicz
Kineutronikon / Cineutronicon, 1975
Fotodokumentation und Objekt |
photo documentation and object
52,5 × 42,5 cm, 25 × 35 × 15 cm
Sammlung | Collection Kozłowski, Poznań

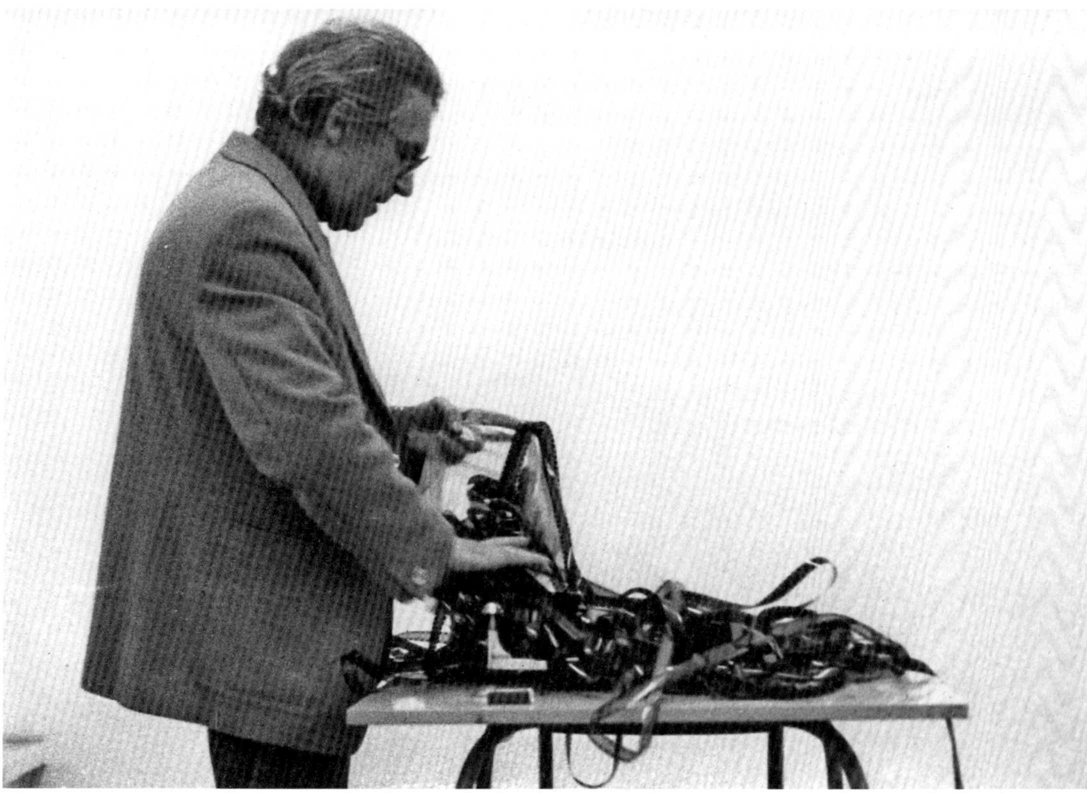

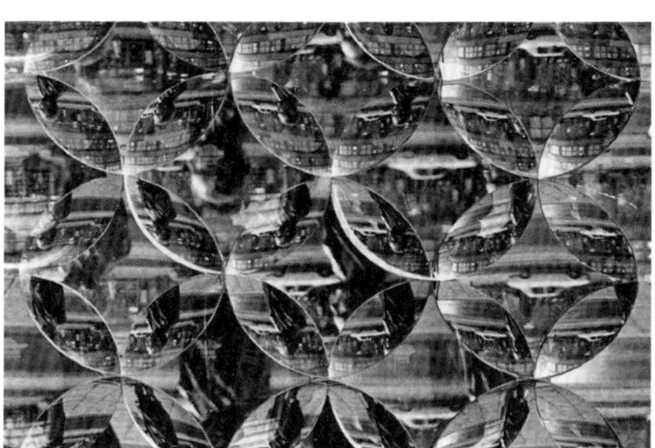

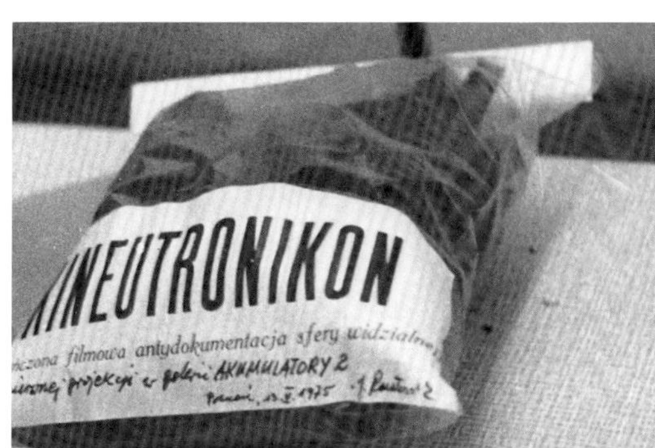

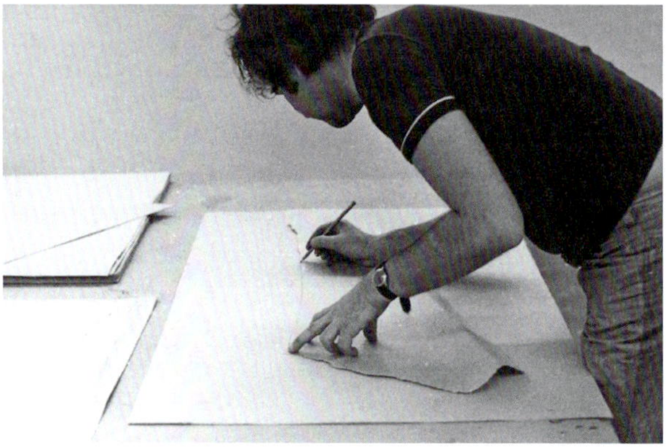

Andrzej Dłużniewski
Proceder | Procedure, 1979
Fotodokumentation, Acryl auf Papier |
photo documentation, acrylic on paper
52,5 × 90 cm; 3 × 43,5 cm
Sammlung | Collection Kozłowski, Poznań

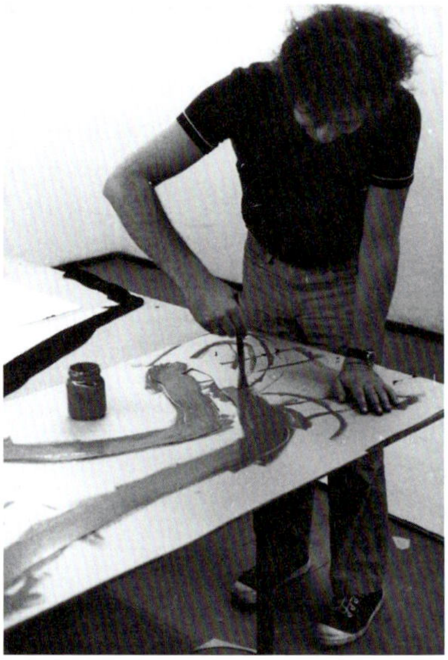

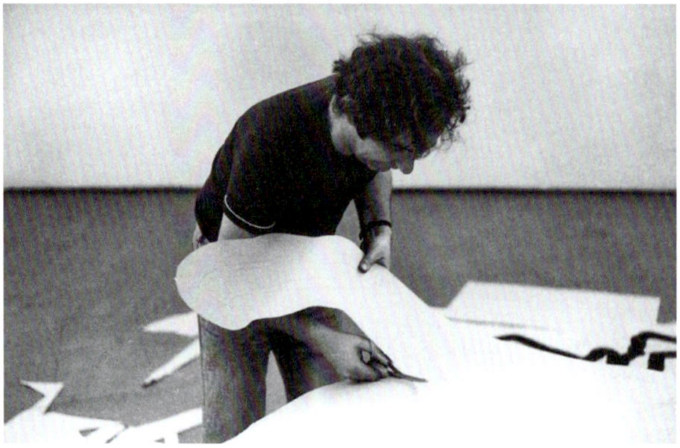

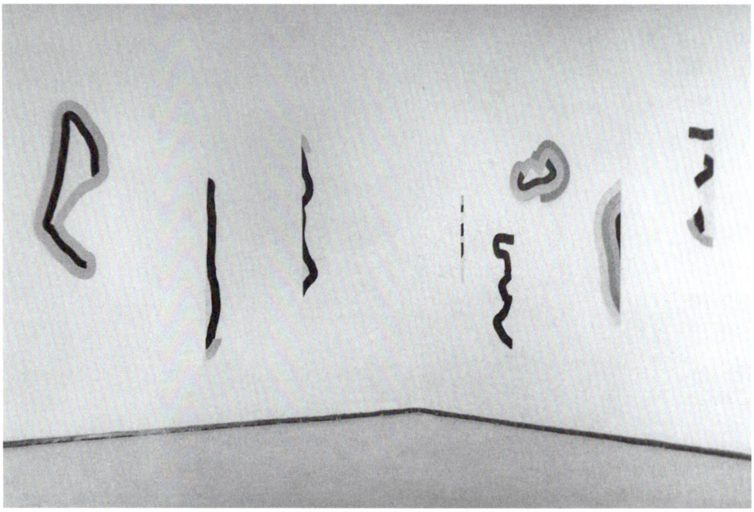

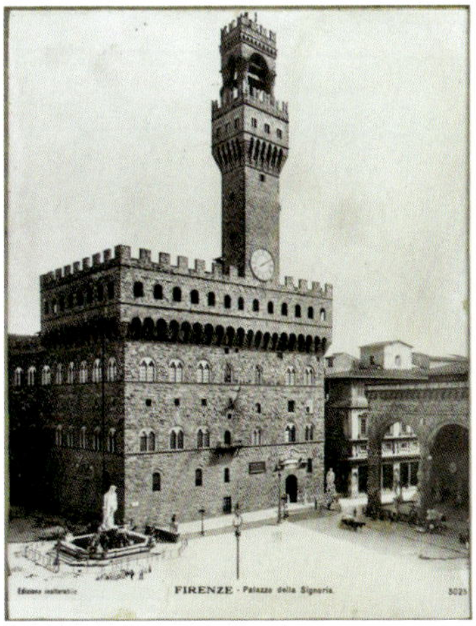

Signore X, o którym wiem, że któregoś dnia w czerwcu lub lipcu 1903 roku stał przed Palazzo della Signoria we Florencji. Utrwaliła to fotografia, na której zobaczyć można sylwetkę tego nieznajomego człowieka. Powiększenie nie wnosi żadnej nowej informacji. Pozwala to sądzić, że moment ten wyrwany z kontekstu wcześniejszych i późniejszych wydarzeń, utrwalony z innych powodów i tak odległy był "c z y s t ą c h w i l ą" leżącą na zewnątrz wszelkiej przydatności. Możemy jedynie wyobrazić sobie to lub owo. Ale czy Signore X prowokuje nas do tego w jakikolwiek sposób? On sobie tam stoi w tym swoim 1903 roku.

Signore X about whom I know that he was standing in front of Palazzo della Signoria in June or July 1903. Thes photograph has preserved the figure of unknown man. The enlargement does not introduce any additional information. This moment seems to have been snatched from the context of some earlier and later events, preserved for other reasons, so distant - just "a p u r e m o m e n t" beyond any practical application. We can only imagine. Does Signore X provoke a flight of our fancy in any way? He is just standing there back in his 1903.

Andrzej Dłużniewski

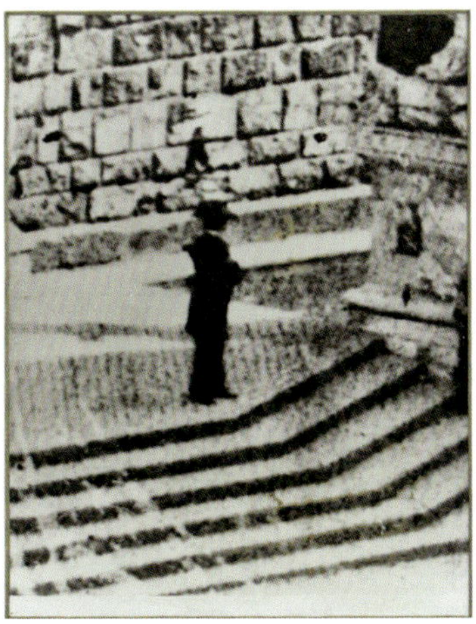

Andrzej Dłużniewski
Signore X, 1973
2 Fotografien, Text | 2 photographs, text
52,2 × 85 cm
Muzeum Sztuki w Łodzi

Andrzej Dłużniewski

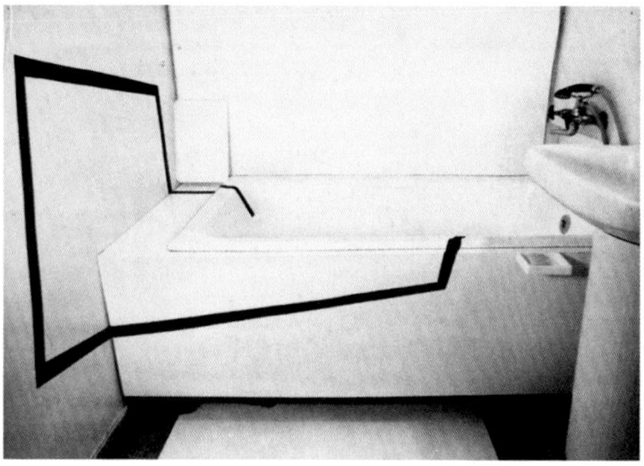

1

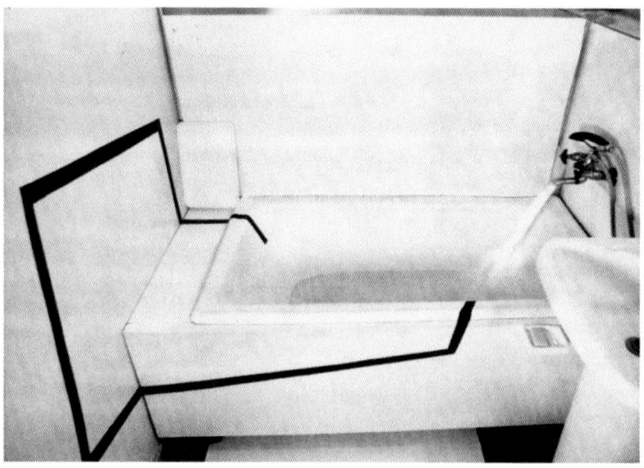

2

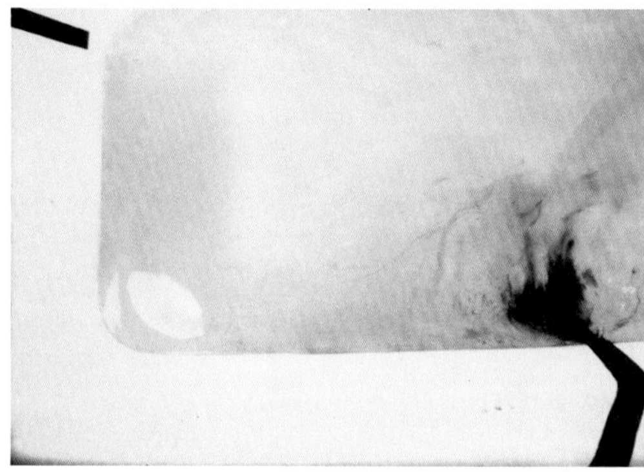

5

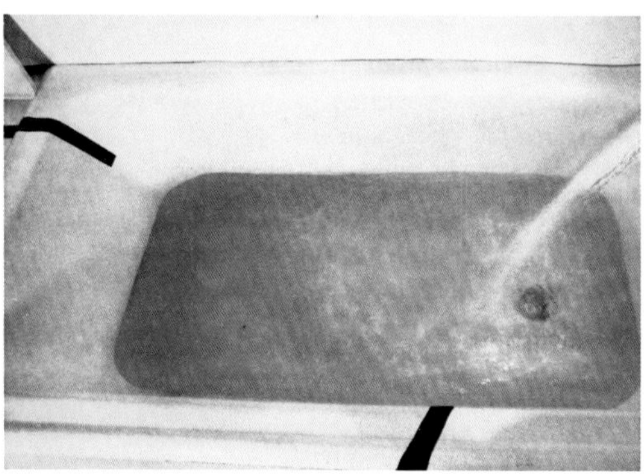

3

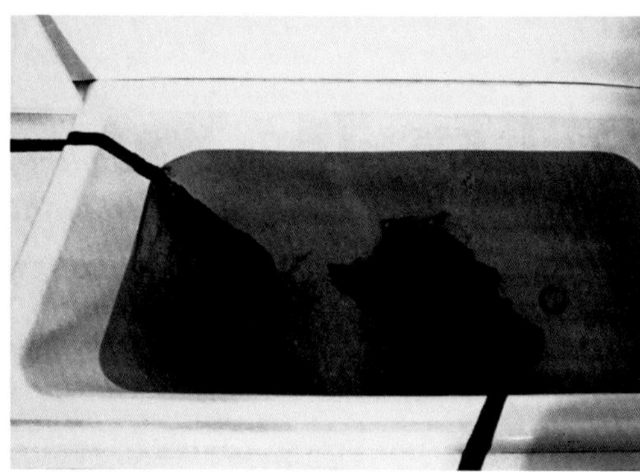

6

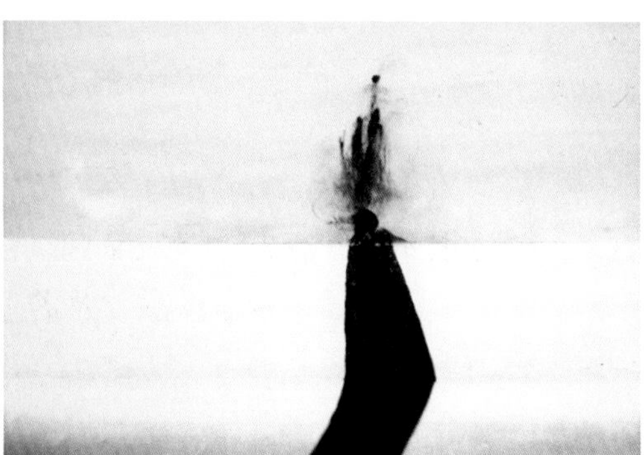

4

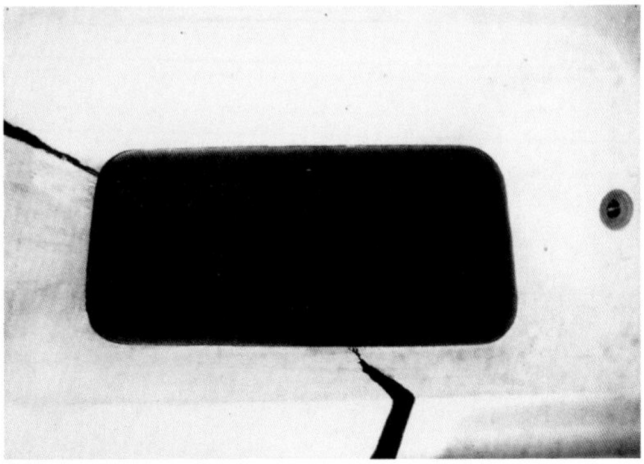

9

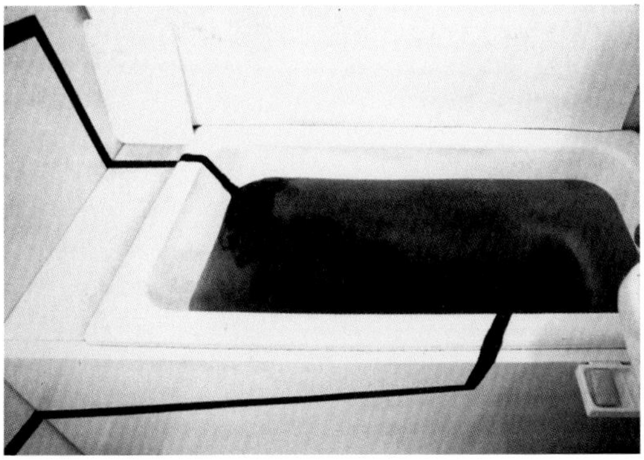

7

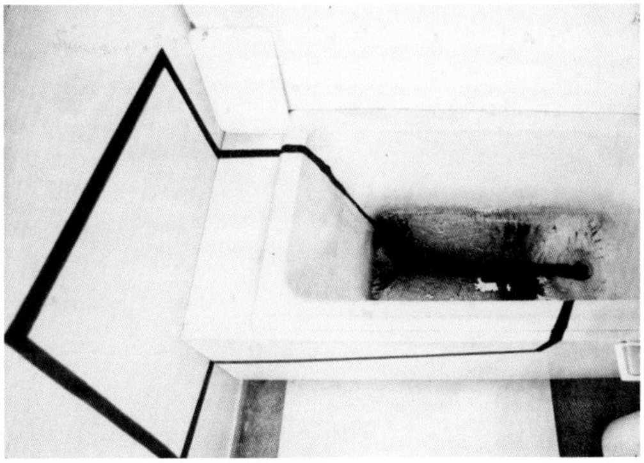

10

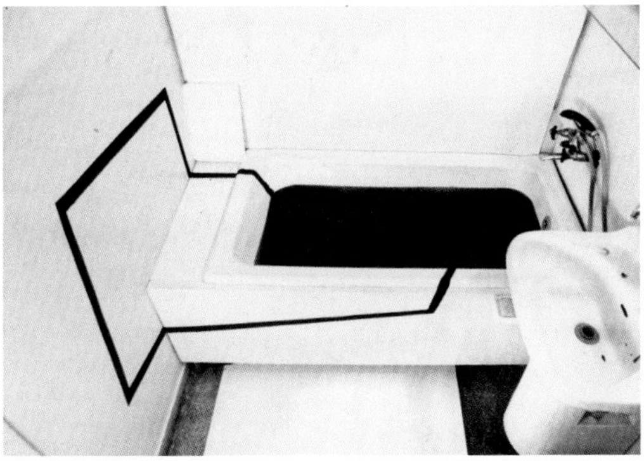

8

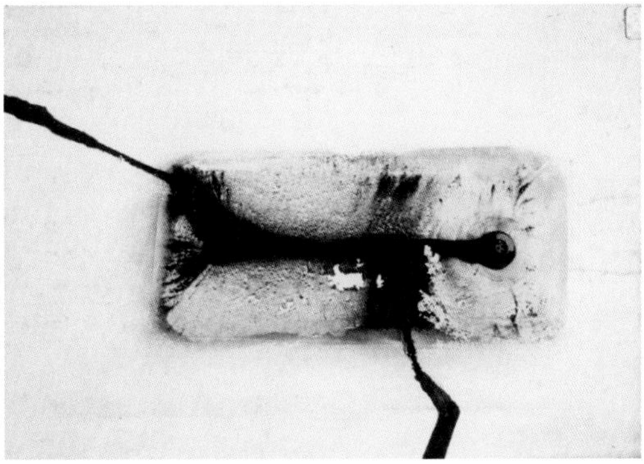

11

Zdzisław Jurkiewicz

Zdzisław Jurkiewicz
Rysunek w łazience / Zeichnung im Badezimmer / Drawing in the Bathroom, 1971
11 Fotografien | 11 photographs
je | each 28 × 38,2 cm
Muzeum Sztuki w Łodzi

CONCEPTUAL ART IN SPITE OF "REAL SOCIALISM": TESTING OTHER LANGUAGES[1]

Paweł Polit

Conceptual art emerged in Poland in the atmosphere of reservations about the principles of composition inherited from the tradition of Constructivism. A weariness with form, symptomatic of European and American art of the 1960s, also manifested itself in the work of Polish artists, leading to decisions which subverted rigorous distinctions between traditional artistic disciplines and provoked a reflection on the notion of art.

The tendency to question the rational principles of construction should not be understood as a complete break with the tradition of the first avant-garde; on the contrary, the special character of Polish conceptual art seems to have emerged in a polemical dialogue with that tradition, among others with the principles of Unism developed in the late 1920s and early 1930s by Władysław Strzemiński. Several decades later, in the 1960s and 1970s, Polish artists and theoreticians, while neutralizing certain aspects of Strzemiński's attitude and developing others, elaborated the conception according to which the work of art opens up to its surrounding reality and acquires the character of a process. In this text, I would like to distinguish and briefly describe the origins, the emergence and the development of this tendency, which culminated around the year 1970.

I

In his programmatic text entitled *Unism in Painting* (*Unizm w malarstwie*, 1928), Władysław Strzemiński formulated the postulate of uniform construction of a work, resulting from the principle of "equal value of space" in the picture: "Each square centimeter of a picture is of equal value and takes part in the construction of a work to the same degree."[2] Strzemiński also proposed to relate the construction of a work to the "innate properties of a picture (rectangular boundaries and a flatness of a picture plane),"[3] which results in a "complete growing together of shapes and their unification with a picture plane."[4] He emphasized the optical character of a painterly work—he defined it as an "organic visual whole"—and its independence from the order of time, which consists, according to him, in a "simultaneity of the spatial-visual phenomenon"[5] (ill. 1, p. 38).

KONZEPTUELLE KUNST, DEM „REALSOZIALISMUS" ZUM TROTZ: EXPERIMENTE IN ANDEREN SPRACHEN[1]

Paweł Polit

Die konzeptuelle Kunst entwickelte sich in Polen in einer Atmosphäre von Skepsis gegenüber den Kompositionsprinzipien, die noch aus der Tradition des Konstruktivismus stammten. Ein Desinteresse an der Form, wie es für die europäische und amerikanische Kunst der 1960er-Jahre symptomatisch war, zeigte sich auch in den Arbeiten im Werk polnischer Künstler*innen und führte zu Entscheidungen, die eine strenge Trennung der überkommenen künstlerischen Disziplinen unterminierten und zum Nachdenken über die Idee der Kunst provozierten.

Die Tendenz einer Infragestellung von rationalen Konstruktionsprinzipien ist allerdings nicht als ein vollständiger Bruch mit der Tradition der ersten Avantgarde zu verstehen; im Gegenteil scheint der besondere Charakter der polnischen konzeptuellen Kunst aus einem polemischen Dialog mit dieser Tradition hervorgegangen zu sein, wobei unter anderem die Prinzipien des im Übergang von den 1920er- zu den 1930er-Jahren durch Władysław Strzemiński entwickelten Unismus zum Tragen kamen. Einige Jahrzehnte später, in den 1960er- und 1970er-Jahren, erarbeiteten polnische Künstler und Theoretiker – indem sie einige Aspekte von Strzemińskis Position tilgten und andere weiterentwickelten – einen Kunstbegriff, demzufolge sich das Kunstwerk seiner Umgebungsrealität öffnet und einen prozesshaften Charakter annimmt. Ich möchte hier die Ursprünge, die Entstehung und die weitere Entwicklung dieser Richtung, die um 1970 ihren Höhepunkt fand, herausarbeiten und in Ansätzen beschreiben.

I

In seinem programmatischen Text mit der Überschrift *Der Unismus in der Malerei* (*Unizm w malarstwie*, 1928) formuliert Władysław Strzemiński das Postulat der uniformen Konstruktion eines Werks, das sich für ihn aus dem Prinzip des „einheitlichen Raums" im Bild ergibt: „Jeder Quadratzentimeter in einem Bild ist gleich viel wert und ist gleichermaßen an der Konstruktion eines Werks beteiligt."[2] Strzemiński legt auch eine Beziehung zwischen der Konstruktion eines Werks und den „elementaren Eigenschaften eines Bildes (rechtwinklige Ränder und eine ebene Bildfläche)"[3] nahe, aus der ein „vollständiges Zusammenwachsen der Formen und deren

Abb. | ill. 1 Władysław Strzemiński
Kompozycja unistyczna / Unistische Komposition / Unistic Composition, 1931
Muzeum Sztuki w Łodzi

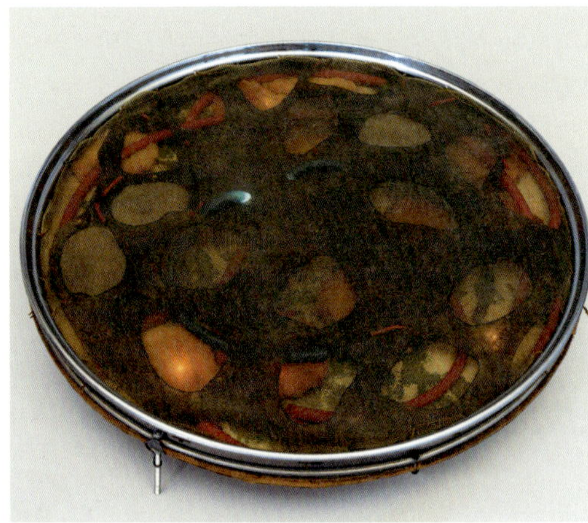

Abb. | ill. 2 Włodzimierz Borowski
Arton B, 1958
Muzeum Sztuki w Łodzi

In his 14 Unistic compositions created in the years 1924–29 and 1931–34, Strzemiński strove to exclude what he called the "Baroque dynamism" in painting, by applying mutually neutral forms and colors of the same intensity. The surfaces of eight paintings in the series are covered with tiny layers of pigment almost identical in shape, which relate the artist's method to a systemic approach. The law of the series and of methodical procedure, resulting in a collection of elements inscribed in the order of repetition, reflects in some sense the central concern of the Unistic project: the very idea of a uniform construction is equally important as each of its particular exemplifications.

What is characteristic of the experiments undertaken at the end of the 1950s and in the 1960s by Polish neo-avant-garde artists, experiments which directly preceded the emergence of conceptual attitudes, is the tendency to literalize the organic metaphor operative in Strzemiński's thinking. This metaphor is evoked by the biomorphism of shapes in the works of representatives of organic abstraction, with their striving to expose the natural qualities of substances applied by them on the surfaces of paintings. These procedures, aiming at—in contradistinction to Strzemiński—the decomposition of a picture, were sometimes intended to emphasize its status

Vereinigung mit der Bildfläche"[4] resultiere. Er betont den optischen Charakter des gemalten Werks – definiert als ein „organisch-visuelles Ganzes" – sowie dessen Unabhängigkeit von der chronologischen Abfolge der Zeit, was sich für ihn in der „Gleichzeitigkeit der räumlich-visuellen Erscheinung" ausdrückt (Abb. 1, S. 38).[5]

In den vierzehn unistischen Kompositionen, die Strzemiński zwischen 1924 und 1929 sowie zwischen 1931 und 1934 schuf, verfolgte er das Ziel, die „barocke Dynamik" in der Malerei, wie er es nannte, hinter sich zu lassen, indem er neutrale Formen sowie Farben von gleicher Intensität benutzte. Die Oberflächen der acht Bilder dieser Reihe bestehen aus hauchdünnen, fast identisch angelegten Pigmentschichten, und darin zeigt sich auch der systematisch-methodische Ansatz des Künstlers. Die Gesetzmäßigkeit der Reihe und das methodische Verfahren, aus dem sich eine Ansammlung von Elementen ergibt, die den Bildern in einer mehrfach wiederholten Reihenfolge eingeschrieben sind, lässt gewissermaßen das zentrale Anliegen des unistischen Projekts erkennen: Der Gedanke der uniformen Konstruktion ist für sich genommen genauso wichtig wie jede einzelne seiner Erscheinungsformen.

Für die Experimente, mit denen sich die Künstler der polnischen Neo-Avantgarde gegen Ende der 1950er und in den 1960er-Jahren beschäftigten – sie gingen den konzeptuellen Ansätzen ganz unmittelbar voraus –, ist die Tendenz charakteristisch, die organische Metapher aus Strzemińskis Denken wörtlich aufzufassen. Die Metapher tritt in den biomorphen Formen der Arbeiten von Vertretern der organischen Abstraktion zutage, die danach strebten, die natürlichen Eigenschaften der verwendeten Substanzen, die sie auf die Oberflächen ihrer Bilder aufbrachten, offen zu zeigen. Diese Verfahren, die im Unterschied zu Strzemiński auf eine Zerlegung des Bildes abzielten, sollten teilweise auch einen Objektstatus hervorheben und das Bild in die unmittelbare Umgebung integrieren. Der zugrundeliegende Gedanke der Experimente, denen sich Włodzimierz Borowski Ende der 1950er-Jahre widmete, bestand darin, das Kunstwerk vom Einfluss überflüssiger, optische Täuschungen hervorbringender Konventionen zu befreien. Er wollte, wie er sagte, „eine organische Realität schaffen", die sich für ihn mit der Idee der Struktur verband: „Eine Struktur – nach seiner Definition – bedeutet iterative Elemente, die Zellen ähneln. Diese Zellen haben ähnliche Merkmale, und deshalb sind sie lebensfähig. Wenn man die Zellen zu verschiedenen Systemen zusammenschließt, schafft man eine Struktur."[6]

Von der grundlegenden Gleichwertigkeit der Elemente in seiner Malerei ausgehend, fühlte sich Borowskis ermutigt, die statische Komposition des Kunstwerks generell infrage zu stellen und das Werk stattdessen mit der Idee des Prozesses in Verbindung zu bringen. Seine frühen *Artons* (*Artony*, Abb. 2, S. 38), flache Objekte, die noch an die Kategorie der Malerei erinnern, ziehen den Blick des Betrachters durch zarte, elektrisch erzeugte Blitze eines sich verändernden und pulsierenden Lichts auf sich. Die nachfolgenden, ab den 1960er-Jahren entstandenen Werke dieser Art sind relativ unzusammenhängende, quasiorganische Objekte aus industriellen und anderen vorgefertigten Materialien, die keinen Bezug mehr zu den traditionellen Kategorien der Malerei und der Skulptur herstellen.

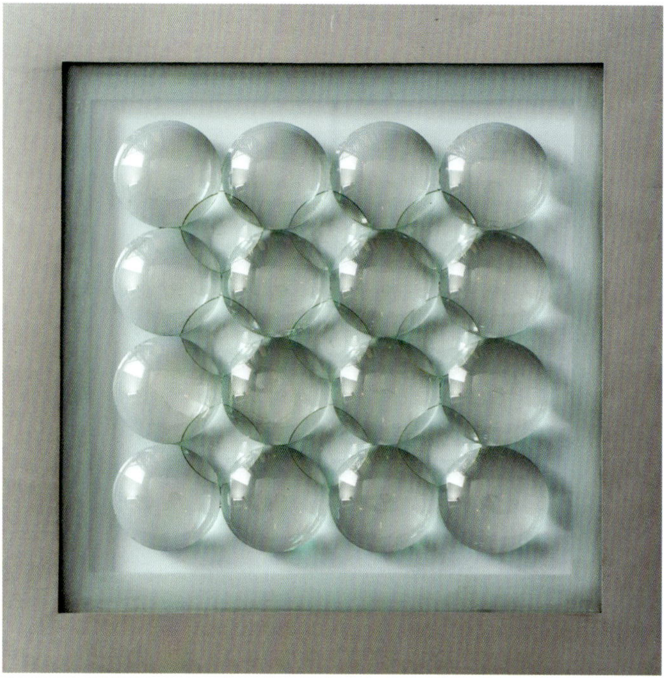

Abb. | ill. 3 Jerzy Rosołowicz
Neutronikon dwustronny / Doppelseitiges Neutronikon / Double-sided Neutronicon, 1969
Muzeum Sztuki w Łodzi

as an object, to integrate it with the direct environment. The idea behind the experiments undertaken at the end of the 1950s by Włodzimierz Borowski was to free an artwork from the impact of superfluous conventions, responsible for effects of optical illusion. He wanted, as he put it, to "create an organic reality," which he associated with the notion of structure; "A structure—as he defined it—means iterative elements which resemble cells. Cells that have similar features and that's why they can live. Connecting these cells into various systems one creates a structure."[6]

The essential equivalence of elements of Borowski's paintings motivated the artist to question the static composition of a work and to associate it with the notion of process. His first *Artons* (*Artony*, ill. 2, p. 38), flat objects still evocative of the category of painting, attract the viewer's eye with gentle flashes (powered by electricity) of shifting and pulsating light; the subsequent ones, created in the early 1960s, are relatively incoherent quasi-organic objects, composed of industrial and readymade materials, which makes them unrelated to the traditional categories of painting and sculpture.

The notion of structure could also be easily applied to the relief compositions of Jerzy Rosołowicz from the early 1960s. Their cell-like pattern brings to mind Unistic compositions by Strzemiński. These works introduce, however, an important modification: the differentiation in size and positioning of tiny elements that are similar in shape gives the impression of convexity and motion. Sometimes these pictures look as if their uniform structure is cracking due to the pressure of some matter from within.

Der Begriff der Struktur lässt sich ebenso leicht auf die Reliefkompositionen von Jerzy Rosołowicz aus den frühen 1960er-Jahren anwenden. Ihr zellenartiges Muster erinnert an unistische Kompositionen von Strzemiński, wobei hier eine wichtige Abwandlung stattgefunden hat: Eine Ausdifferenzierung der Größe und Position kleiner, ähnlich geformter Elemente erweckt den Eindruck einer Wölbung und Bewegung. Bei einigen dieser Bilder gewinnt man den Eindruck, als würde ihre uniforme Struktur durch den Druck einer Substanz im Innern aufreißen.

Werke wie diese verwandeln den Gedanken der uniformen Konstruktion auf bedeutsame Weise. Sie heben die Normen der organischen Einheit und der optischen Gleichzeitigkeit auf. Sie lassen ein gewisses Maß an Zusammenhangslosigkeit zu; sie suggerieren die Möglichkeit der Veränderung, beziehungsweise ihre organische Struktur trägt sie teilweise schon in sich. Jedes einzelne bekommt den Status einer Sammlung heterogener Elemente, die in eine allgemeinere, zeitliche Ordnung von Wiederholungen eingeschrieben ist.

Künstler wie Borowski und Rosołowicz demontierten allmählich den traditionellen Begriff des Kunstwerks als ein in sich geschlossenes Ganzes. Sie stießen die Bürde künstlerischer Konventionen und fester Vorstellungen von sich, die ihrer Ansicht nach zu Verzerrungen der künstlerischen Aussage führten. In der Folge konzentrierten sich die Anstrengungen der radikalsten Künstler in Polen in der Mitte der 1960er-Jahre auf die Suche nach einem „Medium", das im Sinne einer Vermittlung von künstlerischen Ideen möglichst transparent und „neutral" sein sollte. Im Werk von Rosołowicz zum Beispiel weicht die Zellstruktur seiner gemalten Bilder den repetitiven Mustern seiner Reliefs aus optischen Linsen (Abb. 3, S. 40). Diese Objekte, die frei im Galerieraum hängen, scheinen Fragmente lediglich aus ihrer nächsten Umgebung herauszulösen und ständig alle Veränderungen des Umfelds zu registrieren.[7]

II

Der programmatische „Synkretismus" seiner Werke führte Włodzimierz Borowski wiederum dazu, dass er sich die Spiegelfläche als ein Material zu eigen machte, das, wie er in seinem *Spiegelmanifest* (*MANIfest LUStrzany*, 1966) schreibt, „‚Geräusch' reduziert und reine Wahrnehmung ermöglicht."[8] Diese Auffassung stellte eine Radikalisierung des unistischen Projekts der Befreiung des Kunstwerks von überflüssigen und überholten Konventionen dar; in seinen Arbeiten aus der Mitte der 1960er-Jahre verbindet Borowski den Gedanken der Uniformität mit der Kontinuität von nicht chiffrierten, veränderlichen Bildern der Wirklichkeit, wie sie Spiegel bieten. Zur gleichen Zeit reduzierte und neutralisierte er allmählich auch das Erscheinungsbild seiner Arbeiten und verwandelte sie in sprachliche Zeichen.

Borowskis Werk mit dem Titel *Formel* (*Formuła*, 1966), ein Plus- und ein Minuszeichen aus Spiegelglas, in denen sich die Vielfalt der Geschehnisse in der direkten Umgebung spiegeln, kann als eine der ersten Manifestationen einer konzeptuellen Haltung in Polen gelten. Es entspricht

Works of this kind introduce an important transformation into the notion of uniform construction. They suspend the norms of organic unity and optical simultaneity. They allow a degree of incoherence; they suggest or sometimes embrace within their organic structure the possibility of change. Each one of them acquires the status of a collection of heterogeneous elements, inscribed into a more general, temporal order of repetition.

Artists such as Borowski and Rosołowicz gradually dismantled the traditional notion of an artwork as a self-enclosed and coherent whole. They rejected the burden of artistic conventions and preconceptions responsible, in their view, for distortions of an artistic message. Hence, in the mid-1960s, the endeavors of the most radical artists in Poland concentrated on a search for a "medium" which would be most transparent and "neutral" for communicating an artistic idea. For example, in Rosołowicz's work, the cell-like structure of his painterly works gives way to the repetitive pattern of his reliefs constructed of lenses (ill. 3, p. 40). These objects, hanging freely in a gallery space, seem to merely crop fragments of their most direct environment and continuously register all the changes occurring within it.[7]

II

Programmatic "syncretism" of Włodzimierz Borowski's works, in turn, brings him to accept a mirror plane as a material which, as he put it in his *Mirror Manifesto* (*MANIfest LUStrzany*, 1966), "reduces 'noise,' making pure sensation possible."[8] This conception radicalized the Unistic project, which aimed to purify the artwork of superfluous and obsolete conventions; in his works of the mid-1960s Borowski associated the idea of uniformity with a continuity of uncoded and changeable images of reality provided by mirrors. At the same time, he gradually reduced and neutralized the visual aspect of a work, transforming it into a linguistic sign.

Borowski's work entitled *Formula* (*Formuła*, 1966), in which two mirror signs "+" and "–" reflect multiplicity of events occurring in the direct environment, should be considered one of the first manifestations of the conceptual attitude in Poland. It corresponds with the conception of a "singular point" in art as proposed by Jerzy Ludwiński, one of the leading art theoreticians of the period, according to whom the content range of a work of art is inversely proportional to the degree of its formal complexity. Ludwiński said that "art may be concerned with reality as a whole and at the same time its form may be reduced almost to zero."[9] That is why a work of art, understood by the critic as an "artistic fact," should be characterized by maximum conciseness, submitted to the principle of economy of means in formulating a most complex, sometimes even quite illogical, message.

Beginning in 1965, Roman Opałka used arithmetic signs for measuring the lapse of time in a series of numerical paintings entitled *OPAŁKA 1965/1 – ∞* (ill. pp. 28–29). In each one of its *Details*—as he called particular paintings in the series—a sequence of natural numbers

dem künstlerischen Begriff des „singulären Punktes", eingeführt von Jerzy Ludwiński, einem der führenden Kunsttheoretiker jener Zeit, demzufolge sich die inhaltliche Bandbreite eines Kunstwerkes umgekehrt proportional zum Grad seiner formalen Komplexität verhält. In den Worten Ludwińskis: „Die Kunst kann sich mit dem großen Ganzen der Wirklichkeit befassen und die Form lässt sich dabei beinahe auf ein Nichts reduzieren."[9] Das Kunstwerk, das Kritiker als eine „künstlerische Tatsache" verstehen, sollte sich durch ein Maximum an Prägnanz auszeichnen und bei der Formulierung selbst der komplexesten, vielleicht sogar auch unlogischen Aussage dem Prinzip der Sparsamkeit der Mittel gehorchen.

Seit 1965 setzte auch Roman Opałka arithmetische Zeichen ein, um das Verstreichen der Zeit zu messen, namentlich in seiner Reihe von Bildern mit dem Titel *OPAŁKA 1965/1 – ∞* (Abb. S. 28–29). In jedem der „Details", wie er die einzelnen Bilder dieser Reihe nannte, misst eine Reihe von natürlichen Zahlen aufeinanderfolgende Intervalle der zeitlichen Ordnung. Ihr Aufbau ist durch das unistische Prinzip der uniformen Konstruktion bestimmt, das in diesem Fall eine gleichmäßige Verteilung weißer Zahlen auf der Bildfläche bedeutet. Bei diesem Projekt ist auch der systemische Charakter hervorzuheben: Die lineare Zahlenordnung, die auf den Bildoberflächen dieser Arbeiten notiert ist, folgt der linearen Progression von Einerschritten. Zudem gehen die Zahlen graduell in den Hintergrund über, weil dessen Grauton mit jedem weiteren *Detail* um ein Prozent mit Weiß aufgehellt wird. Mit *OPAŁKA 1965/1 – ∞* wurde das Prinzip der uniformen Konstruktion in einen systemischen Ansatz übertragen und inspirierte künstlerische Lösungen, die auf einer breiteren Reflexionsebene wirksam werden.

III

Das Verfahren, einem Kunstwerk Prozesscharakter zu verleihen, dabei jedoch seinen uniformen Aufbau zu bewahren, setzte die Gültigkeit von Strzemińskis Postulat von der „Gleichzeitigkeit der räumlich-visuellen Erscheinung" außer Kraft. Darüber hinaus zog es auch den ikonischen Status des Kunstwerks in Zweifel, da es den Schwerpunkt von der Visualisierung einer Idee auf die Sparsamkeit ihrer Formulierung verschob. Das ganze Spektrum von Zeichen, die polnische konzeptuelle Künstler seit dem Anfang der 1970er-Jahre benutzten – ob es Anordnungen von Buchstaben, Zahlen und Satzzeichen sowie Wörter und Texte, Symbole, Schemata, „Ikonogramme" oder auch komplexere, textlich-visuelle Strukturen waren – sie alle dienten der Untersuchung von Möglichkeiten, wie man jenseits der ordnenden Struktur der Form bedeutsame Aussagen formulieren konnte. Teilweise nahmen sie auch den Charakter von indexikalischen Zeichen an, die im Kunstwerk auf ausgewählte Fragmente der Realität hinwiesen und sie dadurch in den Bereich der Kunst aufnahmen.

Ein Beispiel hierfür ist Zbigniew Gostomskis Werk *Ulysses* (*Ulisses*, 1970), in dem eine aus dem Roman von James Joyce entlehnte Formel Verwendung findet: die unendlich oft wiederholte Handlung des Markierens von Gegenständen in der unmittelbaren Umgebung mit Kreide. Das Zitat,

measures subsequent intervals of the temporal order. Their structure is determined by the Unistic principle of uniform construction determining, in this case, equal distribution of white numbers on the painterly surface. What should also be emphasized in this project is its systemic character: the linear order of numbers noted down on the surfaces of these paintings is determined by the principle of constant progression by the value of one. Moreover, the numbers gradually blend with their background as a result of its grayness being brightened by one percent of white on each consecutive *Detail*. In *OPAŁKA 1965/1 – ∞* the principle of uniform construction has been translated into a systemic approach, inspiring artistic solutions functioning on a more general level of reflection.

III

The operation of endowing a work of art with the character of a process, while at the same time sustaining its uniform structure, suspended the validity of the postulate of a "simultaneity of the spatial-visual phenomenon," as proposed by Strzemiński. Moreover, it also undermines the iconic status of a work, shifting emphasis from the visualization of an idea to its economic formulation. The whole array of signs utilized by Polish conceptual artists from the beginning of the 1970s—arrangements of letters, numbers, and punctuation marks; words, texts; symbols, schemata, "iconograms"; more complex textual-visual structures—they all serve the inquiry into the possibilities of making a meaningful statement beyond the order of form. Sometimes they acquire the character of indexical signs, indicating selected fragments of reality and including them in the domain of art.

This is the case, for example, in Zbigniew Gostomski's *Ulisses* (1970), in which the formula excerpted from James Joyce's novel described an endlessly repeated act of marking with chalk objects encountered in the direct environment. This quotation, noted down on the four panels of which the work consists, reads: "and if ever he went out for a walk he filled his pockets with chalk, to write it up on what took his fancy, the side of a rock or a teahouse table or a bale of cotton or a corkfloat / or / or / or." Artistic decisions make a sign concrete, they reduce its semantic transparency, endowing an artistic message with idiomatic and unique character.

Wiesław Borowski, another critic who provided theoretical grounding for conceptual art in Poland, associated Gostomski's practices with what in a 1971 article he called an "apictorial strand." Borowski understood innovative artistic abstraction not as a "visual (sensual) qualification of the work" but as the "ability to embrace the whole of the creative process, the capacity for thought and consciousness."[10] He privileged the function an artwork performs over the perception of it: "These works are not addressed to any viewer. They assert the constant presence of illegitimate and disinterested actions that do not demand justification now or in the future, nor do they preserve such actions by any means. These actions are immediate, casual, and tied neither to a place nor to any material, or time."[11]

das sich auf den vier Tafeln des Kunstwerks findet, lautet: „Und wann immer er spazieren ging, stopfte er sich die Taschen mit Kreide voll, um alles, was ihm gefiel, vollzuschreiben, sei es die Seite eines Felsens oder ein Teehaustisch oder ein Ballen Baumwolle oder ein Schwimmer aus Kork / oder / oder / oder". Künstlerische Entscheidungen lassen ein Zeichen konkret werden, sie verringern seine semantische Transparenz, verleihen einer künstlerischen Aussage ihren idiomatischen und unverwechselbaren Charakter.

Wiesław Borowski, ein weiterer Kritiker, der zum theoretischen Fundament der konzeptuellen Kunst in Polen beitrug, verband Gostomskis Praktiken mit etwas, was er in einem Artikel von 1971 als einen „unbildhaften Strang" beschrieb. Borowski sah in der innovativen künstlerischen Abstraktion nicht die „visuelle (sinnliche) Eigenschaft eines Werks", sondern die „Fähigkeit, sich des Schaffensprozesses als Ganzes anzunehmen, ein Potential für Denken und Bewusstsein."[10] Er räumte der Funktion eines Kunstwerks mehr Gewicht ein als dessen Wahrnehmung: „Diese Werke richten sich an keinen Betrachter. Sie behaupten die ständige Präsenz illegitimer und unparteiischer Handlungen, die keiner Rechtfertigung bedürfen, weder jetzt noch in der Zukunft, und verleihen solchen Handlungen auch in keiner Weise Dauer. Diese Handlungen sind unmittelbar, zwanglos und weder an einen Ort noch an ein Material oder eine Zeit gebunden."[11]

Die Tendenz, den ikonischen Charakter eines Kunstwerks infrage zu stellen, zeigt sich in Andrzej Dłużniewskis Reihe von Zeichnungen *Ikonogramme* (*Ikonogramy*), die in der ersten Hälfte der 1970er-Jahre entstand (Abb. 4–5, S. 46–47). Die Serie besteht aus verschiedenen Variationen über das Thema des Bildrahmens, der traditionell die Grenzen einer optischen Täuschung definiert. Dłużniewski führt hier verschiedene axonometrische Operationen durch, um in jeder der Zeichnungen den Effekt einer „Implosion" zu erreichen, wobei er einen rechteckigen Rahmen faltet und ihn auf diese Weise in den Hauptprotagonisten des Bildes verwandelt. Anstatt des gemalten „Fensters", das einen Blick auf die Realität freigibt, bietet er eine ganze Vielfalt an Repräsentationssymbolen, die bis dahin noch in keinem Formenlexikon genauer beschrieben waren. Diese Zeichen ordnen sich keinem vorhandenen Modell unter: Einschließlich des Rechtecks, das den Anfang bildet, stellen sie, verbunden durch das Prinzip der Wiederholung, eine Reihe gleichgestellter Elemente dar.

Die systemischen Arbeiten von Jarosław Kozłowski aus den 1970er-Jahren lassen sich am besten über ihre Tendenz beschreiben, alle Möglichkeiten auszuschöpfen, die sich mit einem bestimmten Algorithmus vorhersagen lassen. Die ursprüngliche Idee von *Sprache* (*Język*, 1972), die der Künstler in Buchform konzipierte, setzte die Entwicklung eines riesigen Lexikons voraus, dessen Wörter aus einer Kombination der Buchstaben des lateinischen Alphabets resultierten. Jeder Buchstabe durfte jeweils nur einmal in einem Wort vorkommen. Damit war die Länge der Wörter dieser „Sprache" durch die Anzahl der Buchstaben im Alphabet begrenzt. Im Lexikon, das Kozłowski anlegte, waren die Einträge in fortlaufend nummerierten Abschnitten zusammengefasst, wobei die Abschnittsnummer der Anzahl der Buchstaben in den Wörtern entsprach. Kozłowskis Werk beginnt im Abschnitt I

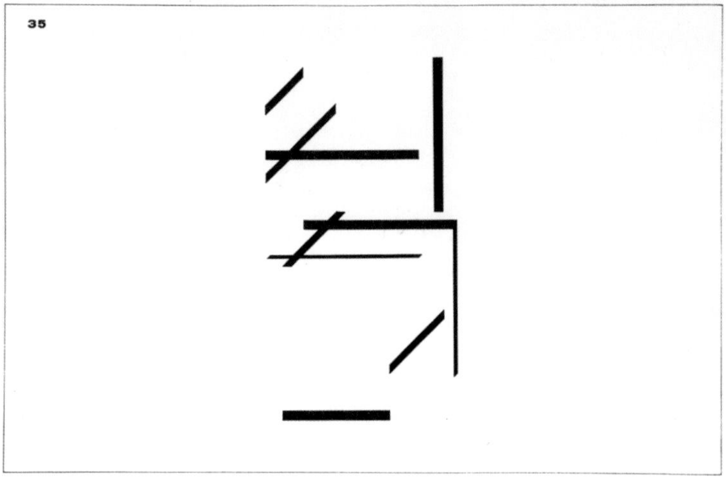

Abb. | ill. 4 Andrzej Dłużniewski
Aus der Serie | from the series
Iconograms, no. 35, 1975
Courtesy Emilia Małgorzata Dłużniewska und | and Kajetan Dłużniewski

The tendency to question the iconic character of a work is manifested in Andrzej Dłużniewski's series of drawings entitled *Iconograms* (*Ikonogramy*, ill. 4–5, pp. 46–47), created in the first half of the 1970s. This series consists of a number of variations on the theme of a picture frame, traditionally delimiting a space of optical illusion. Dłużniewski applied a number of axonometric operations in order to achieve in each drawing an effect of "implosion," folding a rectangle of frame and transforming it into the main protagonist of a picture. Instead of a painterly "window" onto outside reality, he proposed the whole multiplicity of symbols of representation, which were not specified before by any known lexicon of forms. These signs are not subservient to any pre-existing model; inclusive of the initial rectangle of the frame, they constitute a series of equivalent elements, tied together by the very principle of repeated operation.

Systemic works by Jarosław Kozłowski of the 1970s could be best described by their tendency to exhaust all possibilities anticipated by a given algorithm. The initial idea behind *Language* (*Język*, 1972), conceived by the artist as a book, presumed the creation of a gigantic lexicon consisting of words that resulted from putting together Latin alphabet letters. Each letter was planned to appear in a single word only once. As a result of this, the longest words of the "language" had to be those limited by the number of letters in the alphabet. The lexicon begun by Kozłowski implied the ordering of terms in sections marked by consecutive numbers, according to the number of contained letters. Kozłowski's work begins in section I with the word "a" and is interrupted in section IV with the significant word "idea." The significance of these terms, like the significance of Dłużniewski's "iconograms," is not determined by any of the codes functioning in culture; the effect of signification arises here as a result of punctuation—the interruption of a chain of signs ordered in a logical sequence.

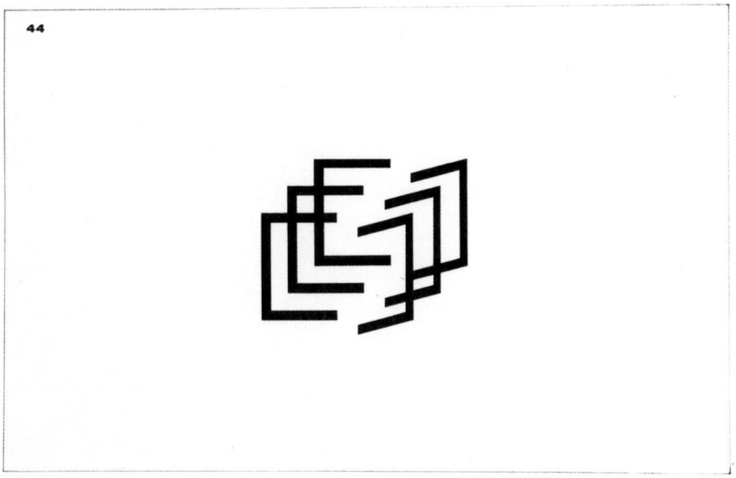

Abb. | ill. 5 Andrzej Dłużniewski
Aus der Serie | from the series
Iconograms, no. 44, 1975
Courtesy Emilia Małgorzata
Dłużniewska und | and
Kajetan Dłużniewski

mit dem Wort „a" („ein") und wird im Abschnitt IV mit dem bedeutenden Wort „idea" („Idee") unterbrochen. Wie die Bedeutung von Dłużniewskis *Ikonogrammen* ist auch die Bedeutung dieser Begriffe durch keine kulturell gültigen Chiffren festgelegt. Der Effekt der Signifikation ergibt sich aus der Interpunktion, aus der Unterbrechung einer logisch geordneten Zeichenkette.

Kozłowskis systemische Werke übertragen das unistische Prinzip der uniformen Konstruktion auf die Idee der Vollständigkeit, was sich in seinem Bestreben offenbart, die Bandbreite der möglichen Operationen genau zu bestimmen. Letztere wurden vorerst als Denkspiele erprobt und fanden dann, ab den späten 1970er-Jahren, in seinen Performances und ortsgebundenen Arbeiten Ausdruck. In seinem Werk *Unterricht* (*Lekcja*, 1972) führt der Künstler eine methodische, gründliche Analyse der diversen Beziehungen zwischen vier Elementen durch: ein Textabsatz mit dazugehöriger Zeichnung (beides einem englischsprachigen Handbuch entnommen), eine Fotografie, die an der Zeichnung orientiert ist, sowie etwas, was er als „Gedanken" beschreibt. In einem theoretischen Begleittext listet Kozłowski 22 verschiedene Arten von Beziehungen zwischen den Elementen auf, darunter semantische, syntaktische sowie Ähnlichkeits- und Repräsentationsbeziehungen. Indem er eine ironische Haltung gegenüber dem Didaktischen und Autoritären der Schulerziehung und, im weiteren Sinne, gegenüber der politischen Propaganda einnimmt, bietet der Künstler dem Betrachter keine fertige Aussage, sondern lädt ihn zu einer Reflexion über die Komplexität von semiotischen Beziehungen ein, aus denen Bedeutung hergestellt wird.

Theoretische Überlegungen zur Semiose und zum damit verbundenen Aspekt der Möglichkeiten von Bedeutungsbildung werden auch im Werk von Zdzisław Jurkiewicz angestellt, zum Beispiel in seiner Assemblage *Form der Kontinuität: ‚Stuhl' – ‚Stuhl' Stuhl – Stuhl* (*Kształt ciągłości: „Krzesło" – „krzesło" krzesło – krzesło*, 1971). Mit Hinweis auf die berüchtigte Tautologie von

Kozłowski's systemic works translate the Unistic principle of uniform construction into the idea of completeness, manifested in his endeavor to precisely determine the range of possible operations, enacted initially within a mental sphere, and later, beginning in the late 1970s, in his performances and site-specific works. In his *Lesson* (*Lekcja*, 1972) the artist conducted a methodical and thorough analysis of a range of relations between four elements: the paragraph of text and the accompanying drawing—both excerpted from an English language handbook, the photograph modeled on the drawing, and what he specified as "thought." In an accompanying theoretical statement, the artist listed 22 kinds of relations between the elements, among others: semantic, syntactical, relations of similitude, and representation. Being ironic about the didacticism and authoritarianism of a school education, and—by extension—of political propaganda, the artist did not propose a ready message, inviting the viewer to reflect on the complexity of semiotic relations responsible for the construction of meaning.

Theoretical consideration of semiosis and the related issue of the possibility of meaning is also undertaken with regard to the work of Zdzisław Jurkiewicz, for example in the arrangement *The Shape of Continuity: "Chair"—"chair"chair—chair* (*Kształt ciągłości: „Krzesło"—„krzesło"krzesło—krzesło*, 1971). Referring to the notorious tautology of *One and Three Chairs* (1965) by Joseph Kosuth, this work stages the relationship between the sign (in this case the simplified narrowed down version of the chair, its referent (the chair in its full shape), and something in between (its meaning denominated with the phrase "'chair' chair" and described by Jurkiewicz in terms of continuity) (ill. 6, p. 49). What determines the special character of Jurkiewicz's endeavors is the impulse to search for new and unique "shapes of continuity" (*kształtu ciągłości*). Throughout the 1970s the artist made use of quite a range of means (painting, drawing, text, photography, object, film) for defining this notion anew.

A distinguished kind of sign, among the ones listed so far, is the blue stripe of Scotch Tape employed by Edward Krasinski in his *Interventions* (*Interwencje*, ill. p. 30). Leading the viewer's gaze along the walls at the height of 130 cm, moving over the surfaces of representations hanging there, be they reproductions of paintings or photographs, and entering the interiors presented in the axonometric structures, which the artist started to create in 1973, the blue stripe effaces the differences between real and fictitious space. Krasiński endowed it with the paradoxical character of an indexical sign, which adjusts itself to the nature of the space that it explores; characteristic of it is a kind of mimicry—it may be transparent on some occasions and opaque on others. When penetrating illusory spaces of axonometric structures, the blue stripe seems to lose its material qualifications, aligning itself with abstract patterns of lines. When crawling across the walls and encountering uneven surfaces of assemblages, it intensifies its sensual qualities, exposing the richness and diversity of the environment within which it operates. As Krasiński commented upon the nature of its operation, the blue stripe "intervenes with the real, reveals the real which was not noticed (obvious) before."[12]

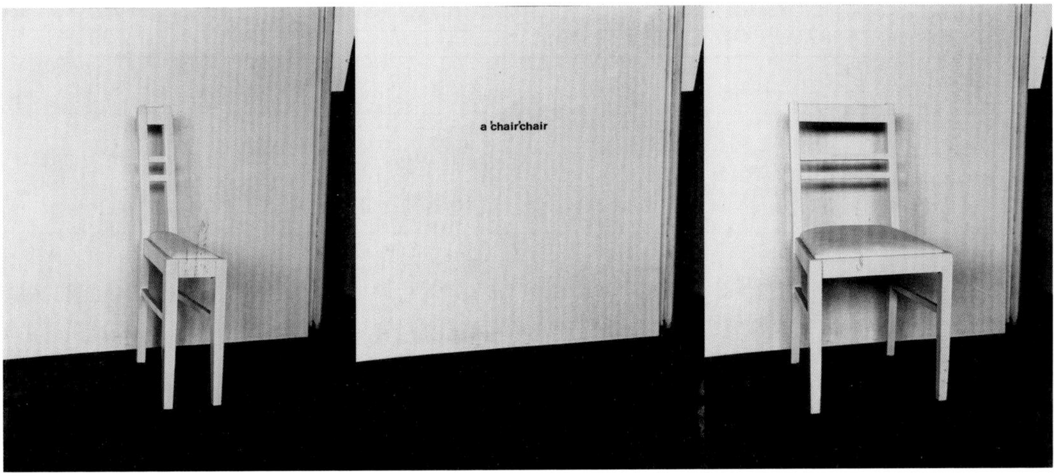

Abb. | ill. 6 Zdzisław Jurkiewicz
The Shape of Continuity: "chair" – "chair"chair – chair, 1971–1973, Muzeum Współczesne, Wrocław

Joseph Kosuths *One and Three Chairs* (1965) inszeniert diese Arbeit die Beziehung zwischen dem Zeichen (in diesem Fall eine vereinfachte, schmale Version des Stuhls), dem Referenten (dem Stuhl in seiner ganzen Form) und etwas Dazwischenliegendem (dessen Bedeutung, mit der Formulierung *Stuhl' Stuhl* benannt und von Jurkiewicz als Kontinuität beschrieben wird) (Abb. 6). Die Besonderheit der Bemühungen von Jurkiewicz ist durch den Impuls gekennzeichnet, stets nach neuen und einzigartigen „Formen von Kontinuität" (*kształtu ciągłości*) zu suchen. Im Laufe der 1970er-Jahre griff der Künstler auf eine beachtliche Bandbreite an verschiedenen Medien zurück (Malerei, Zeichnung, Text, Fotografie, Objekt, Film), um diese Vorstellung neu zu definieren.

Ein Zeichen, das unter den bisher genannten besonders herausragt, ist der blaue Streifen aus Klebeband, den Edward Krasiński in seinen *Interventionen* (*Interwencje*) einsetzt (Abb. S. 30). Auf einer Höhe von 130 Zentimetern führt der blaue Streifen das Auge des Betrachters an den Wänden entlang, über die Oberflächen von dort hängenden Darstellungen (Reproduktionen gemalter Bilder oder Fotografien etwa) und in Innenräume, die durch axonometrische Strukturen dargestellt sind, die der Künstler ab 1973 schuf, so dass die Unterschiede zwischen realer und fiktiver Räumlichkeit zum Verschwinden gebracht werden. Krasiński verleiht dem Werk den paradoxen Charakter eines indexikalischen Zeichens, das sich an die Eigenschaften des Raums, den es erforscht, anpasst, wobei es sich durch eine Art Mimikry auszeichnet: Mal ist es durchsichtig, mal wieder undurchsichtig. Wenn er in die imaginären Räume der axonometrischen Strukturen eindringt, scheint der blaue Streifen seine materiellen Eigenschaften zu verlieren und sich an den abstrakten Mustern von Linien auszurichten. Wenn er sich über die Wände zieht und dabei auf die unebenen Oberflächen von Assemblagen trifft, treten seine sinnlich wahrnehmbaren Qualitäten stärker hervor, wodurch der Reichtum und die Vielfalt der Umgebung, in der er agiert, betont werden. Krasiński sagte über die Funktion des blauen Streifens, dass dieser „in das Reale eingreift, etwas Reales zeigt, das zuvor unbemerkt geblieben (nicht offenkundig) war."[12]

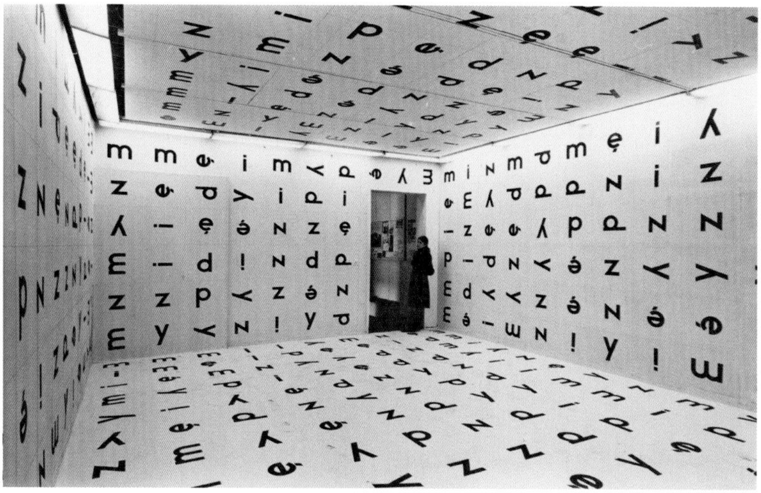

Abb. | ill. 7 Stanisław Dróżdż
Między / Zwischen / Between, 1977
Installationsansicht | installation view
Galeria Foksal, Warschau / Warsaw
Muzeum Sztuki w Łodzi

IV

Artistic phenomena associated with the idiom of conceptual art abounded in the growing political repressiveness of the era. The political crisis at the end of the year 1970,[13] epitomized by bloody events in Gdańsk and other coastal cities, to some extent muffled the social repercussions of an artistic revolution that had been enacted, in several stages, during a series of events which took place that year.[14] The crisis stimulated the gradual transformation of the conception of art as process, coextensive with reality and unlimited in time and space, for the sake of a more restrained model focused on securing integrity of art and celebrating its autonomy.[15] Reality turned out to be "disloyal with regard to art," as Jerzy Ludwiński commented in retrospect.[16] Although autonomous, new art did not detach itself from social reality completely, making repeated attempts at addressing it in covert and allusive ways.

When commenting upon institutional practices aimed at securing the integrity of the artistic message, Andrzej Turowski associated them with resistance against the pressure of "ideosis"—an ideologized space of political discourse striving to control the whole of artistic life and to exploit it for propagandistic purposes. According to Turowski, the political regime's allowance of a proliferation of the avant-garde art formula in Poland in the 1970s served to legitimize the Gierek era's policy of cultural liberalism. That involved "political acceptance for art using certain gestures, formulas, avant-garde categories, but already 'tamed,' devoid of autonomous artistic values."[17]

The recognition of the mechanism of the instrumentalization of art for political purposes generated the need to oppose it. Consequently, throughout the 1970s conceptual artists tended to undertake a covert game with the ideological codification of social space. The tendency manifested itself in artistic proposals aimed at unfastening the strict bond between the verbal and the visual components of a work. Such procedures were typical for Stanisław Dróżdż's concrete poetry pieces. The visual aspect

IV

Künstlerische Phänomene, die mit dem Idiom der konzeptuellen Kunst in Zusammenhang standen, gab es in dieser politisch zunehmend repressiven Ära zuhauf. Die politische Krise von Ende 1970[13], die sich in den blutigen Ereignissen in Danzig und anderen Küstenstädten darstellte, dämpfte gewissermaßen die gesellschaftlichen Auswirkungen einer künstlerischen Revolution, die sich im selben Jahr etappenweise in einer Reihe von Ereignissen abgespielt hatte.[14] Die Krise leistete der allmählichen Verwandlung des prozessualen Kunstbegriffs Vorschub, eine Begrifflichkeit, die sich mit der Realität deckte und zeitlich wie räumlich unbegrenzt war, und begünstigte ein gemäßigteres Modell, bei dem es hauptsächlich darum ging, die Integrität der Kunst zu bewahren und ihre Unabhängigkeit zu zelebrieren.[15] Es sollte sich herausstellen, dass die Realität sich, „was die Kunst anging, illoyal" verhielt, wie Jerzy Ludwiński rückblickend kommentierte.[16] Die neue Kunst war zwar unabhängig, doch sie löste sich nicht vollständig von der gesellschaftlichen Realität, sondern unternahm immer wieder Versuche, sich verdeckt und über Anspielungen mit ihr auseinanderzusetzen.

In seiner Auseinandersetzung mit den institutionellen Praktiken, die darauf abzielten, die Integrität der künstlerischen Aussage zu sichern, stellte Andrzej Turowski diese mit einem Akt des Widerstands gegen den Druck der „Ideosis" in Zusammenhang – gegen einen ideologisierten Raum des politischen Diskurses, der danach strebte, das Kunstschaffen insgesamt zu kontrollieren und es für propagandistische Zwecke auszunutzen. Turowski zufolge diente das Zulassen einer Verbreitung der Avantgarde-Formel in der Kunst im Polen der 1970er-Jahre durch das Regime einer Legitimierung der Politik des kulturellen Liberalismus, die in der Ära Gierek praktiziert wurde. Das bedeutete die „politische Akzeptanz einer Kunst, die bestimmte Gesten, Formeln, Kategorien der Avantgarde verwendete, welche aber schon ‚zahm' waren, frei von unabhängigen künstlerischen Werten."[17]

Aus der Einsicht, dass die Kunst für politische Zwecke instrumentalisiert wurde, erwuchs das Bedürfnis, sich zu widersetzen. Dementsprechend tendierten konzeptuelle Künstler im Verlauf der 1970er-Jahre dazu, sich auf ein verdecktes Spiel mit der ideologischen Kodifizierung der gesellschaftlichen Sphäre einzulassen. Diese Tendenz kam in künstlerischen Positionen zum Ausdruck, die es sich zum Ziel machten, die strenge Verbindung zwischen den sprachlichen und den visuellen Komponenten eines Werkes zu lockern. Typisch waren solche Verfahren für die konkrete Poesie von Stanisław Dróżdż. Der visuelle Aspekt seiner Anordnungen von sprachlichen Zeichen ist hier die notwendige Voraussetzung für ein Verständnis der Bedeutungen, deren Träger sie sind. Dróżdż' *Begriffsgestalten* (*pojęciokształty*) waren der radikale Versuch, einen Sinngehalt in eine sprachliche Inschrift zu integrieren und dabei gleichzeitig die Frage der Repräsentation zu problematisieren. In seinen Arbeiten benutzte Dróżdż eine offene Struktur, die das Prinzip der uniformen Verteilung von Zeichen auf einer ebenen Fläche widerspiegelte[18], und eine mittels systemischer oder tautologischer Formeln festgelegte Struktur fand ebenfalls Verwendung.

of his arrangements of linguistic signs was a necessary condition of recognizing the meanings written into them; Dróżdż's 'ideaforms' (*pojęciokształty*) were a radical attempt to integrate meaning with the verbal inscription, while at the same time problematizing the question of representation. In his works, Dróżdż employed an open structure reflective of the principle of uniform distribution of signs on a flat surface[18] or a structure determined by systemic or tautological formulas.

Dróżdż's installation *Between* (*Między*, ill. 7, p. 50) played a game with the conception of the work classified as autonomous, left in a state of isolation. In that work, it seems, Dróżdż performed a kind of implosion of such parameters, effecting—as Jacek Wesołowski suggested—a semantic inversion of the word used. The artist permutated the letters constitutive of the word "between" to fix their precise location and angular position. The uniform, systematic distribution of the letters on the walls and ceiling thus comments in a self-reflective manner on the complex relationships "between" the individual letters and sequences of letters, as well as defining the position of the viewer as he moves across the space of the work.

The disintegration of the linear order of the title word and the writing of its constituent letters into a spatial structure was to result, according to Wesołowski, in an inversion of the initial meaning: "Between" as "Nothing (Not This)"[19] changes into "Something" in the process of the work's active interpretation by the recipient. This kind of "double negation" gesture is to express a striving towards the "defalsification of the word" and to give the piece the character of a "remedy, a cure, for the state of inequality between the artist and his public."[20]

What Dróżdż's installation proves is that the status of autonomy ascribed to conceptual works in the 1970s did not make them devoid of contextual references. What was manifest in them were attitudes critical of the order of representation written into the ideological space of "ideosis." These critical comments were not direct; described by the seemingly politically "safe" formula of analytical art, they performed the function of deluding the regime's "evil eye." The optical experiments effected by Krzysztof Wodiczko in *Ladder* (*Drabina*) and in *Drawing of a Stool* (*Rysunek taboretu*) and *Drawing of a Line* (*Rysunek linii*) made possible points of view other than just those determined by the rules of representation in 1974. They prescribed no particular order in which they should be visited, instead situating the viewer inside an ambiguous space defined only by the physical dimensions of the room. The technical aspect of Wodiczko's works, including his *Vehicle* (*Pojazd*, 1973), suggested an attitude of disobedience towards the social life-regulating mechanism of socialist production.

In the late 1960s and early 1970s, Jerzy Ludwiński described the "shrinking" of artistic process—its ongoing reduction to the initial phase of formulating an idea for an action or to the final phase of presenting its documentation.[21] If Władysław Strzemiński emphasized several decades earlier the opticality of a work of art—the above-mentioned "simultaneity of the spatial-visual phenomenon"—Jerzy Ludwiński questioned its purely visual character by describing it with a

Dróżdż' Installation *Zwischen* (*Między*, Abb. 7, S. 50) spielte mit dem Begriff des als unabhängig klassifizierten Werks, das in einem Zustand der Isolierung verbleibt. Hier scheint es, als hätte Dróżdż eine Art Implosion bestimmter Parameter zur Aufführung gebracht, um eine semantische Umkehrung des verwendeten Wortes zu bewirken, wie Jacek Wesołowski nahelegte. Der Künstler vertauschte die Buchstaben, aus denen das Wort „zwischen" besteht, miteinander und legte ihre Lage und ihren Winkel präzise fest. Die uniforme, systematische Verteilung der Lettern über Wände und Decke ist damit als ein selbstreflektierender Kommentar zu den komplexen Beziehungen „zwischen" den einzelnen Buchstaben und Buchstabenfolgen zu lesen sowie als eine Positionsbestimmung des Betrachters, während sich dieser durch den Raum des Werks bewegt.

Die Auflösung der linearen Ordnung des Titelwortes und das Einschreiben seiner Buchstaben in eine räumliche Struktur sollte laut Wesołowski zur Umkehrung der ursprünglichen Wortbedeutung führen: „Zwischen", verstanden als „nichts (nicht dies)"[19], verändert sich im Laufe der aktiven Rezeption durch den Betrachter zu „etwas". In dieser Geste einer „doppelten Verneinung" drückt sich das Streben nach einer „Entfalsifizierung des Wortes" aus; sie soll dem Werk den Charakter einer „Arznei, eines Heilmittels, gegen die Ungleichheit zwischen dem Künstler und seiner Öffentlichkeit" verleihen.[20]

Die Installation von Dróżdż belegt, dass der Status der Unabhängigkeit, der konzeptuellen Werken in den 1970er-Jahren zugesprochen wurde, ihnen nicht alle kontextuellen Verweise nahm. In ihnen manifestierten sich kritische Haltungen gegenüber der im ideologischen Raum der „Ideosis" festgeschriebenen Darstellungsordnung. Diese kritischen Kommentare waren nicht direkter Natur: Charakterisiert durch die scheinbar politisch „sichere" Formel der analytischen Kunst, erfüllten sie die Aufgabe, den „bösen Blick" des Regimes zu täuschen. Die optischen Experimente, die Krzysztof Wodiczko 1974 in *Leiter* (*Drabina*), in *Zeichnung eines Hockers* (*Rysunek taboretu*) und in *Zeichnung einer Linie* (*Rysunek linii*) durchführte, machten andere Sichtweisen möglich, als nur jene, die durch die sanktionierten Repräsentationsformen festgelegt waren. Sie gaben keine Reihenfolge der Betrachtung vor, sondern platzierten den Betrachter an einem mehrdeutigen Ort, der lediglich durch die physische Ausdehnung des Raums definiert war. Der technische Aspekt von Wodiczkos Arbeiten, zum Beispiel sein *Fahrzeug* (*Pojazd*, 1973), verriet eine Widerstandshaltung gegenüber der sozialistischen Produktion als einem Mechanismus, der das gesellschaftliche Leben regelte.

Ende der 1960er-, Anfang der 1970er-Jahre sprach Jerzy Ludwiński von einem „Schrumpfen" des künstlerischen Prozesses, von seiner stetigen Reduzierung entweder auf die Anfangsphase der Formulierung einer Idee für eine Aktion oder auf die Schlussphase, auf die Präsentation der Dokumentation zum Werk.[21] Wenn Władysław Strzemiński einige Jahrzehnte zuvor die Optik des Kunstwerks hervorgehoben hatte – die oben genannte „Gleichzeitigkeit der räumlich-visuellen Erscheinung" –, so hinterfragte Jerzy Ludwiński nun dessen rein visuellen Charakter, indem er ihn mit der Kategorie der Abwesenheit beschrieb: Für ihn entfaltete ein Kunstwerk seine Wirkung

category of absence. For him, a work of art functioned "between" the formula for an action and its documentation. Hence the proposals of conceptual artists are characterized by the tendency to isolate the meaning of a work; freed from the postulate of defining the special character of a particular artistic discipline, they neutralize the optical status of a work. Their interest in the neutrality of the artistic medium and in the purity of the artistic message motivated practices which subverted politically sanctioned modes of representation.

Notes:

1 This essay is a modified version of Paweł Polit's text published in Polish as "Odpowiedź Strzemińskiemu. Idea jednolitości w twórczości polskich artystów konceptualnych," in *Artium Quaestiones XVI* (2005). It includes excerpts from other texts by Polit: "Can one be late for the end of the history of Foksal Gallery?" in *We See You: Foksal Gallery Activities 1966–1989*, ed. Karolina Łabowicz Dymanus (Warsaw: Galeria Foksal MCKiS, 2009); "Shattering the Monoliths of Meaning. On Conceptual Art in Foksal Gallery," in *Galeria Foksal 1966–2016*, ed. Michał Jachuła, Justyna Wesołowska (Warsaw: Galeria Foksal, Mazowiecki Instytut Kultury, 2016).

2 Władysław Strzemiński, *Unizm w malarstwie* (Warszawa: Biblioteka „Praesens," Nr. 3, 1928), 11. In fact, Strzemiński's program anticipated certain solutions proposed by American critic Clement Greenberg in the 1930s, according to whom the arrangement of forms and colors in a painting should serve the function of defining the specificity of the painterly medium. See Clement Greenberg, "Towards a Newer Laocoon," in *Partisan Review*, Vol. VII, Nr. 4, July–August 1940.

3 Strzemiński, *Unizm w malarstwie*, op. cit.

4 Ibid., 12.

5 Ibid.

6 "Struktura, Wyobraźnia, Wszechświat. O problemie strukturalizmu z Włodzimierzem Borowskim rozmawia Luiza Nader," in *Grupa Zamek. Włodzimierz Borowski*, exh. cat., (Muzeum Sztuki w Łodzi 2002), 17.

7 This interpretation has been proposed by Jerzy Ludwiński, "The Mimicry of Neutrdrome," in Ludwiński, *Notes from the Future of Art: Selected Writings by Jerzy Ludwiński*, ed. Magdalena Ziółkowska (Eindhoven: Van Abbemuseum Public Research # 1, 2007).

8 Włodzimierz Borowski, "Mirror Manifesto," in *Włodzimierz Borowski. Ślady / Traces 1956–1992*, exh. cat., ed. Jarosław Kozłowski, Centre for Contemporary Art Ujazdowski Castle (Warsaw, 1998), 46.

9 Zygmunt Korus, "Rozmowa z Jerzym Ludwińskim," in *Integracje*, Vol. VII, 1979, 52.

10 Wiesław Borowski, "Nurt apikturalny w Galerii Foksal PSP," *Poezja*, Vol. 5, 1971, 104.

11 Ibid., 104.

12 Joanna Mytkowska, "Interview with Edward Krasiński," in *Edward Krasiński*, exh. cat., Fundacja Galerii Foksal (Warsaw, 1997), 69.

13 The crisis in question was the turning point between two consecutive phases of "real socialism" in Poland: Władysław Gomułka's era (1956–1970) and Edward Gierek's era (1970–1980).

14 These events were, in chronological order, *Wrocław '70* artists' symposium (March 1970), the seventh meeting of artists in Osieki (August 1970) and the exhibition *Conceptual Art* (*Sztuka pojęciowa*) at Wrocław's Mona Liza Gallery (December 1970).

„zwischen" der Formel für eine Aktion und deren Dokumentation. So zeichneten sich die Positionen der konzeptuellen Künstler durch die Tendenz aus, die Bedeutung einer Arbeit zu isolieren; befreit von der Forderung, die besondere Eigenschaft einer bestimmten künstlerischen Disziplin definieren zu müssen, neutralisierten sie den visuellen Status des Werks. Ihr Interesse an der Neutralität des Mediums und an der Reinheit der künstlerischen Aussage regte zu Praktiken an, die politisch sanktionierte Repräsentationsformen unterminierten.

Anmerkungen:

1 Dieser Essay ist eine überarbeitete Fassung eines Texts von Paweł Polit, der in polnischer Sprache erschienen ist: „Odpowiedź Strzemińskiemu. Idea jednolitości w twórczości polskich artystów konceptualnych", *Artium Quaestiones XVI*, 2005. Er enthält auch Ausschnitte aus anderen Texten von Polit: „Can one be late for the end of the history of Foksal Gallery?", in: *We See You: Foksal Gallery Activities 1966–1989*, hrsg. von Karolina Łabowicz Dymanus, Galeria Foksal MCKiS, Warschau 2009; „Shattering the Monoliths of Meaning. On Conceptual Art in Foksal Gallery", in: *Galeria Foksal 1966–2016*, hrsg. von Michał Jachuła, Justyna Wesołowska, Galeria Foksal, Mazowiecki Instytut Kultury, Warschau 2016.

2 Władysław Strzemiński, *Unizm w malarstwie*, Biblioteka „Praesens" Nr. 3, Warschau 1928, S. 11. Tatsächlich nahm Strzemińskis Programm bestimmte Lösungsansätze des amerikanischen Kritikers Clement Greenberg aus den 1930er-Jahren vorweg. Ihnen zufolge sollte die Anordnung von Formen und Farben in einem Bild die Funktion haben, die Besonderheit des Mediums der Malerei zu definieren. Siehe Clement Greenberg, „Towards a Newer Laocoon", Partisan Review, VII, Nr. 4, Juli–August 1940.

3 Strzemiński, *Unizm w malarstwie*, op. cit.

4 Ibidem, S. 12.

5 Ibidem.

6 „Struktura, Wyobraźnia, Wszechświat. O problemie strukturalizmu z Włodzimierzem Borowskim rozmawia Luiza Nader", in: *Grupa Zamek. Włodzimierz Borowski*, exh. cat., Muzeum Sztuki, Łódź 2002, S. 17.

7 Der Vorschlag zu dieser Interpretation stammt von Jerzy Ludwiński, „The Mimicry of Neutrdrome", in: Ludwiński, *Notes from the Future of Art: Selected Writings by Jerzy Ludwiński*, hrsg. von Magdalena Ziółkowska, Van Abbemuseum, Eindhoven, Public Research # 1, 2007.

8 Włodzimierz Borowski, „Mirror Manifesto", in: *Włodzimierz Borowski. Ślady / Traces 1956–1992*, Ausst.-Kat., hrsg. von Jarosław Kozłowski, Centre for Contemporary Art Ujazdowski Castle, Warschau 1998, S. 46.

9 Zygmunt Korus, „Rozmowa z Jerzym Ludwińskim", *Integracje* VII, 1979, S. 52.

10 Wiesław Borowski, „Nurt apikturalny w Galerii Foksal PSP", *Poezja 5*, 1971, S. 104

11 Ibidem, S. 104.

12 Joanna Mytkowska, „Interview with Edward Krasiński," in: *Edward Krasiński*, Ausst.-Kat. Fundacja Galerii Foksal, Warschau 1997, S. 69.

13 Die Krise, von der hier die Rede ist, war der Wendepunkt zwischen zwei aufeinanderfolgenden Phasen des „Realsozialismus" in Polen: der Ära Władysław Gomułka (1956–1970) und der Ära Edward Gierek (1970–1980).

15 Symptomatic of this turn was the conception of art as "isolated message" announced in 1971 by Foksal Gallery critics Wiesław Borowski and Andrzej Turowski in their statements "Dokumentacja" and "Żywe archiwum," in *Tadeusz Kantor w Archiwum Galerii Foksal*, ed. Małgorzata Jurkiewicz, Joanna Mytkowska, Andrzej Przywara (Warszawa: Galeria Foksal SBWA, 1998).

16 Jerzy Ludwiński, Paweł Polit, "Nowość w sztuce jest miarą wyobraźni artysty," in *Obieg*, 19.01.2006, http://archiwum-obieg.u-jazdowski.pl/rozmowy/5726, last accessed 08.04.2018.

17 Andrzej Turowski, "Polska ideoza," in *Sztuka polska po 1945 roku*, Association of Art Historians symposium materials, Warsaw, November 1984 (Warsaw: PWN, 1987), 36.

18 O związkach "pojęciokształtów" Dróżdża z unizmem Strzemińskiego pisał Adam Szymczyk, "Means More, Before It Means," in *Stanisław Dróżdż: Conceptiforms. Concrete Poetry 1967–2003*, ed. Andrzej Przywara (Fundacja Galerii Foksal, Warsaw 2014).

19 Jacek Wesołowski, "Between," typescript, Galeria Foksal archive.

20 Ibid.

21 See Jerzy Ludwiński, "Art in the Postartistic Age," "Unidentified Art" and "Neutralization of Criteria," in Ludwiński, *Notes from the Future of Art*, op. cit.

14 Diese Ereignisse waren, in chronologischer Reinfolge, *Wrocław '70* (ein Künstlersymposion im März 1970), das 7. Künstlertreffen Osieki (im August 1970) und die Ausstellung „Konzeptuelle Kunst" (*Sztuka pojęciowa*) in der Galerie Mona Lisa, Wrocław (Dezember 1970).

15 Symptomatisch für diese Wende war der Begriff der Kunst als eine „isolierte Aussage", so benannt durch die Kritiker der Galerie Foksal Wiesław Borowski und Andrzej Turowski in ihren Stellungnahmen „Dokumentacja" und „Żywe archiwum" im Jahr 1971, in: *Tadeusz Kantor w Archiwum Galerii Foksal*, hrsg. von Małgorzata Jurkiewicz, Joanna Mytkowska, Andrzej Przywara, Galeria Foksal SBWA, Warschau 1998.

16 Jerzy Ludwiński, Paweł Polit, „Nowość w sztuce jest miarą wyobraźni artysty", *Obieg*, 19.01.2006, http://archiwum-obieg.u-jazdowski.pl/rozmowy/5726, abgerufen am 08.04.2018.

17 Andrzej Turowski, „Polska ideoza", in: *Sztuka polska po 1945 roku*, Materialien des Kunsthistoriker-Symposions in Warschau im November 1984, Warschau 1987, S. 36.

18 O związkach „pojęciokształtów" Dróżdża z unizmem Strzemińskiego pisał Adam Szymczyk, „Means More, Before It Means", in: *Stanisław Dróżdż: Conceptiforms. Concrete Poetry 1967–2003*, hrsg. von Andrzej Przywara, Fundacja Galerii Foksal, Warschau 2014.

19 Jacek Wesołowski, „Between", Manuskript, Archiv Galeria Foksal.

20 Ibidem.

21 Siehe Jerzy Ludwiński, „Art in the Postartistic Age", „Unidentified Art" und „Neutralization of Criteria", in: Ludwiński, *Notes from the Future of Art*, op. cit.

SPRACH- UND BILDANALYSE 1

LANGUAGE AND IMAGE ANALYSIS 1

Stanisław Dróżdż

Barbara Kozłowska

Natalia LL

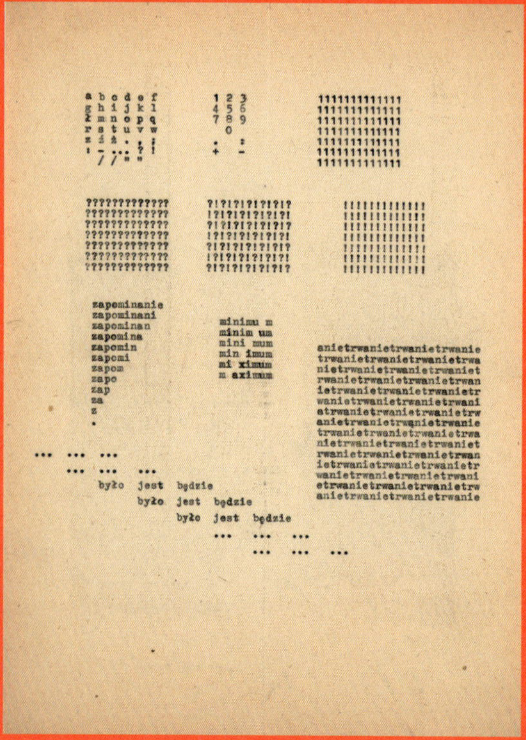

Stanisław Dróżdż
Ohne Titel / Untitled, ca. | around 1969
Schreibmaschine auf Papier |
typescript on paper
29,7 × 21 cm
Staatliche Kunstsammlungen Dresden,
Archiv der Avantgarden – Egidio Marzona

Konkrete Poesie und Performance

Concrete Poetry and Performance

In concrete poetry, words, letters and punctuation are freed from everyday usage. Since the late 1960s, Stanisław Dróżdż has playfully developed his poetry with radically abbreviated symbols, emphasising their visual form. He made his mark both theoretically, with his idea for *Concept Shapes* (*Pojęciokształty*), which constitutes a seminal artistic direction for Wrocław, as well as with his work, as in *Untitled* (*Forgetting*, 1967/1972). His walk-in installation *In Between* (*Między*, 1977) expanded the practice of experimental language with a typewriter-printed sheet of paper. The artist Barbara Kozłowska took up this theme. In addition to arranging ideograms (image poetry), she addressed norms and naming practices in her text-based performances *Point of View* (*Punkt Widzenia*, 1977/78) and *Arrythmia, Anatomy Lesson* (*Arytmia, Lekcja anatomii*, 1980) She uses her body as a medium for a critique of language and perception. Analytical-conceptual processes such as listing, repetition and reduction, also featured in the photography of Natalia LL. At the same time, she boycotted these processes through conscious exaggeration and provocation. In her series on *Consumer Art* (*Sztuka konsumpcyjna*, 1970s) she played with the Western pornography aesthetic, having an actress excessively parse the fetishization of women as advertising objects and food as consumer items.

K. K.

In der Konkreten Poesie sind Wörter, Buchstaben und Satzzeichen von ihrem alltäglichen Gebrauch losgelöst. Ab den späten 1960er-Jahren entwickelte Stanisław Dróżdż spielerisch seine Poesien mit radikal verknappten Zeichen und betonte ihre visuelle Gestaltung. Er prägte sowohl theoretisch mit seinem Konzept der *Begriffsgestalten* (*Pojęciokształty*) maßgeblich diese für Wrocław so wegweisende künstlerische Richtung als auch mit seinen Arbeiten wie *Ohne Titel* (*Vergessen*, 1967/1972). Mit seiner begehbaren Installation *Zwischen* (*Między*, 1977) erweitert er die experimentelle Sprachpraxis über das mit Schreibmaschine bedruckte Blatt Papier hinaus. Hieran knüpfte die Künstlerin Barbara Kozłowska an. Neben dem Arrangieren von Kaligrammen (Bildgedichten) verhandelte sie in ihren textbasierten Performances *Point of View* (*Punkt Widzenia*, 1977/78) und *Arrhythmie, Anatomiestunde* (*Arytmia, Lekcja anatomii*, 1980) Normen und Benennungspraktiken. Ihren Körper setzte sie dabei als ein Medium zur Sprach- und Erkenntniskritik ein. Mit den analytisch-konzeptuellen Verfahren wie Reihung, Wiederholung und Reduktion arbeitete auch Natalia LL in ihren Fotoarbeiten, boykottierte diese allerdings zugleich durch bewusstes Übertreiben und Provozieren. In ihren Serien zur *Consumer Art* (*Sztuka konsumpcyjna*, 1970er-Jahre) spielte sie mit der westlichen Porno-Ästhetik und ließ exzessiv eine Schauspielerin das Fetischisieren von Frauen als Werbe-Objekt und von Nahrungsmitteln als Konsumartikel durchdeklinieren.

K. K.

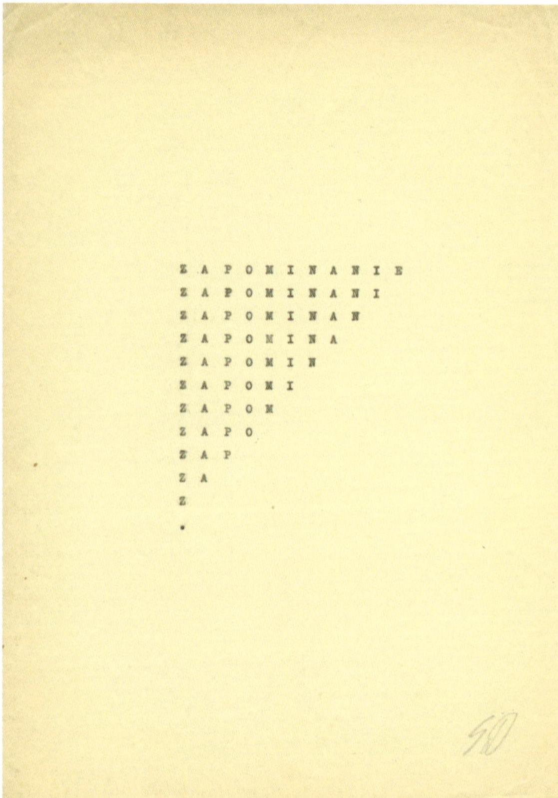

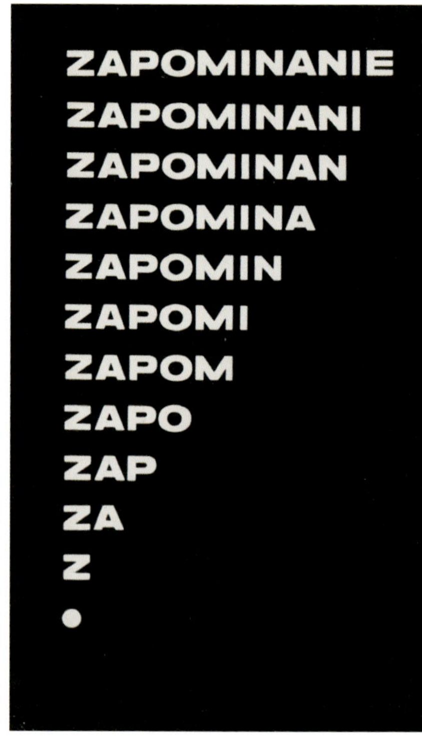

Stanisław Dróżdż

Stanisław Dróżdż
Bez tytułu (Zapominanie) / Ohne Titel (Vergessen) / Untitled (Forgetting), 1967
Schreibmaschine auf Papier | typescript on paper
29,6 × 21 cm
Courtesy ŻAK | BRANICKA, Berlin

Stanisław Dróżdż
Bez tytułu (Zapominanie) / Ohne Titel (Vergessen) / Untitled (Forgetting), 1972
Fotografie | photograph
17,2 × 10,8 cm
Courtesy ŻAK | BRANICKA, Berlin

Stanisław Dróżdż
Ohne Titel (Vergessen), 2018
Installationsansicht | installation view
Kupferstich-Kabinett, Dresden
Courtesy ŻAK | BRANICKA, Berlin

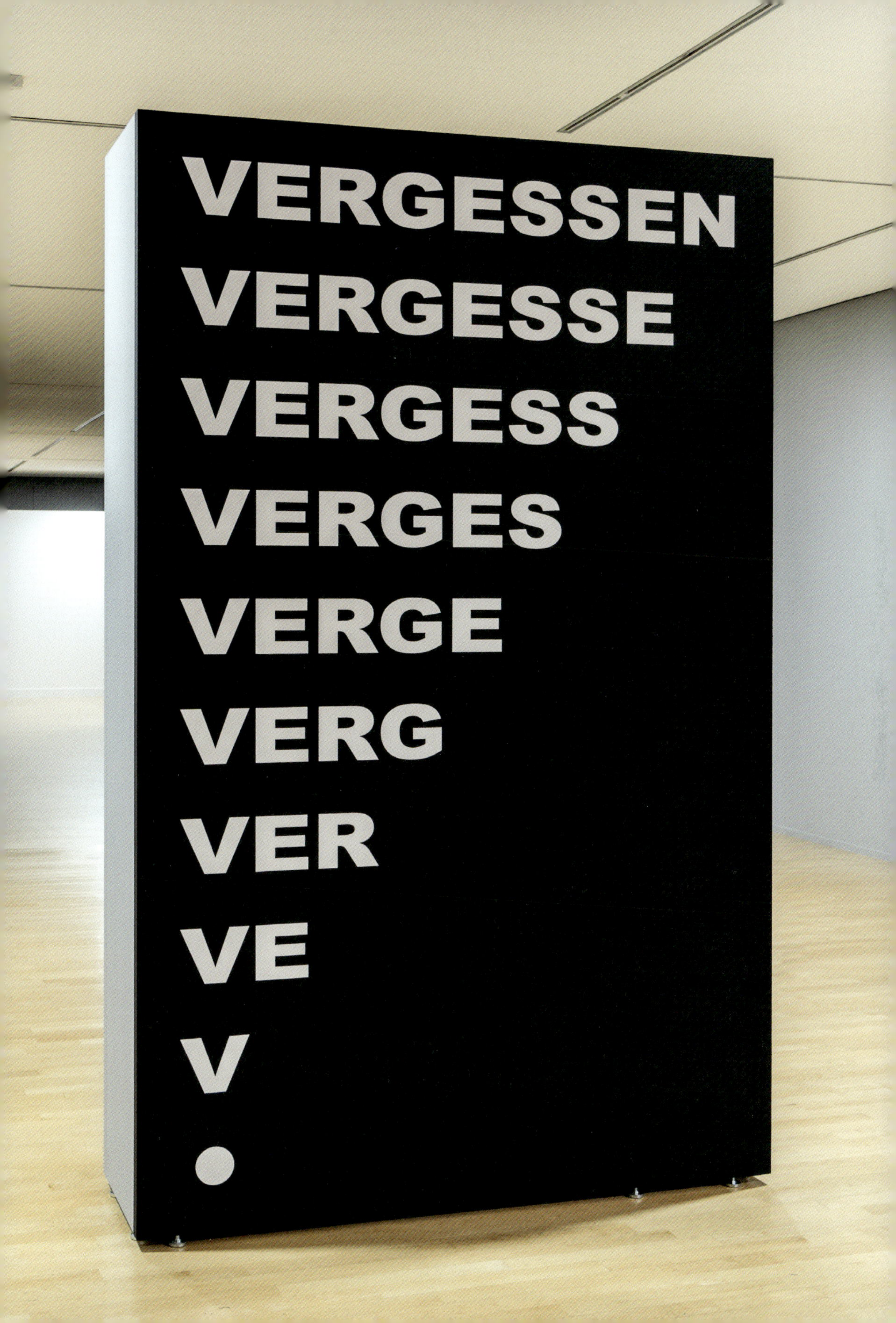
VERGESSEN
VERGESSE
VERGESS
VERGES
VERGE
VERG
VER
VE
V

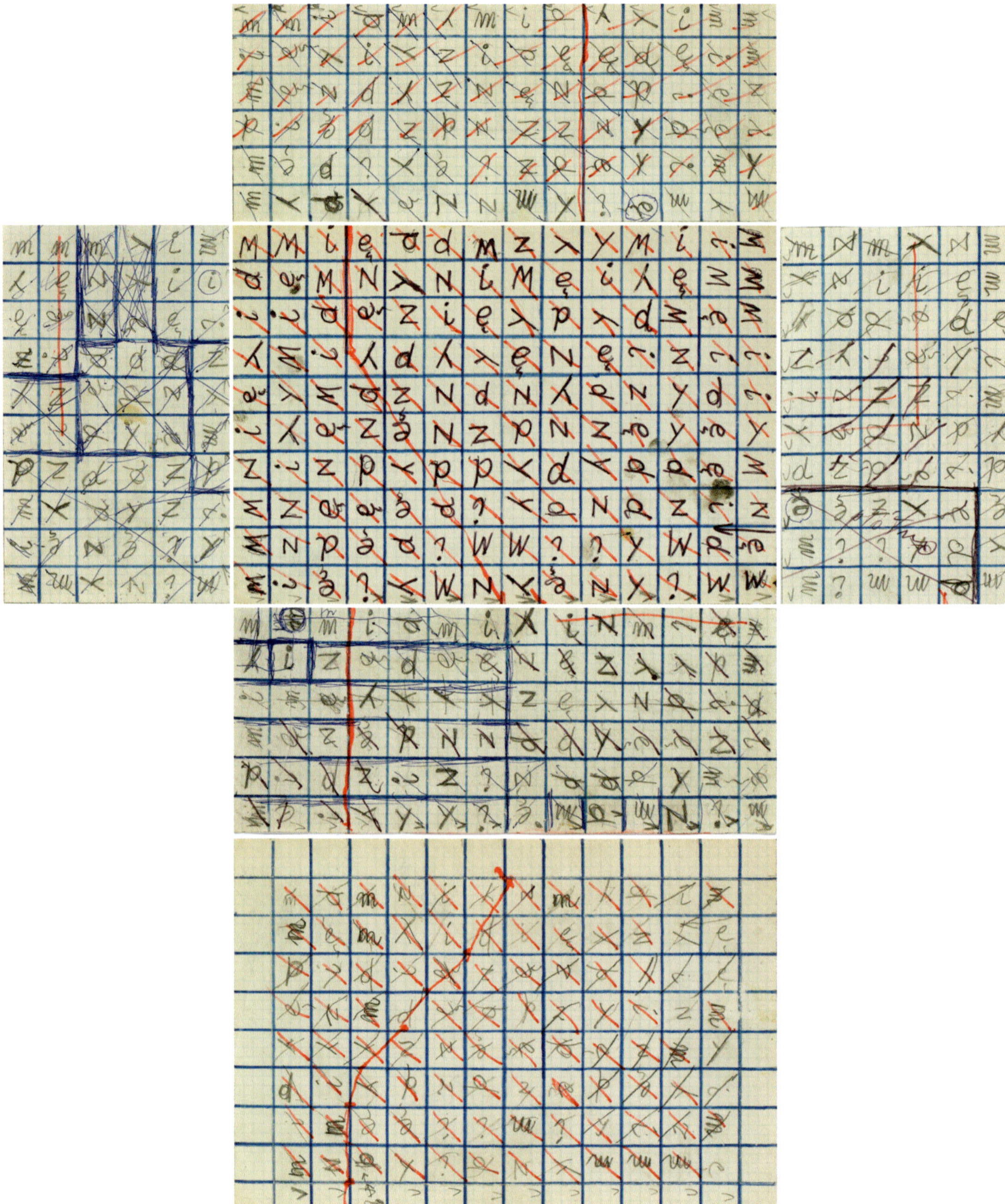

Stanisław Dróżdż
Entwurf zu *Między* | draft of *Między*, 1973
Bleistift und Filzstifte auf Papier |
pencil and felt-tip pens on paper
6 Blätter | 6 sheets
Muzeum Sztuki w Łodzi
Installationsansicht 1977, S. 50, Abb. 7 |
installation view 1977, p. 50, ill. 7

Stanisław Dróżdż

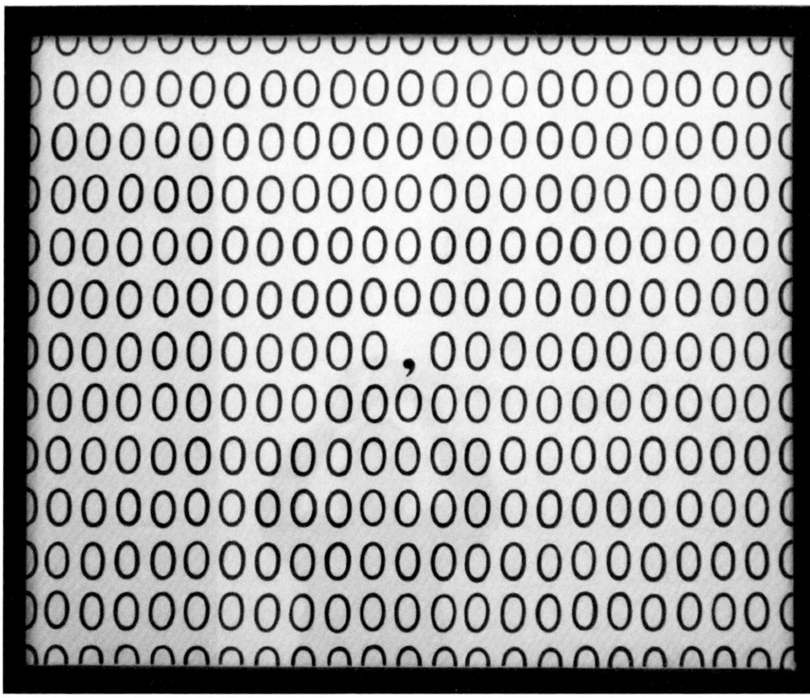

Stanisław Dróżdż
Continuum, 1973
Fotografie | photograph
71 × 83,5 cm
Courtesy ŻAK | BRANICKA, Berlin

Stanisław Dróżdż

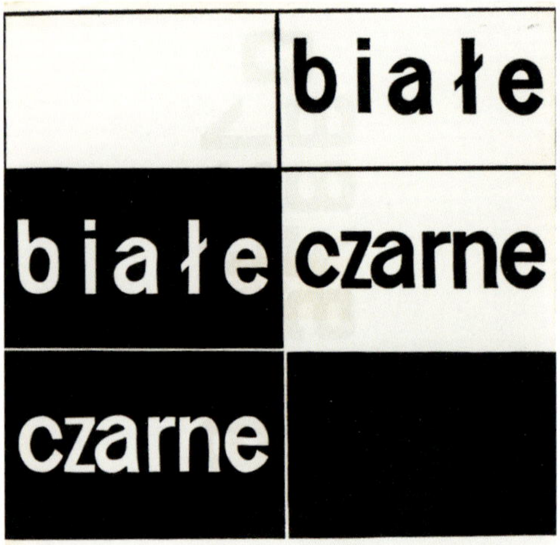

Stanisław Dróżdż
Pojęciokształty-poezja konkretna / Begriffsgestalten – Konkrete Poesie / Concept-Shapes – Concrete Poetry
Ausschnitt | detail, Katalog | catalogue, Galeria Foksal, o. J. | n. d.
Staatliche Kunstsammlungen Dresden, Archiv der Avantgarden – Egidio Marzona

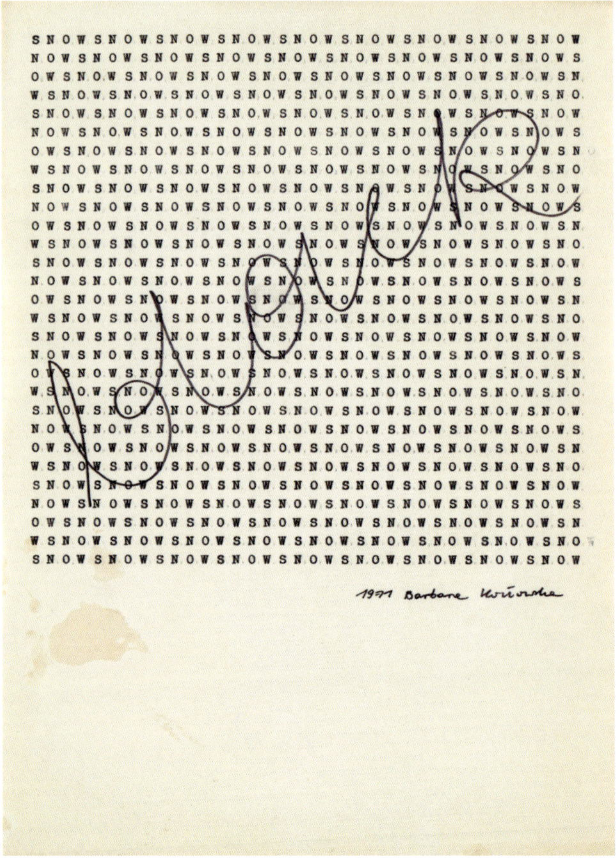

Barbara Kozłowska
Ohne Titel / Untitled, 1971
Schreibmaschine und Handschrift auf Papier | typescript and handwriting on paper
29,4 × 20,7 cm
Staatliche Kunstsammlungen Dresden, Archiv der Avantgarden – Egidio Marzona

Barbara Kozłowska
Arytmia, Lekcja anatomii / Arrhythmie, Anatomiestunde / Arrhythmia, Anatomy Lesson, 1980
3 Fotografien | 3 photographs
je | each 23,5 × 18 cm
Courtesy ŻAK | BRANICKA, Berlin

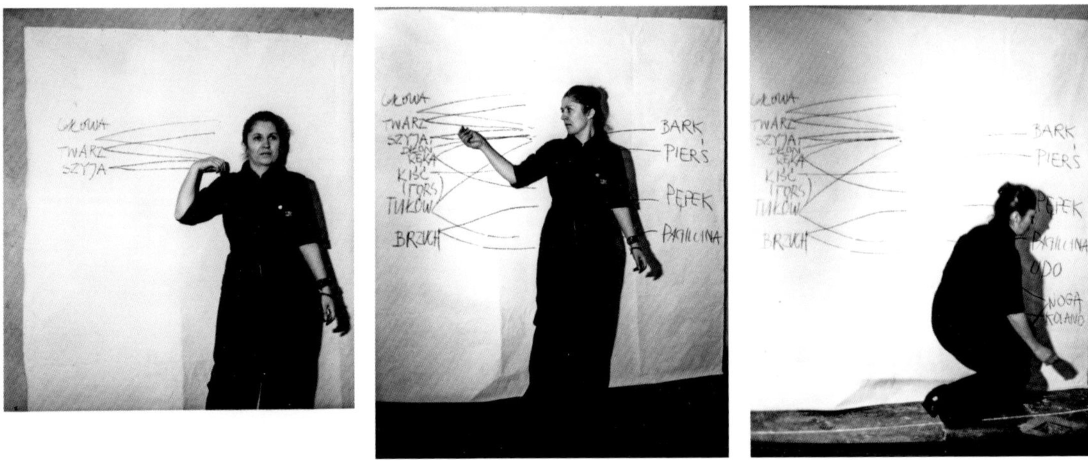

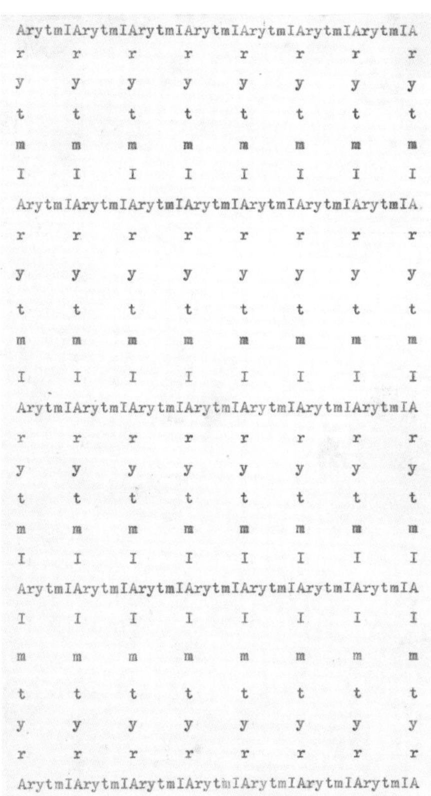

Barbara Kozłowska

Barbara Kozłowska
Arytmia / Arrhythmie / Arrhythmia, 1980
Schreibmaschine auf Papier | typescript on paper
22,3 × 12,3 cm
Staatliche Kunstsammlungen Dresden, Archiv der Avantgarden – Egidio Marzona

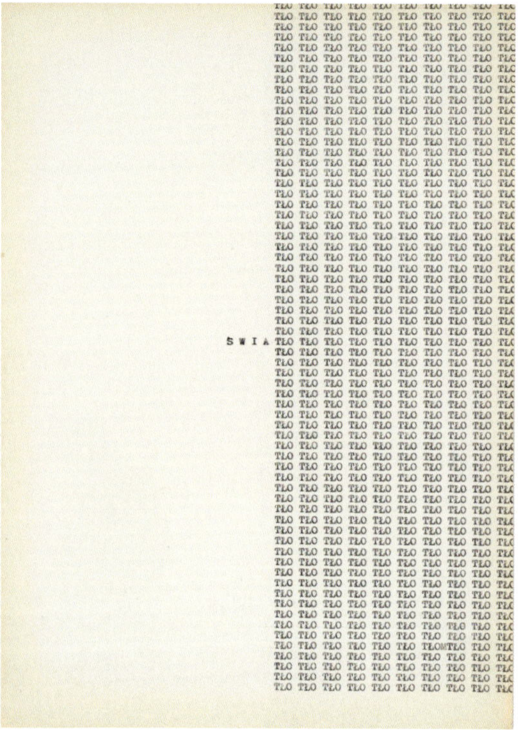

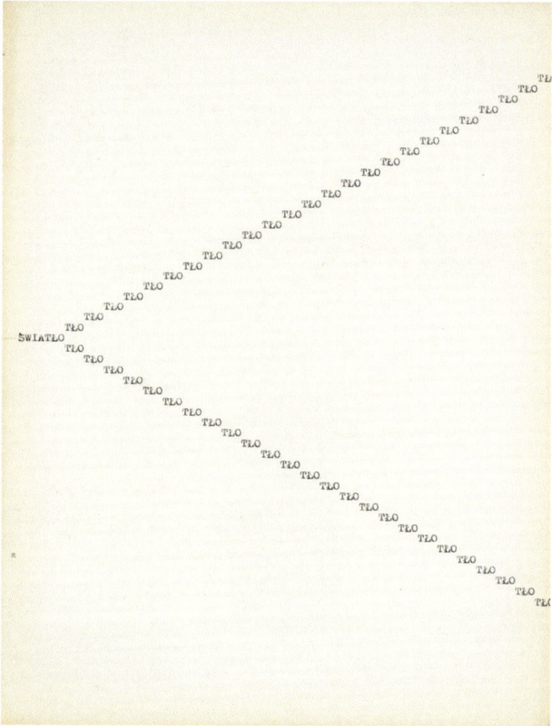

Barbara Kozłowska

Barbara Kozłowska
Swiatło-Tło / Licht-Hintergrund / Light-Background, 1973
Schreibmaschine auf Papier | typescript on paper
2 Blätter | 2 sheets, je | each 29,7 × 21 cm
Staatliche Kunstsammlungen Dresden,
Archiv der Avantgarden – Egidio Marzona

Natalia LL

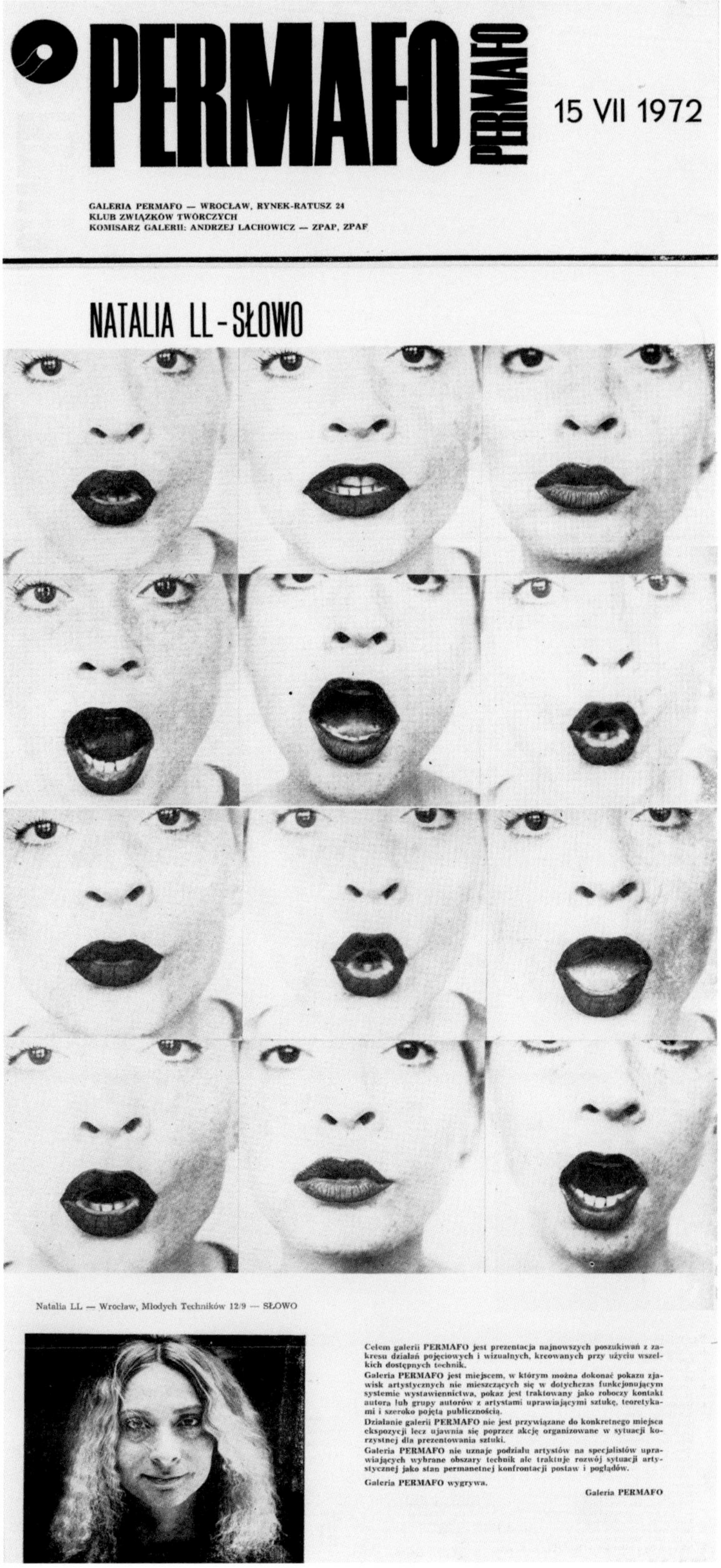

PERMAFO PERMAFO

15 VII 1972

GALERIA PERMAFO — WROCŁAW, RYNEK-RATUSZ 24
KLUB ZWIĄZKÓW TWÓRCZYCH
KOMISARZ GALERII: ANDRZEJ LACHOWICZ — ZPAP, ZPAF

NATALIA LL-SŁOWO

Natalia LL — Wrocław, Młodych Techników 12/9 — SŁOWO

Celem galerii PERMAFO jest prezentacja najnowszych poszukiwań z zakresu działań pojęciowych i wizualnych, kreowanych przy użyciu wszelkich dostępnych technik.

Galeria PERMAFO jest miejscem, w którym można dokonać pokazu zjawisk artystycznych nie mieszczących się w dotychczas funkcjonującym systemie wystawiennictwa, pokaz jest traktowany jako roboczy kontakt autora lub grupy autorów z artystami uprawiającymi sztukę, teoretykami i szeroko pojętą publicznością.

Działanie galerii PERMAFO nie jest przywiązane do konkretnego miejsca ekspozycji lecz ujawnia się poprzez akcję organizowane w sytuacji korzystnej dla prezentowania sztuki.

Galeria PERMAFO nie uznaje podziału artystów na specjalistów uprawiających wybrane obszary technik ale traktuje rozwój sytuacji artystycznej jako stan permanetnej konfrontacji postaw i poglądów.

Galeria PERMAFO wygrywa.

Galeria PERMAFO

Natalia LL
Słowo / A Word, 1972
Faltblatt | foldout
Galeria Permafo, Wrocław
66 × 29,5 cm
Staatliche Kunstsammlungen Dresden,
Archiv der Avantgarden – Egidio Marzona

Natalia LL

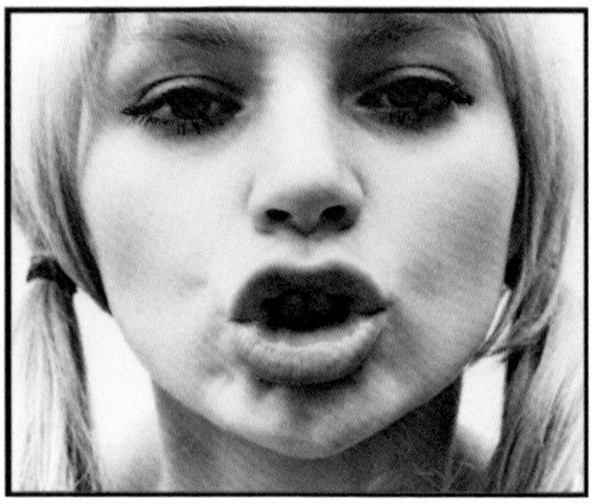
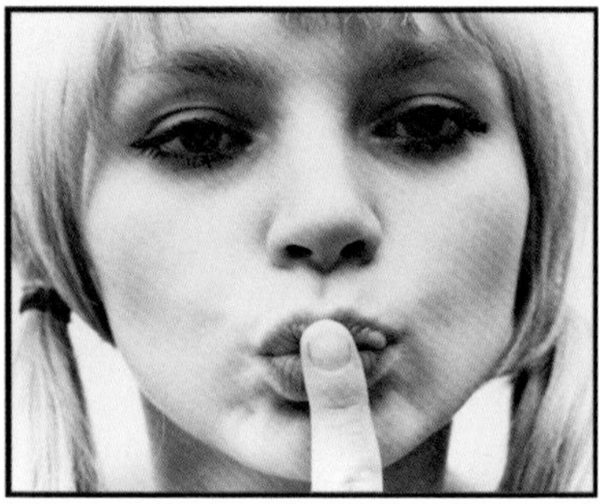
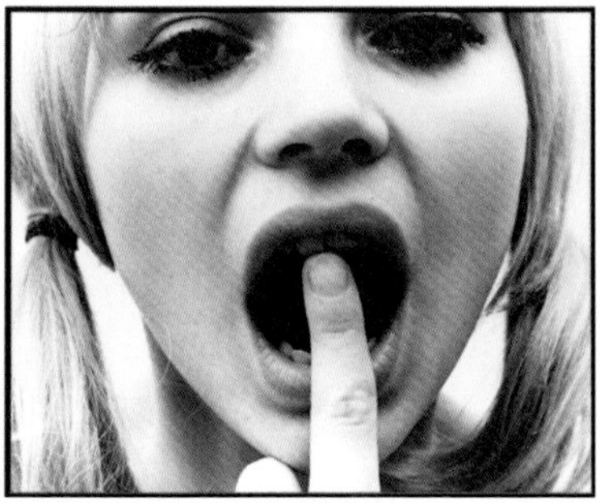

Natalia LL
Sztuka konsumpcyjna / Consumer Art, 1972
6 Fotografien | 6 photographs
je | each 50 × 60 cm
Staatliche Kunstsammlungen Dresden,
Schenkung Sammlung Hoffmann

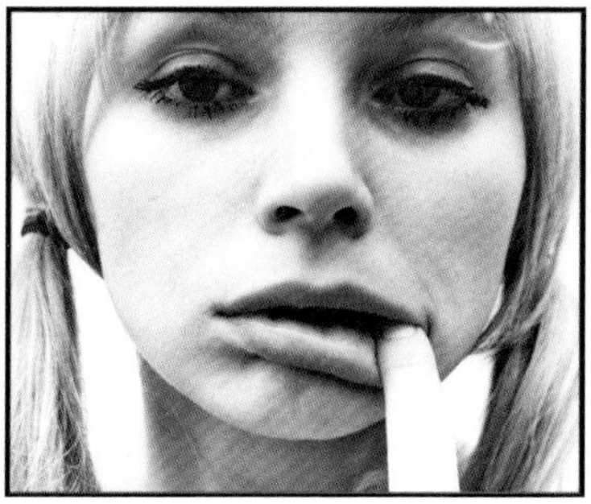
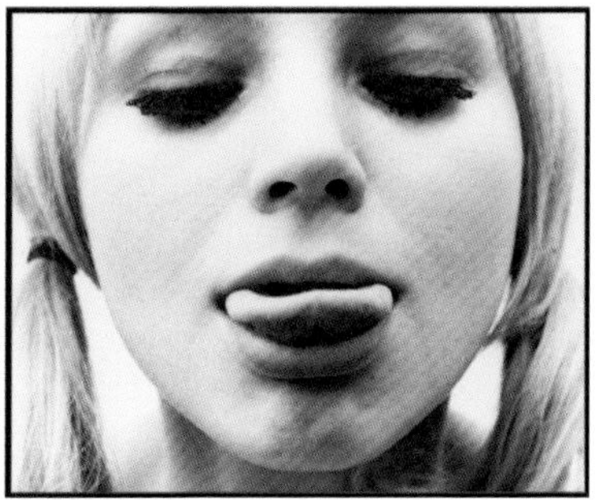
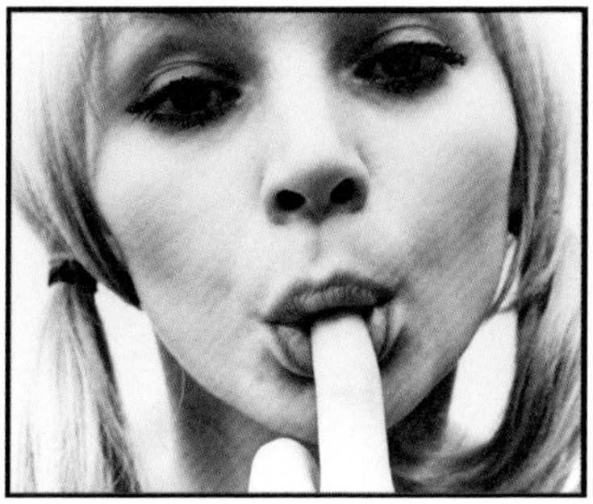

THE SELF-INTERROGATION OF THE ARTIST. REMARKS ON FEMINIST ART IN THE POLISH PEOPLE'S REPUBLIC

Constance Krüger

In her nine-part photo series *Categorical Statements from the Sphere of Post-Consumer Art, October 1975*, (ill. 1, p. 71) Natalia LL occupies the full image, sitting in different positions: comfortably leaning back, provocatively spreading her legs, looking inquiringly into the camera, eating a banana, or swinging with her legs casually. The artist appears to ask, "Which positions suit me as a woman? Which are appropriate, erotic, obscene? Which poses count as masculine, which as feminine?" Natalia LL conjugates an everyday, internalized, and highly gendered bodily language through her own body, adopting masculine-connoted attitudes in the process. She presents herself as a self-confident female artist, on the same level with her male colleagues. This self-confidence was present in a lot of Polish women artists of the 1970s. They put themselves into the picture and develop their own artistic programs, which are necessarily individual, private, and personal. Essentialist concepts, in which the female body is assigned an innate power are treated here in the exact same way as structural concepts, in which the role of the female artist as part of society is reflected.

In the performance *Lady's Smock. Rzeżucha* (1975), Teresa Murak wears a linen shirt sprinkled with cress seeds (ill. 2, p. 72). Through proximity to her bodily warmth and constant watering, a green plant dress emerged, which Murak subsequently presented in urban space and then exhibited in a gallery. The female body functions here as a creator of life and art. Through the reference to the life-giving quality of the female body, the artist ascribes an *ur*-female creative power to herself—a feminist alternative to the myth of male demiurges.

The female body also brings forth art in Ewa Partum's work. *The Poem by Ewa* (1975) refers to the authentic proportions of Partum's female body as the origin of art. Language emerges here through the performative act of pressing the strongly red painted lips of the artist on paper. Here, Partum announces a woman artist who speaks with female means. In her work *Change* (*Zmiana*, 1974), the artist had a professional make-up artist artificially alter half of her face (ill. p. 76). Partum takes on the conceptual work, the execution she puts in someone else's hands. Her body functions

DIE SELBSTBEFRAGUNG DER KÜNSTLERIN. ANMERKUNGEN ZUR FEMINISTISCHEN KUNST IN DER VOLKSREPUBLIK POLEN

Constance Krüger

In ihrer neunteiligen Fotografie-Serie *Categorical Statements from the Sphere of Post-Consumer Art, October 1975* (Abb. 1) nimmt Natalia LL bildfüllend verschiedene Sitzpositionen ein: einmal gemütlich zurückgelehnt, dann aufreizend die Beine gespreizt, einmal forsch in die Kamera blickend oder eine Banane essend, dann lässig mit den Beinen schlenkernd. Die Künstlerin scheint hier zu fragen: Welche Positionen stehen mir als Frau zu, welche gelten als angemessen, als erotisch, als obszön? Welche Posen gelten als männlich, welche als weiblich? Natalia LL dekliniert die alltägliche verinnerlichte und hochgradig geschlechtsspezifische Körpersprache am eigenen Leib durch und eignet sich dabei auch männlich konnotierte Haltungen an. Sie präsentiert sich als selbstbewusste Künstlerin auf Augenhöhe mit ihren männlichen Kollegen. Dieses Selbstbewusstsein zeigt sich bei vielen polnischen Künstlerinnen der 1970er-Jahre. Sie setzen sich selbst ins Bild und entwickeln ihr eigenes künstlerisches Programm. Und dieses kann gar nicht anders sein als individuell, privat und persönlich. Essentialistische Ansätze, in denen dem weiblichen Körper eine ureigene Kraft zugeschrieben wird, werden dabei genauso verhandelt wie strukturelle Ansätze, in denen die Rolle der Künstlerin als Teil der Gesellschaft reflektiert wird.

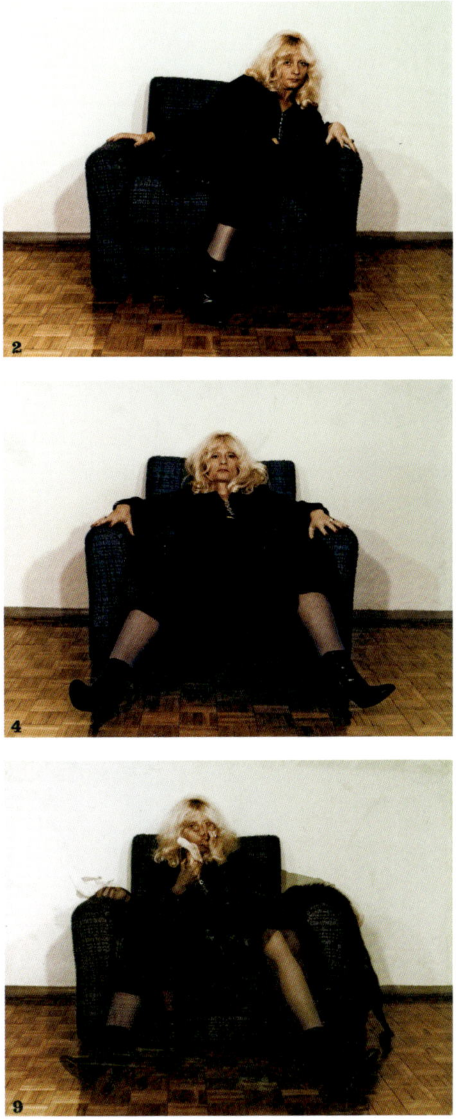

Abb. | ill. 1 Natalia LL, *Zdania kategoryczne w obszaru sztuki postkonsumpcyjnej, październik 1975 / Categorical Statements from the Sphere of Post-Consumer Art, October 1975**, Courtesy Lokal_30 Galerie, Warschau; Natalia LL

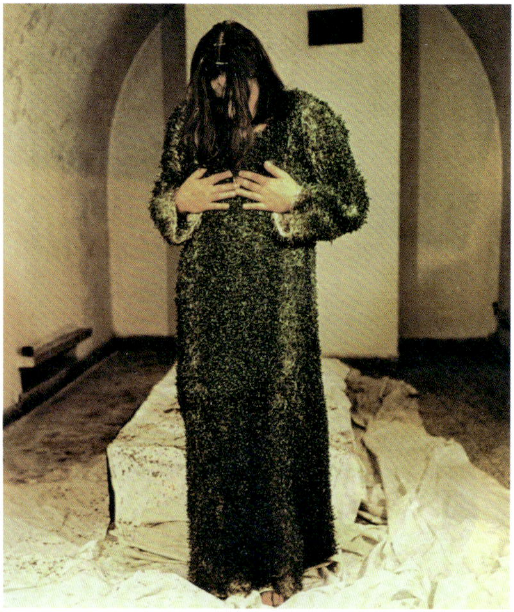

Abb. | ill. 2 Teresa Murak
Lady's Smock. Rzeżucha, 1975
Performance
Fotografie von | photograph by Andrzej Polakowski
Archiv Teresa Murak

as quasi-sculptural raw material on which the impermanence of (the beauty of) the artist is inscribed. Her body, in its physical state, is the subject of, and venue for, art; it becomes an artwork itself. In the performance *Change. My Problem is the Problem of a Woman* (*Zmiana. Mój problem jest problemem kobiety*, 1978), she combines the cosmetic alteration process with her own statements as well as texts by other feminists, such as VALIE EXPORT, about the oppression of women in the patriarchy. The female body becomes here a metaphor of social conditions.

The emergence of feminist art in the Polish People's Republic differs fundamentally from the developments in the USA and Western Europe, where feminist positions were imbedded in the social transformation of the civil rights and student movements. In socialist Poland, artists could neither organize themselves[1] as a movement nor be politically engaged. Feminist standpoints manifested themselves in the natural engagement with artistic questions from specifically female, or artistic, perspectives. More precisely formulated: feminists were a genuine part of the Polish neo-avant-garde.

With female artists asserting themselves to be the object of their art, the personal becomes socially visible. With female artists declaring their own bodies to be their medium, they asserted self-determination. They liberated "woman" as an object from male artists' centuries-old monopoly of meaning; in the works, active women—namely active women artists—become perceivable. Feminist art in the Polish People's Republic in the 1970s was an act of self-empowerment. "For me, the most important thing was to make women's work of high quality,"[2] is how Maria Pinińska-Bereś described it. Self-empowerment in this sense means not only bringing personal, autobiographical experiences and opinions into art, but also formulating these into a particular artistic program that emphasizes

In der Performance *Lady's Smock. Rzeżucha* (Wiesenschaumkraut / Der Mantel der Dame. Kresse, 1975) trägt Teresa Murak ein mit Kressesamen bestreutes Leinenhemd (Abb. 2, S. 72). Durch ihre Körperwärme und ständiges Gießen entsteht ein grünes Pflanzenkleid, das Murak anschließend im Stadtraum präsentiert und im Galerieraum ausstellt. Der weibliche Körper fungiert hier als Hervorbringer von Leben und von Kunst. Durch die Bezugnahme auf die lebenspendende Eigenschaft des weiblichen Körpers schreibt sich die Künstlerin eine „urweibliche" Schöpfungskraft zu – eine feministische Alternative zum Mythos des männlichen Demiurgen.

Auch bei Ewa Partum bringt der weibliche Körper Kunst hervor: Die *Poems by Ewa* verweisen auf den genuinen Anteil ihres weiblichen Körpers für die Entstehung von Kunst. Sprache entsteht hier durch den performativen Akt des Aufdrückens der stark rot geschminkten Lippen der Künstlerin auf das Papier. Partum proklamiert hier eine mit weiblichen Mitteln sprechende Künstlerin. In ihrer Arbeit *Change* (*Zmiana*, 1974) lässt die Künstlerin die Hälfte ihres Gesichtes von professionellen Maskenbildnerinnen künstlich altern (Abb. S. 76). Partum übernimmt die konzeptionelle Arbeit, die Ausführung gibt sie in andere Hände. Ihr Körper fungiert als quasi bildhauerisches Rohmaterial, in das sich die Vergänglichkeit der (Schönheit der) Künstlerin einschreibt. Ihr Körper in seiner leiblichen Verfassung ist Thema und Austragungsort von Kunst, er wird selbst zum Kunstwerk. In der Performance *Change. My Problem is the Problem of a Woman* (*Zmiana. Mój problem jest problemem kobiety*, 1978) kombiniert sie den maskenbildnerischen Alterungsprozess mit eigenen Äußerungen sowie Texten anderer Feministinnen wie VALIE EXPORT über die Unterdrückung der Frau im Patriarchat. Der Frauenkörper wird nun zur Metapher gesellschaftlicher Zustände.

Das Aufkommen feministischer Kunst in der Volksrepublik Polen unterscheidet sich grundlegend von den Entwicklungen in den USA und in Westeuropa, wo feministische Positionen in den gesellschaftlichen Aufbruchsprozess der Bürgerrechts- und Studentenbewegungen eingebettet waren. Im sozialistischen Polen konnten sich Künstlerinnen weder als Bewegung organisieren[1] noch politisch engagieren. In der selbstverständlichen Beschäftigung mit künstlerischen Fragestellungen aus einer spezifischen Frauen- bzw. Künstlerinnenperspektive manifestierten sich feministische Standpunkte. Zugespitzt formuliert: Feministische Positionen sind genuiner Bestandteil der polnischen Neo-Avantgarde.

Indem sich Künstlerinnen selbst zum Gegenstand ihrer Kunst erklären, wird das Persönliche gesellschaftlich sichtbar. Indem Künstlerinnen ihren eigenen Körper zu ihrem Medium deklarieren, bestimmen sie über ihn. Sie befreien „die Frau" als Objekt aus dem jahrhundertealten Deutungsmonopol der männlichen Künstler. Denn in den Arbeiten werden handelnde Frauen, nämlich handelnde Künstlerinnen sichtbar. Feministische Kunst in der Volksrepublik Polen der 1970er-Jahre ist ein Akt der Selbstermächtigung. „For me, the most important thing was to make women's work of high quality"[2], formuliert es Maria Pinińska-Bereś. Selbstermächtigung in diesem Sinne bedeutet also nicht nur, persönliche, autobiografische Erlebnisse, Erfahrungen

its gender-specific origin. In this way, feminist art in Poland was simultaneously locally grounded and globally comprehensible. Instead of measuring regional particularities against the presumed primacy of Western European or North American feminism, we can look to the perspective of "global feminisms"—since this is precisely feminist art: a global phenomenon, which is integrated into respective regional, socio-political settings as a genuine, socially critical art form.

Notes:

1 The exhibition *Sztuka Kobiet* (*Art of Women*) organized by Izabella Gustowska and Krystyna Piotrowska in the Posener Galeria O. N. can be seen as the first attempt of this kind of group building. Izabella Gustowska could only follow up on this idea with the exhibition cycle *Obecność* (*Presence*) after the lifting of martial law in the mid-1980s.

2 Pinińska-Bereś in an interview with Wiesława Wierzowska, with an English translation in Maria Pinińska-Bereś, exh. cat. Galeria Studio (Warsaw 1997).

***** Natalia LL, *Categorical Statements from the Sphere of Post-Consumer Art,* October 1975, 9 photographs, text, courtesy Lokal_30 Galerie, Warsaw; Natalia LL
CATEGORICAL STATEMENTS FROM THE SPHERE OF POST-CONSUMER ART
1. Art is a result of intellectual abilities of the human mind.
2. Art is the method of formalizing actuality. This formalizing is based on the apparent illogicality of the result and enters into the multi-valued logic.
3. The specific and separate way in which art functions makes it impossible for scientific methods to be introduced into the study of its motivation.
4. The kinds and styles of art: realistic, abstract, deformational correspond to the level of consciousness of the social group and artists working within the group.
5. Post-consumer art is an attempt to go beyond the sphere of experiences and manipulations of art which are the work of critics, the history of art, institutions, etc, these manipulations being an attempt at integrating the world of objects with the world of ideals.
6. Post-consumer art bases itself on creating visual and mental formulas which, though not contradictory in themselves, are as 'artificial' as possible and constitute a projection of complicated intellectual and intuitive processes.
7. Post-consumer art, remaining an alogical or extralogical structure, is self-definable, which means that any valid opinions on this art can be formulated only from the position of art.
8. Post-consumer art is a permanent dialogue within the consciousness of the social group represented b.
9. Art becomes post-consumer art only when it has been defined by art.
Text published by PERMAFO editions Translated by Henryk Holzhausen

und Anschauungen in die Kunst einzubringen, sondern diese in einem eigenen künstlerischen Programm zu formulieren, das seine geschlechtsspezifische Herkunft herausstellt. Feministische Kunst in Polen ist also regional fundiert und zugleich global verständlich. Anstatt regionale Spezifika am vermeintlichen Primat des westeuropäischen und nordamerikanischen Feminismus zu messen, empfiehlt sich die Perspektive der „Global Feminisms". Denn genau dies ist feministische Kunst: eine globale Erscheinung, die als genuin gesellschaftskritische Kunstform in die jeweils regionalen sozio-politischen Settings eingebunden ist.

Anmerkungen:

1 Die 1980 von Izabella Gustowska und Krystyna Piotrowska organisierte Ausstellung *Sztuka Kobiet* (*Kunst von Frauen*) in der Posener Galeria O. N. kann als erster Versuch einer solchen Gruppenbildung verstanden werden. Izabella Gustowska konnte erst nach der Aufhebung des Kriegsrechts Mitte der 1980er-Jahre mit dem Ausstellungszyklus *Obecność* (Anwesenheit) an diese Idee anknüpfen.

2 Pinińska-Bereś in einem Interview mit Wiesława Wierzowska, in englischer Übersetzung in Maria Pinińska-Bereś, Ausst. - Kat. Galeria Studio, Warschau 1997.

INDIVIDUUM UND GESELLSCHAFT

THE INDIVIDUAL AND SOCIETY

KwieKulik

Ewa Partum

Krzysztof Wodiczko

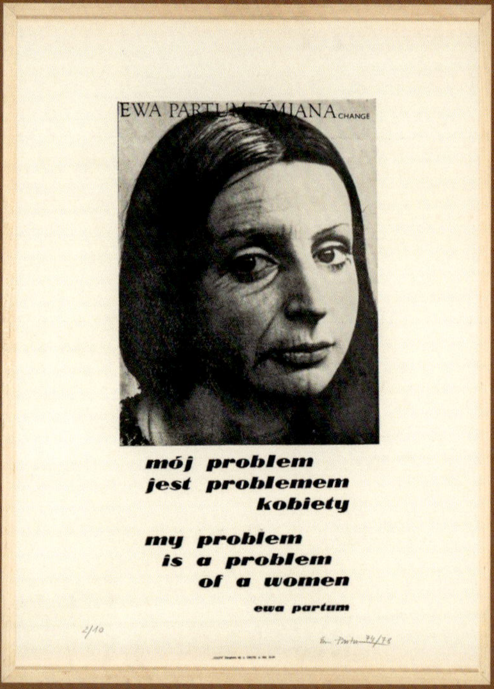

Ewa Partum
Zmiana. Mój problem jest problemem kobiety / Change. My Problem is a Problem of a Woman, 1974–1978
Offsetdruck auf Offsetpapier | offset print on offset paper
Aufl. 10 Exemplare | edition of 10
68,5 × 48,5 cm
Courtesy Galerie M+R Fricke Berlin

At the end of the 1960s, Krzysztof Wodiczko began to articulate his theme of individual language and voicelessness by perceiving and discerning his environment via sensors (*Personal Instrument*, 1969/1972). No less ironic and also in direct conflict with the communist state, he started designing vehicles in the 1970s that produced energy from the shifting weight of the artist as he stepped forward and back, but could only be driven straight ahead. The drawing *Vehicle for Workers* (1980) was based on the same laborious principle: Sisyphus-like, the vehicle would start only by moving a weight, and its direction could not be changed.

The border between art and life is completely erased by the artistic duo KwieKulik (Zofia Kulik and Przemysław Kwiek). In performances, photo-graphy and films (*The Monument without a Passport*, 1978), they take as their subject the experience of having personal documents revoked by the state. Impressed by the happy life packaged and distributed quarterly in the pages of the magazine *Ameryka* by the American embassy in Poland, they have, since 1972, been acting out their own American Dream as a journalistic profile: KwieKulik on a walk with their son, KwieKulik at an exhibition opening, KwieKulik in front of the Cologne Cathedral, etc. Their *Ameryka* is an artistic contribution to the propaganda machinery of the Cold War.

Ewa Partum operated as a feminist artist using her body in works such as *Change* (1974–1978) and offered a critique of the invisibility of women in public discourse with her statement, "My Problem is a Problem of a Woman." In the photo collage *Self-Identification* (1980), she used her nakedness as a medium to assert herself in public space and to become visible beyond assigned, socially acceptable women's roles. In the works of all four artists, the socio-political approach is clear, making self-empowerment independent of state doctrine possible only through reflection on their own artistic existence.

K. K.

Ende der 1960er-Jahre thematisierte Krzysztof Wodiczko seine individuelle Sprach- und Stimmlosigkeit, indem er begann, sein Umfeld über Sensoren abzutasten und wahrzunehmen (*Personal Instrument*, 1969/1972). Nicht weniger ironisch und ebenfalls in direkter Auseinandersetzung mit dem kommunistischen Staat, entwarf er seit den 1970er-Jahren Fahrzeuge, die durch Gewichtsverlagerung beim Auf- und Abgehen des Künstlers zwar Energie erzeugen, aber sich nur geradeaus fahren lassen. Die Zeichnungen *Vehicle for Workers* (1980) basieren auf demselben mühsamen Prinzip, sisyphosgleich lässt sich das Vehikel nur durch das Verschieben eines Gewichtes in Gang setzen, die Richtung ändert es nicht.

Die Grenzziehung zwischen Kunst und Leben hob das Künstler-Duo KwieKulik (Zofia Kulik und Przemysław Kwiek) vollständig auf. Sie verarbeiteten die Erfahrung von staatlich entzogenen Ausweispapieren in Performances, Fotoarbeiten und Filmen (*The Monument without a Passport*, 1978) und imitierten ab 1972 – beeindruckt von dem glücklichen Leben, das im Magazin *Ameryka* aufbereitet und vierteljährlich von der amerikanischen Botschaft in Polen verteilt wurde – ihren eigenen amerikanischen Traum als Homestory: KwieKulik beim Spaziergang mit ihrem Sohn, KwieKulik bei einer Ausstellungseröffnung, KwieKulik vor dem Kölner Dom usw. Ihr *Ameryka* ist ein künstlerischer Beitrag zur Propaganda-Maschinerie des Kalten Krieges.

Als feministische Künstlerin agierte Ewa Partum in Arbeiten wie *Change* (1974–1978) mit ihrem Körper und kritisierte mit ihrem Statement „My Problem is a Problem of a Woman" die fehlende Sichtbarkeit von Frauen im öffentlichen Diskurs. In den Foto-Collagen *Self-Identification* (1980) benutzte sie ihre Nacktheit als Medium, um sich als Subjekt im öffentlichen Raum behaupten und über die zugeschriebenen, gesellschaftlich akzeptierten Frauenrollen hinaus begreifen zu können. In den Arbeiten aller vier Künstler*Innen wird ein politisch-gesellschaftlicher Ansatz deutlich, der erst durch die Reflexion über das eigene, künstlerische Dasein eine Selbstermächtigung unabhängig von staatlicher Doktrin ermöglicht.

K. K.

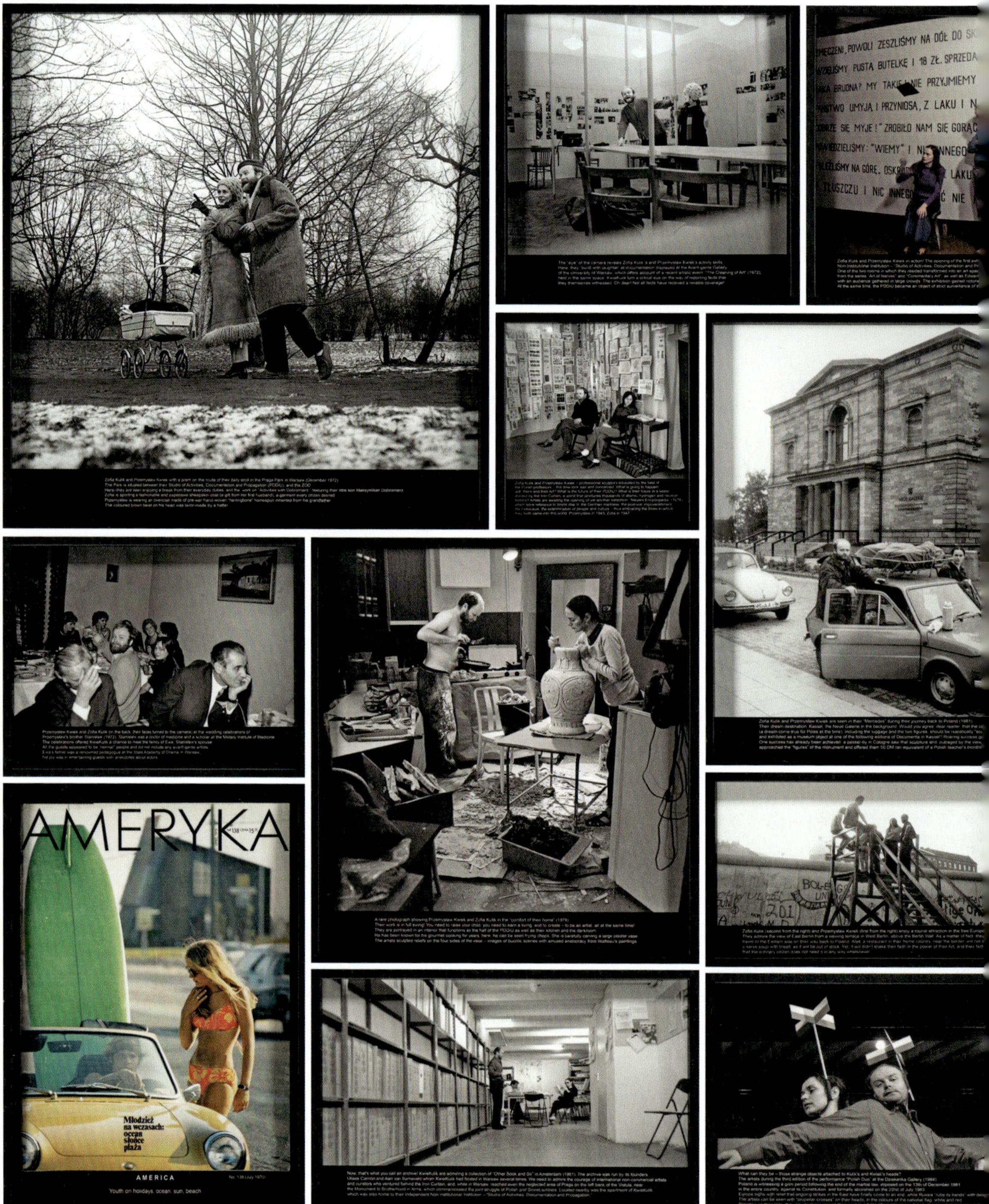

KwieKulik

KwieKulik
Ameryka, ab | from 1972
16 Fotografien, 1 Zeitschrift |
16 photographs, 1 magazine
115 × 168 cm
Courtesy ŻAK | BRANICKA, Berlin

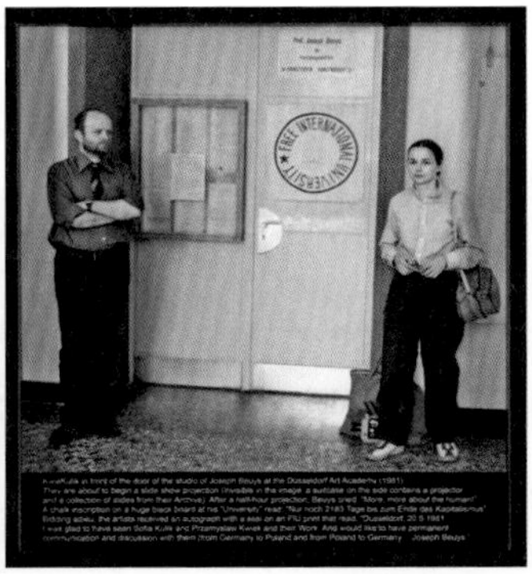

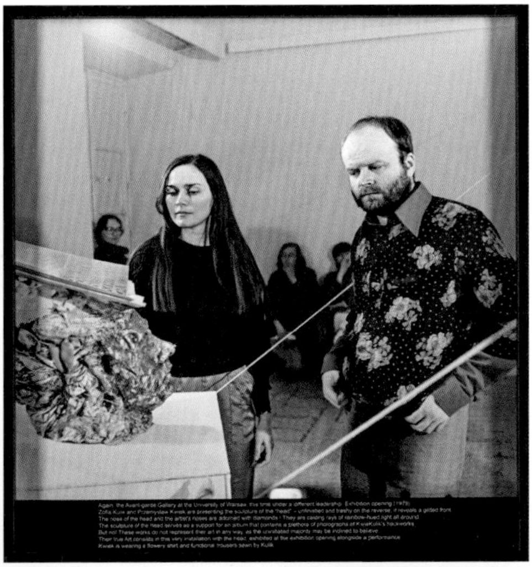

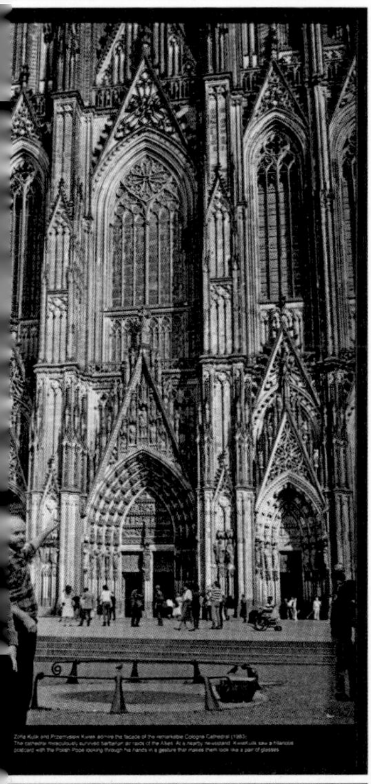

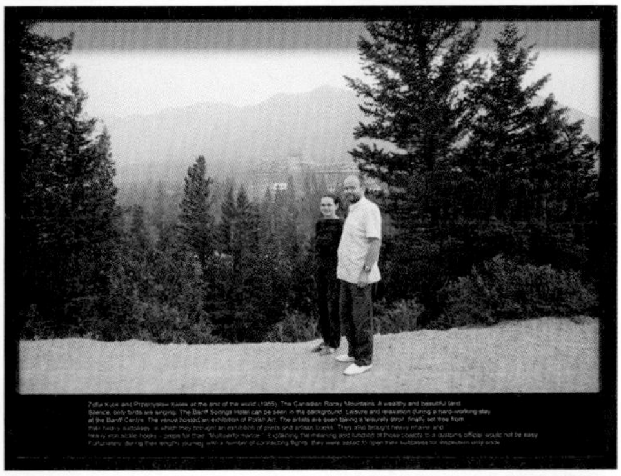

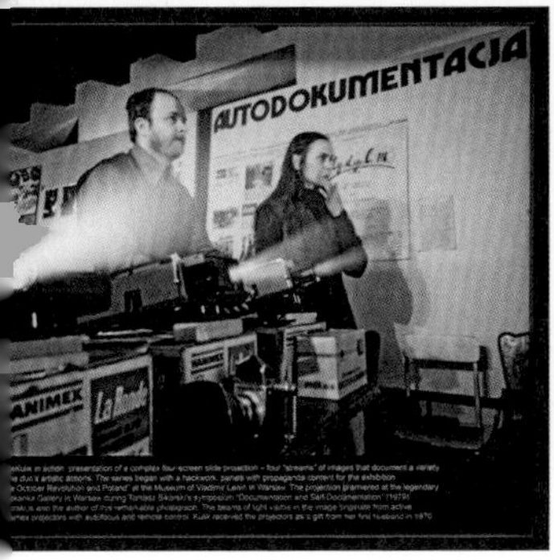
AUTODOKUMENTACJA

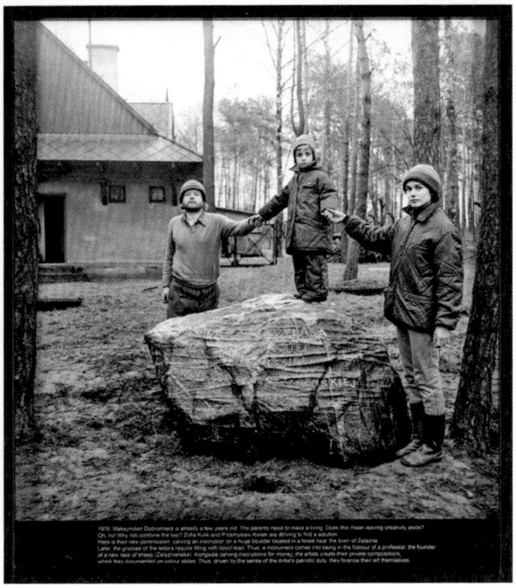

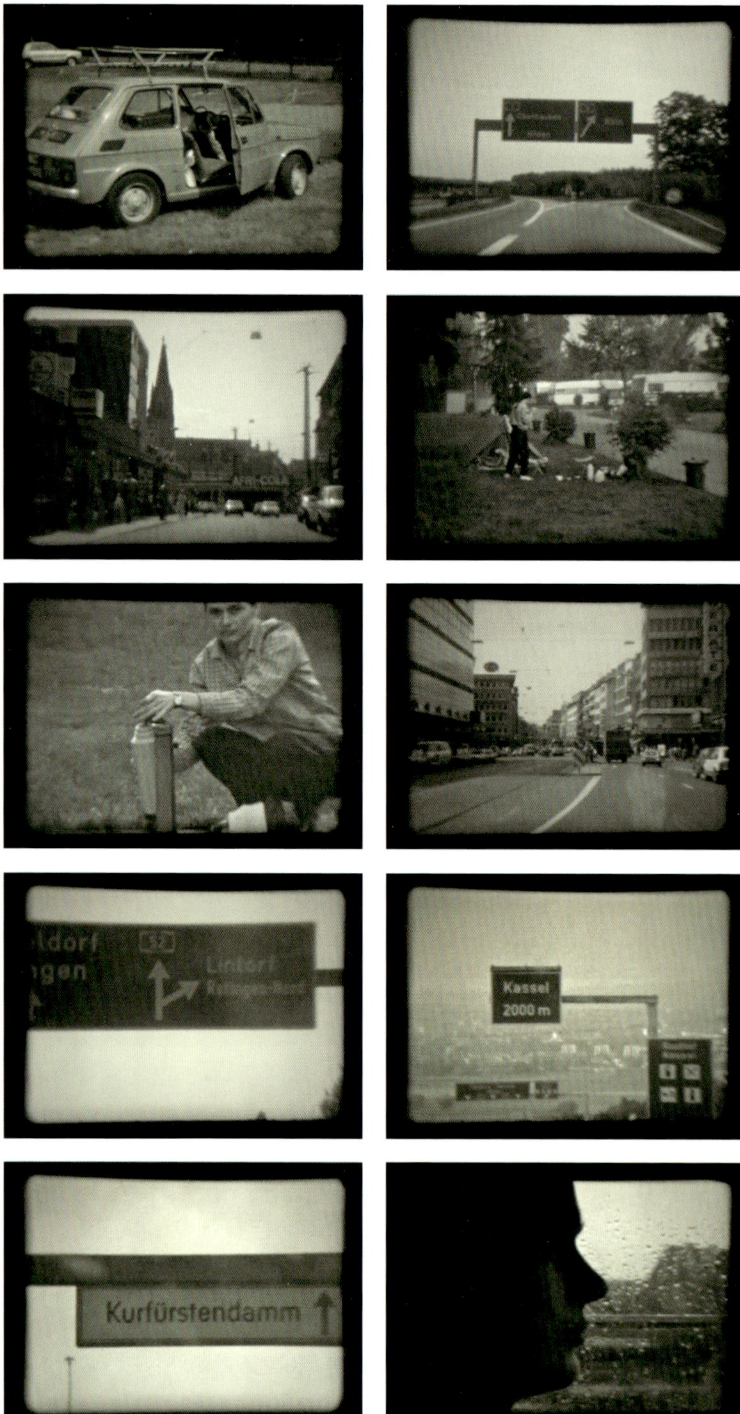

KwieKulik
Trip around Europe, 1981, Video, 9:19 min.
Courtesy ŻAK | BRANICKA, Berlin

KwieKulik
Pomnik bez paszportu / Das Denkmal ohne Pass / The Monument without a Passport, 1978
Diashow | slide show HD, 4:31 min.
Courtesy ŻAK | BRANICKA, Berlin

KwieKulik

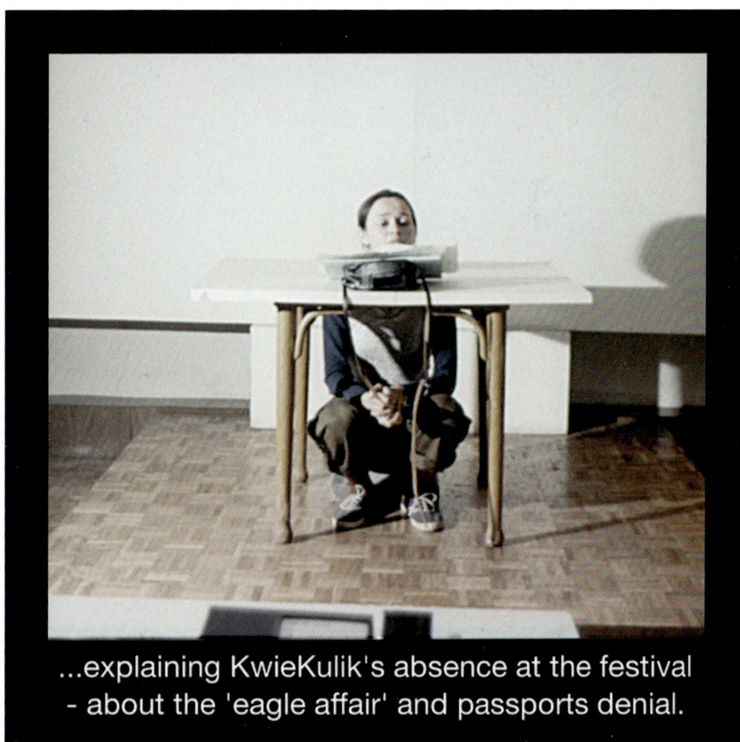

Ewa Partum

Ewa Partum
Tautological Cinema, 1973–1974
Video, 4:12 min.
Courtesy Galerie M+R Fricke, Berlin

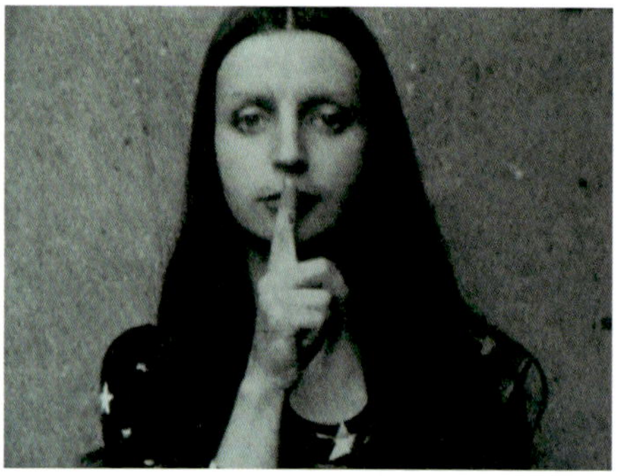
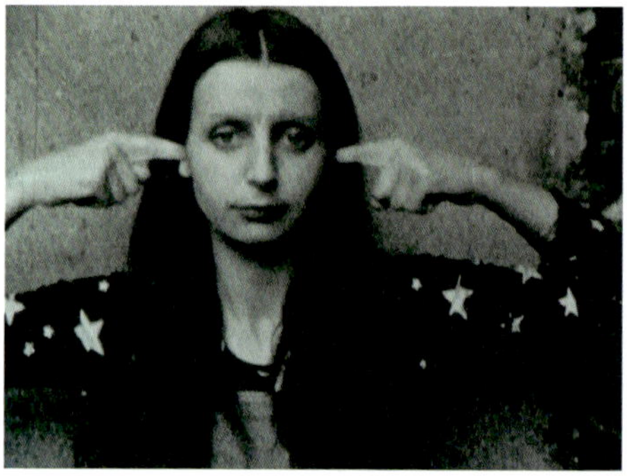
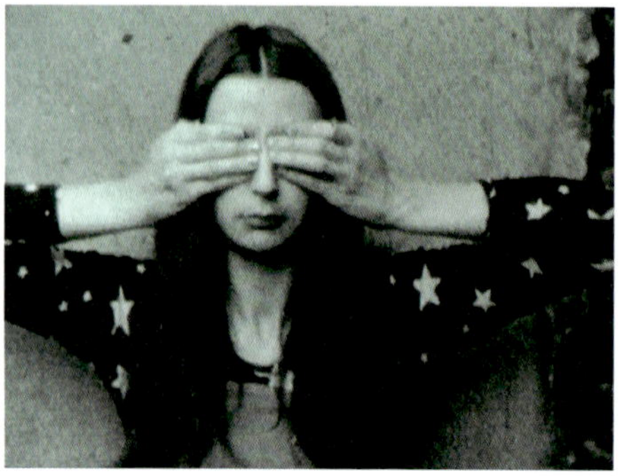
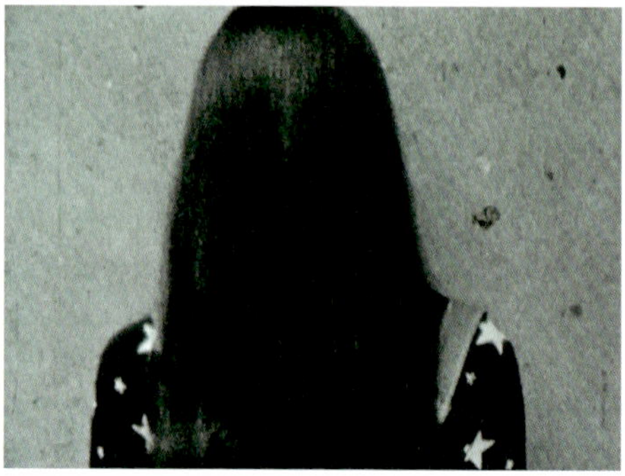

Ewa Partum
Samoidentyfikacja / Selbstidentifikation / Self-Identification, 1980
6 Fotografien | 6 photographs
Serie 8-teilig | series of 8 pieces
je | each ca. 40 × 49 cm,
1 Abzug | print 36 × 50 cm,
1 Abzug | print 34 × 48,6 cm
Courtesy Galerie M+R Fricke, Berlin

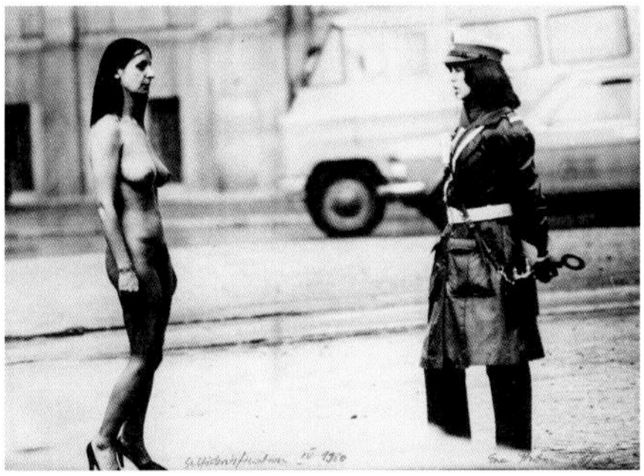
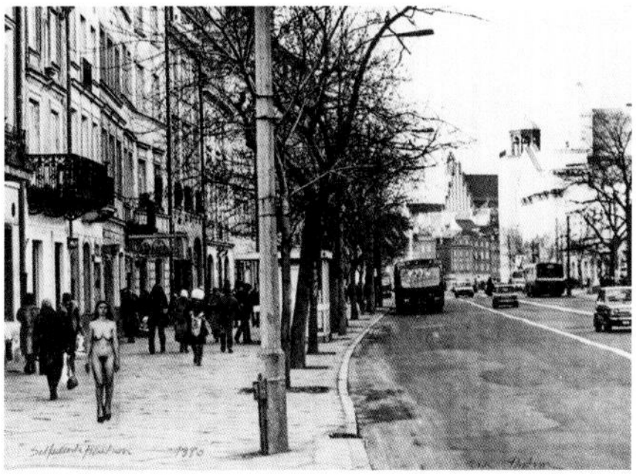
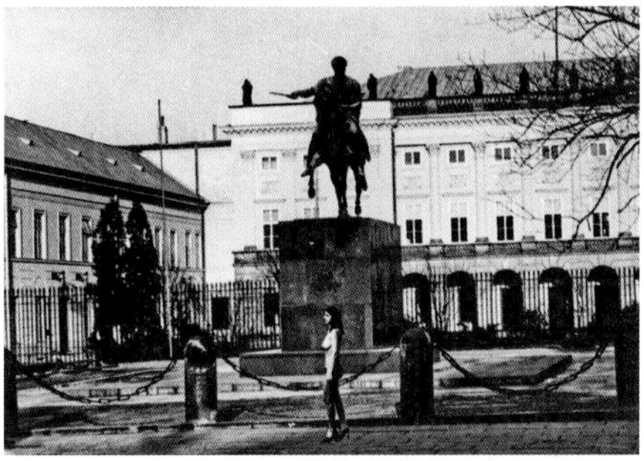
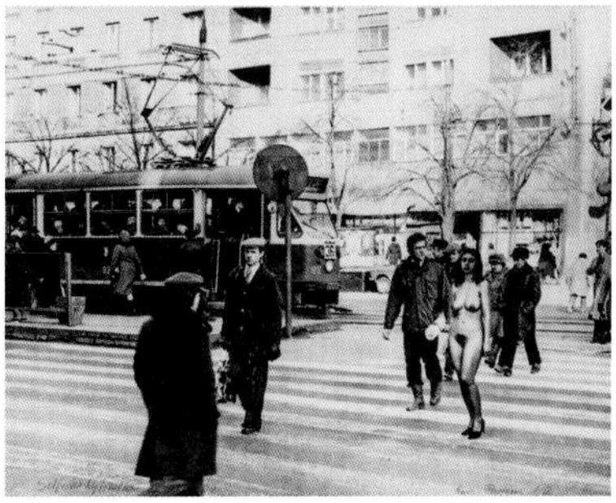
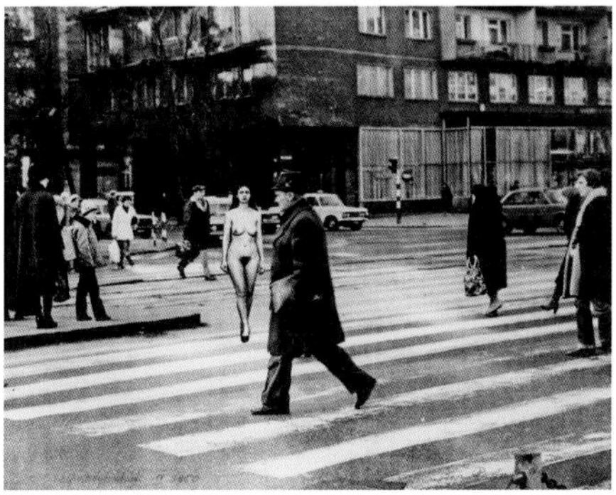
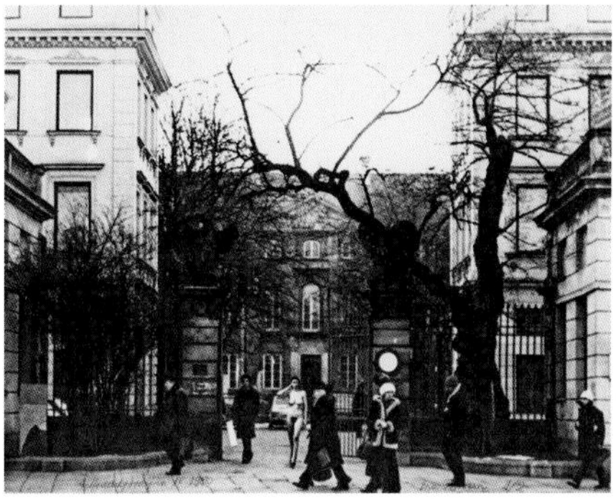

Self-identification
These photographs inform about the existence of a special relationship between the factual facts and what they represent. Here the indicators of social life, a certain series of patterns of the functioning of the individual in his social and cultural role are revealed. In this case, it is the role of the WOMAN—the concept of role (the existence as a woman, as a mother, as a housewife, as an employed person, as a member of a concrete social group) is thereby understood as the sum of roles, as a model created and cemented by tradition and therefore deeply rooted in the subconscious of today's society, as the "WOMAN" par excellence. These patterns are a direct product of the patriarchal culture of life and have been sanctioned by the norms of interpersonal interaction. They humiliate the woman while at the same time showing respect for her. The events—noted as my own intervention—barely exhaust the problem and are merely intended as a signal and sketch.

Ewa Partum, 1980

Selbstidentifikation
Diese Fotografien informieren über die Existenz einer besonderen Beziehung zwischen dem faktischen Tatbestand und dem, was sie darstellen. Die Indikatoren des gesellschaftlichen Lebens, eine bestimmte Reihe von Mustern des Funktionierens des Einzelnen in seiner sozialen und kulturellen Rolle werden hier entlarvt. In diesem Fall handelt es sich um die der FRAU – wobei der Begriff der Rolle (das Existieren als Frau, Mutter, Hausfrau, als berufstätige, als das Mitglied einer konkreten sozialen Gruppe) verstanden wird als die Summe von Rollen, als ein Modell, das durch die Tradition geschaffen und zementiert wurde und deshalb tief mit dem Unterbewusstsein der heutigen Gesellschaft verankert ist, als Muster der „FRAU" schlechthin. Diese Muster sind ein direktes Produkt der patriarchalen Lebenskultur und wurden durch die Normen des zwischenmenschlichen Umgangs sanktioniert. Sie erniedrigen die Frau bei gleichzeitigem Anschein von Respekt für sie. Die Ereignisse – notiert als meine eigene Intervention – erschöpfen die Problematik kaum, sind lediglich gedacht als Signal und Skizze.

Ewa Partum, 1980

Krzysztof Wodiczko

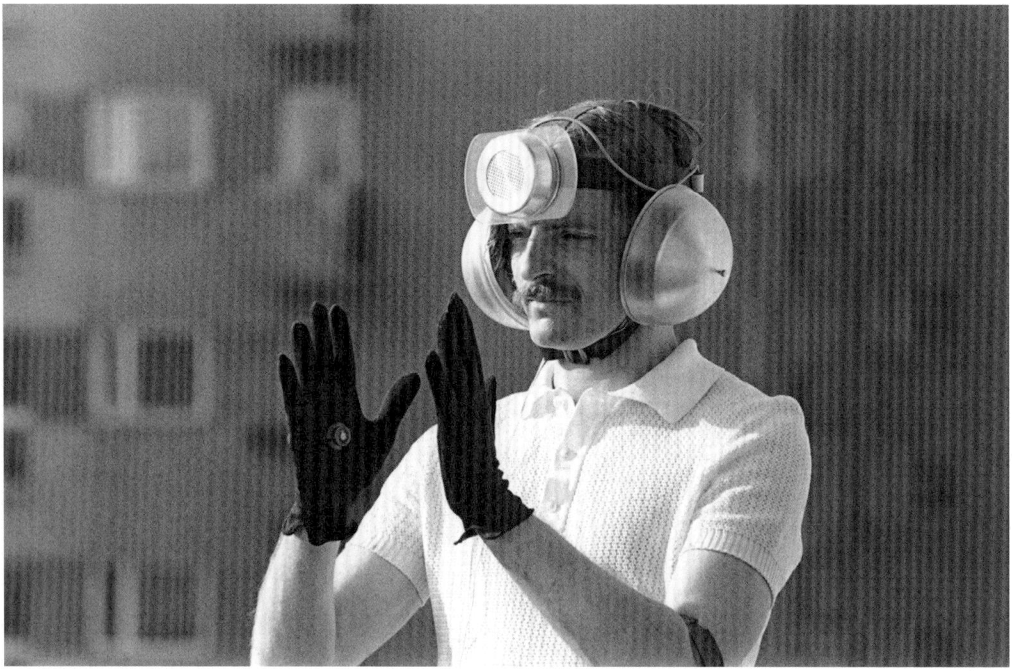

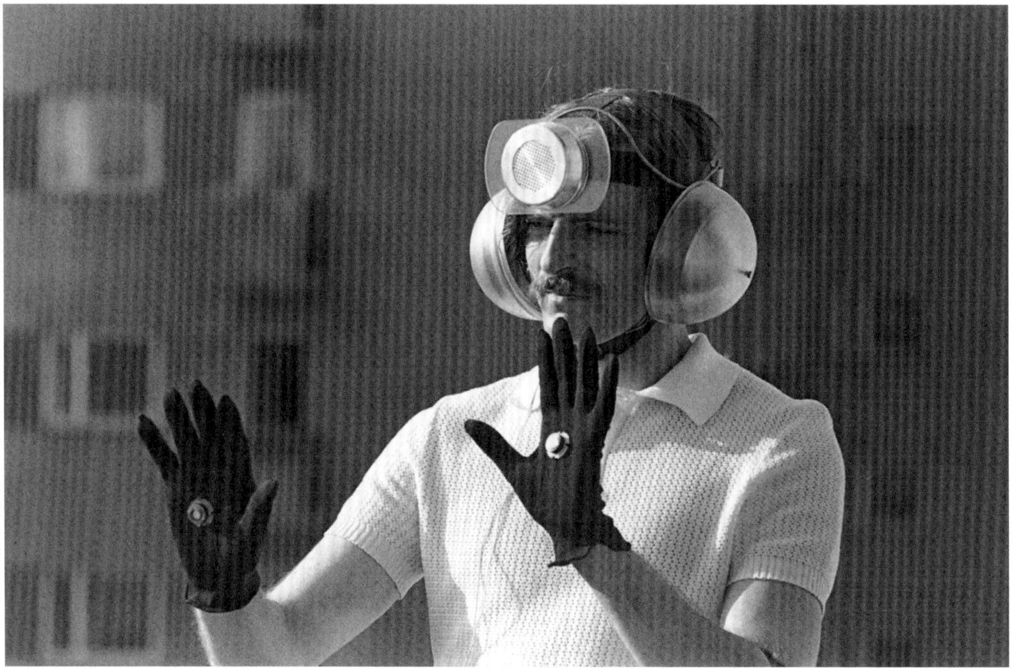

Krzysztof Wodiczko
Personal Instrument, 1972
Performance, 4 Fotografien von |
4 photographs by Jerzy Surwiło
je | each 22 × 33 cm
Profile Foundation, Warschau

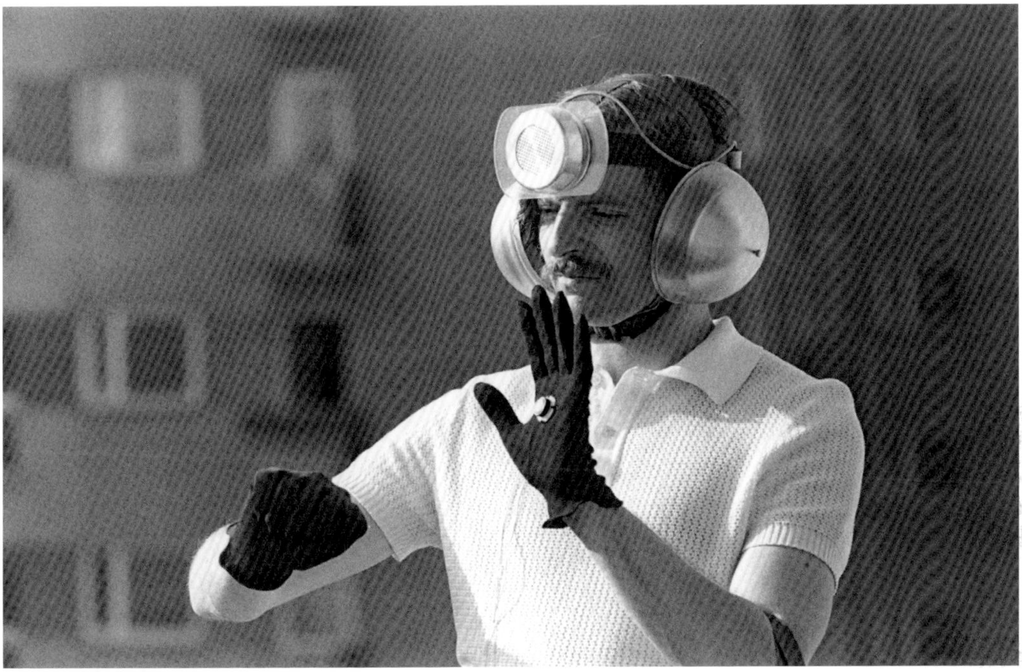

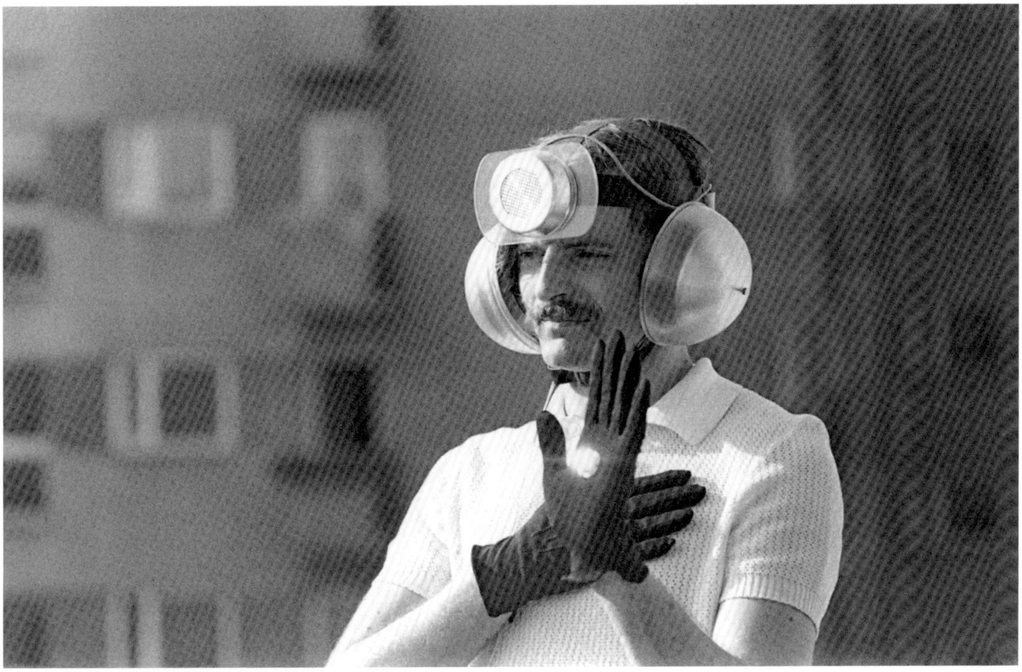

Krzysztof Wodiczko

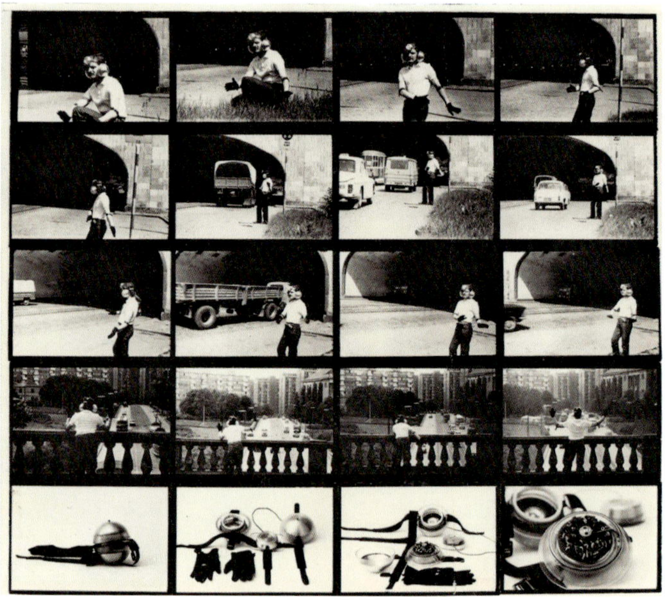

Krzysztof Wodiczko
Personal Instrument, 1972
Kontaktabzug | contact sheet
16,3 × 17,9 cm
Profile Foundation, Warschau

Personal Instrument, 1969

The instrument transforms the sounds of the environment.
The instrument functions in response to hand movements.
The instrument reacts to sunlight.
The instrument is portable.
The instrument can be used any place and any time.
The instrument is for exclusive use of its author.
The instrument permits the author to attain virtuosity.
Krzysztof Wodiczko, 1969

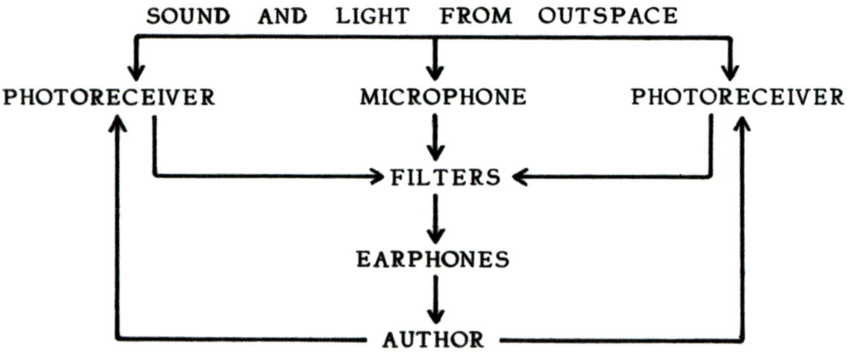

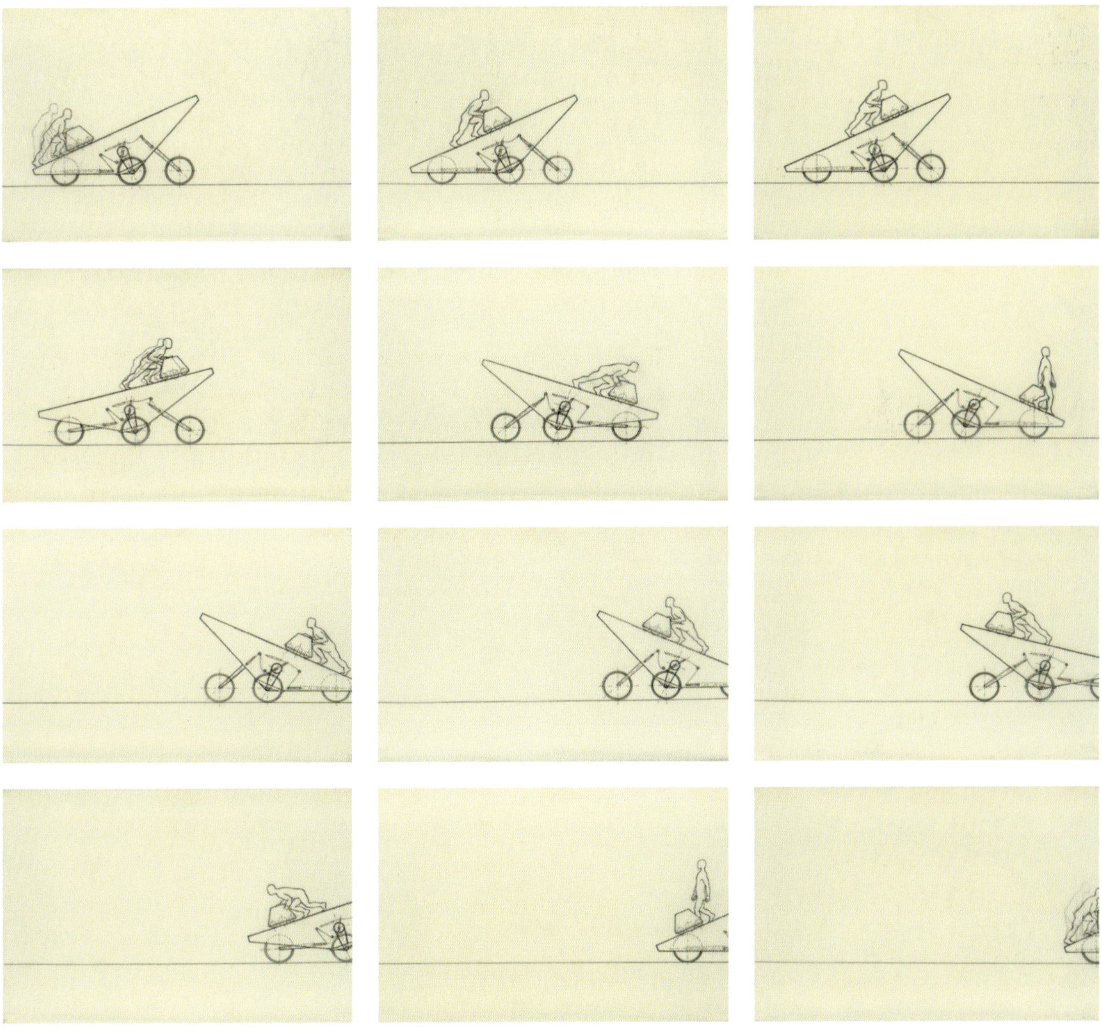

Krzysztof Wodiczko
Projekty pojazdów: Pojazd 2 / Vehicle for Workers, 1980
12 Tuschzeichnungen | 12 ink drawings
je | each 30 × 45 cm
Muzeum Sztuki w Łodzi

WERKSTATT FÜR FILMFORM / ANALYTISCHE FOTOGRAFIE

WORKSHOP FOR FILMFORM / ANALYTICAL PHOTOGRAPHY

Józef Robakowski

Ryszard Waśko

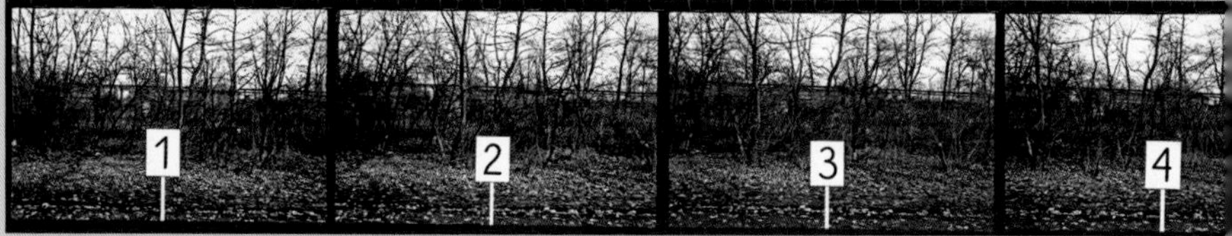

Ryszard Waśko
Making an Inventory of Space with the Numbers 1–8, 1976
9 Fotografien | 9 photographs
je | each 24,3 × 33 cm
Courtesy ŻAK | BRANICKA, Berlin

The Workshop for Filmform existed from 1970 to 1977 at the State Academy for Film, Television and Theatre in Łódź. A group of students and alumni founded the largely independent working group out of dissatisfaction with the instruction there. They directed their criticism at the uninspiring education of directors and camera operators for commercial films. Józef Robakowski and Ryszard Waśko, in addition to Wojciech Bruszewski and Paweł Kwiek, were among the most significant members of the workshop. The group demanded a departure from conventional motion pictures with their deceptive narrative forms. Inspired by the experimental films of the 1920s, they subjected the medium to a fundamental formal-aesthetic analysis. Their interest in the manipulative possibilities of film, which the state used for ideological purposes, gave the workshop a political bent.

In both their minimalistic films as well as in their photography from the same period, Robakowski and Waśko eschew the usual narrative and visual functions and instead concentrate on medium-specific techniques. In their photography, for instance, series of images, fragmented representations and identical settings with varying shutter speeds are used to explore spatial and chronological dimensions and provide information about image production and perception. In their films, familiar visual habits are targeted and questioned in various ways: by replacing the director's handwriting with the shared authorship of 22 students; by manipulating the cut so that the action is divided into opposing sequences; by eliminating the synchronicity of image and sound; or ceasing to project images, but rather only points of light created by puncturing the film.

B. E.

Die Werkstatt für Filmform existierte von 1970 bis 1977 an der Staatlichen Hochschule für Film, Fernsehen und Theater in Łódź. Eine Gruppe von Studierenden und Absolventen hatte die weitgehend unabhängige Arbeitsgemeinschaft aus Unzufriedenheit über den dortigen Unterricht gegründet. Die Kritik richtete sich gegen die uninspirierte Ausbildung von Regisseuren und Kameraleuten für den kommerziellen Kinofilm. Józef Robakowski und Ryszard Waśko zählten neben Wojciech Bruszewski und Paweł Kwiek zu den bedeutendsten Mitgliedern der Werkstatt. Die Akteure forderten die Abkehr vom herkömmlichen Spielfilm mit seinen illusionserzeugenden Erzählformen. Inspiriert von den experimentellen Filmen der 1920er-Jahre, unterzogen sie das Medium Film einer grundlegenden formalästhetischen Analyse. Das Interesse an den vom Staat für ideologische Zwecke genutzten, manipulativen Möglichkeiten des Films gab der Werkstatt für Filmform eine politische Dimension.

Robakowski und Waśko verzichten sowohl in ihren minimalistischen Filmen, als auch in den zeitgleich entstandenen fotografischen Arbeiten auf die gewohnte Erzähl- und Abbildfunktion und konzentrieren sich stattdessen auf die jeweiligen medienspezifischen Techniken. In der Fotografie etwa erforschen Bildserien, fragmentierte Darstellungen und identische Einstellungen mit verschiedenen Verschlusszeiten räumliche und zeitliche Aspekte und geben Auskunft über Bilderzeugung und -wahrnehmung. Vertraute Sehgewohnheiten werden in den Filmen beispielsweise dadurch gezielt infrage gestellt, dass die Handschrift des Regisseurs durch die gleichberechtigte Autorschaft von 22 Studierenden ersetzt wird, der Schnitt den Handlungsverlauf in widerläufige Sequenzen zerteilt, die Synchronität von Bild und Ton aufgehoben wird oder ein Film keine Abbildungen mehr zeigt, sondern nur helle Punkte durch die Perforation der Filmrolle.

B. E.

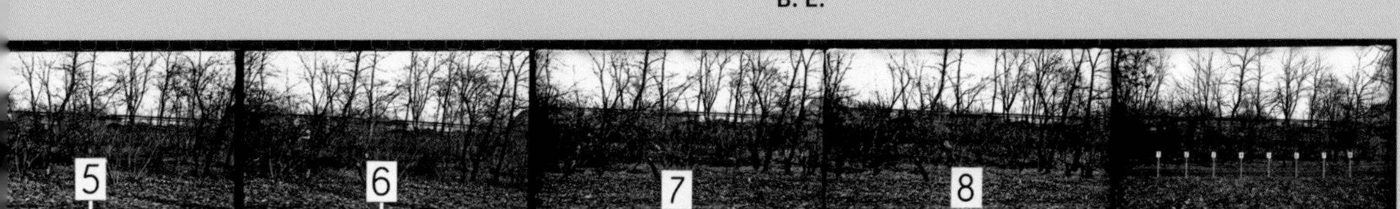

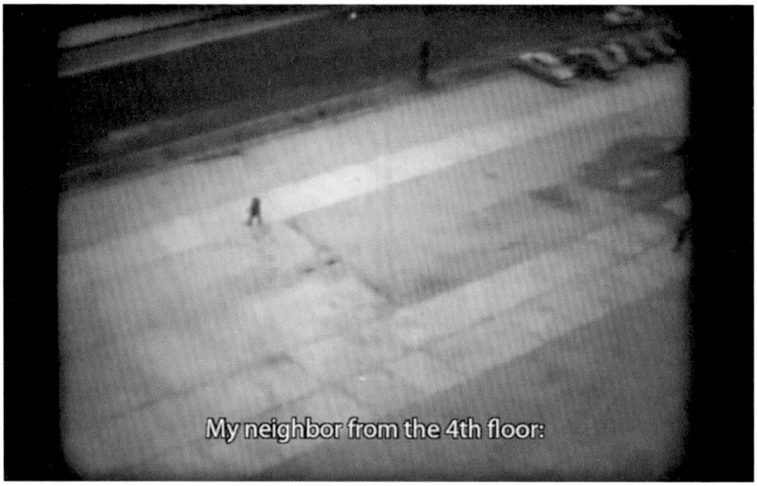

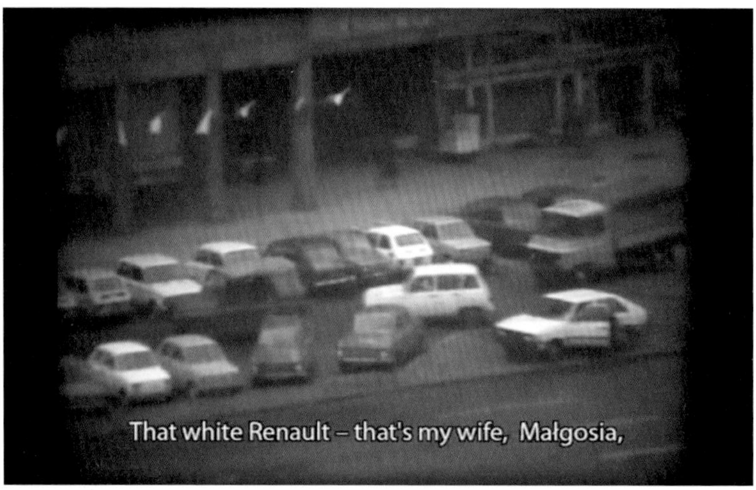

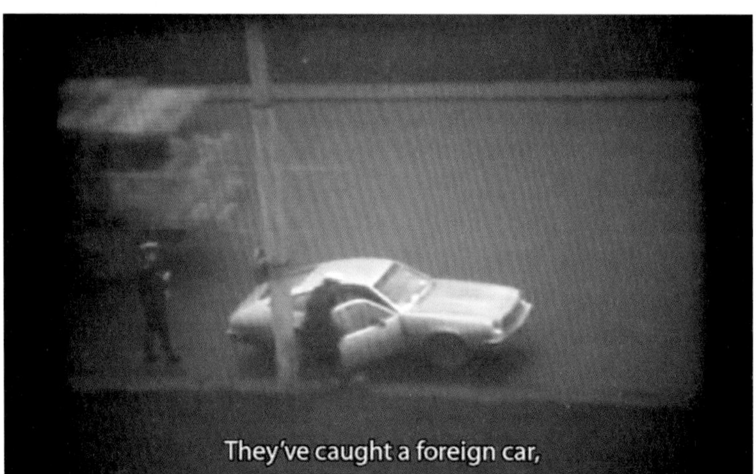

Józef Robakowski
Widok z mojego okna /
Von meinem Fenster aus /
From my Window, 1978–1999
Video, 20:00 min.
Profile Foundation, Warschau

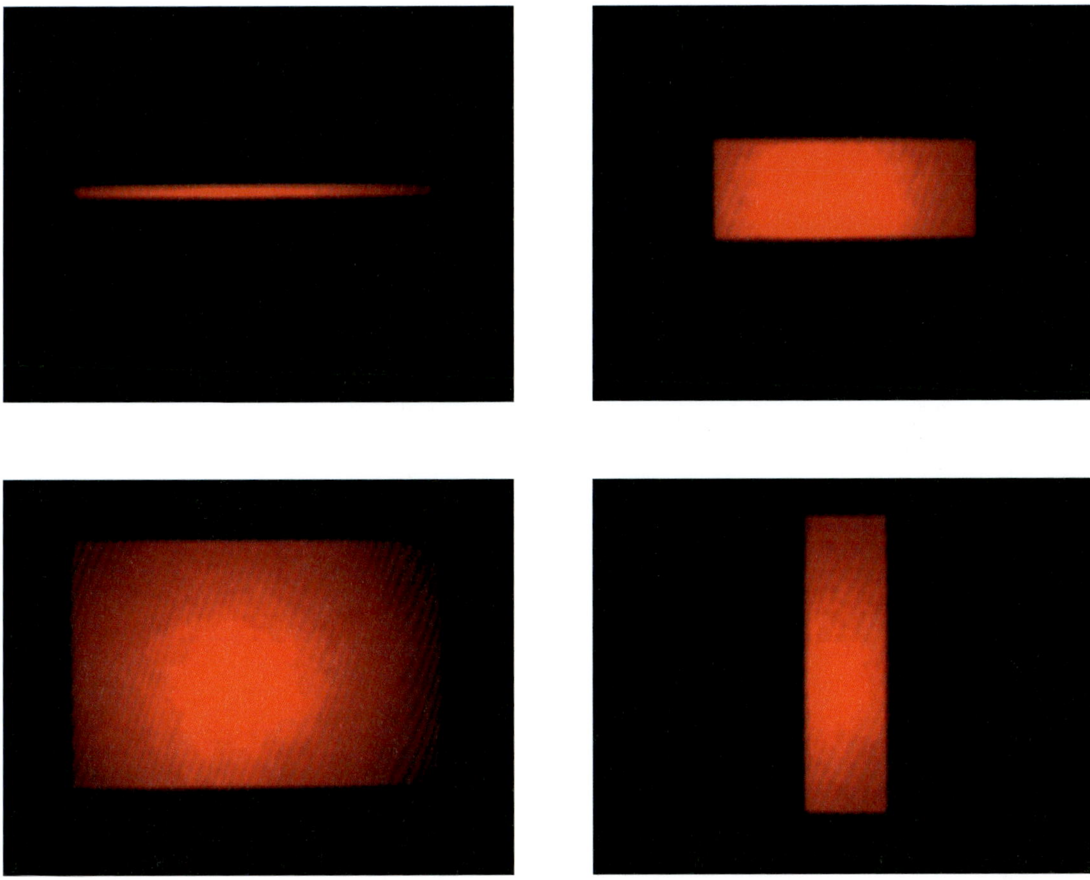

Józef Robakowski

Józef Robakowski
Dynamisches Rechteck / Dynamic Rectangle, 1971
35 mm Film, digitalisiert | digitized, 5:00 min.
Profile Foundation, Warschau

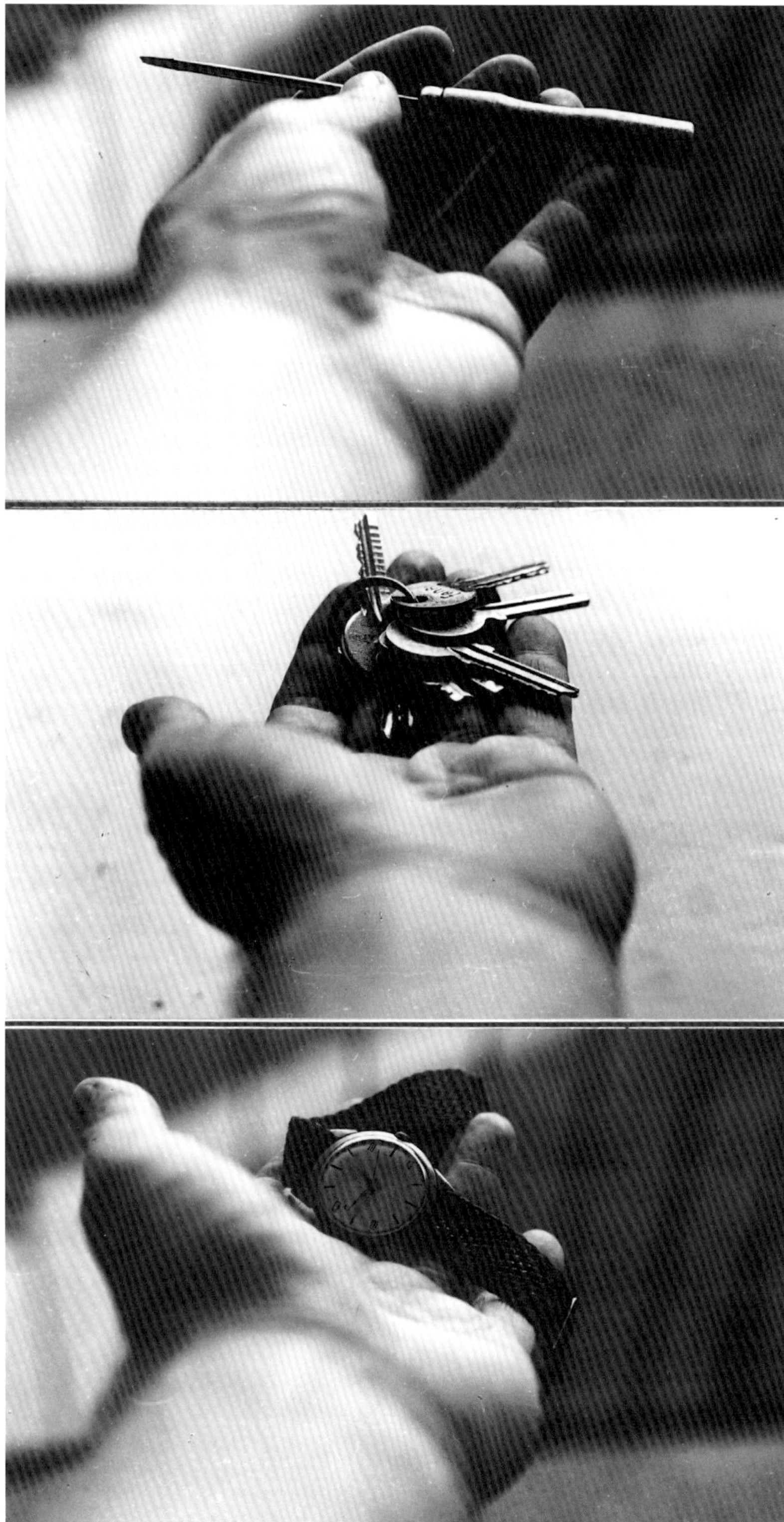

Józef Robakowski
Aus der Serie | from the series
Objective Photography, 1973
3 Fotografien | 3 photographs
je | each 20 × 28 cm
Profile Foundation, Warschau

Józef Robakowski
t=1/100, t=1/50, t=1/10, aus der Serie | from the series
Objective Photography, 1973
3 Fotografien | 3 photographs
je | each 24 × 18 cm
Profile Foundation, Warschau

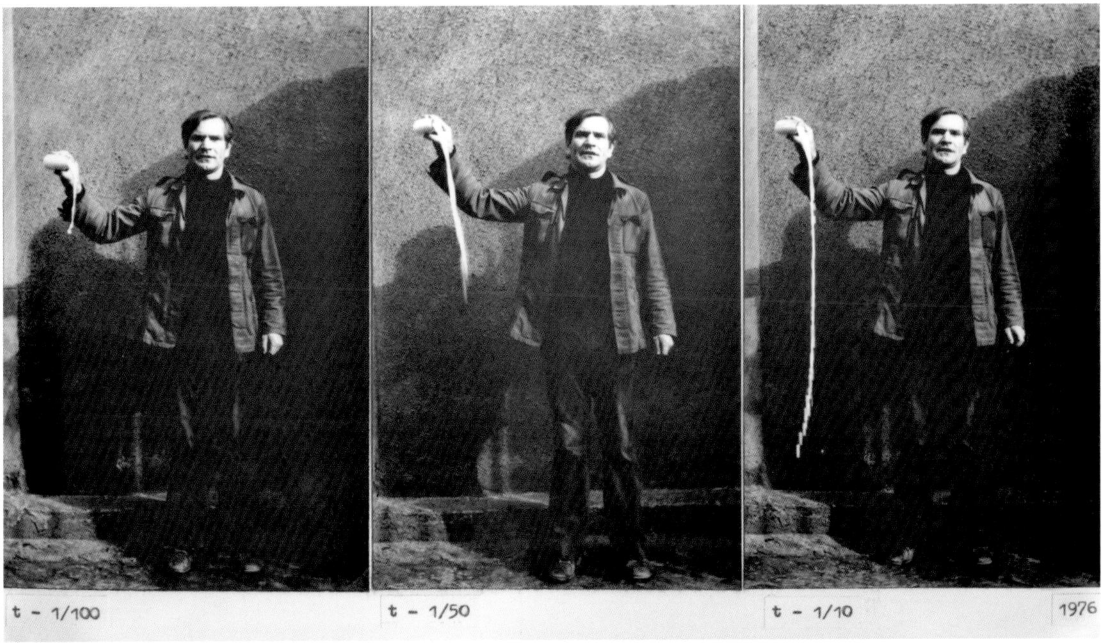

Józef Robakowski

Ryszard Waśko

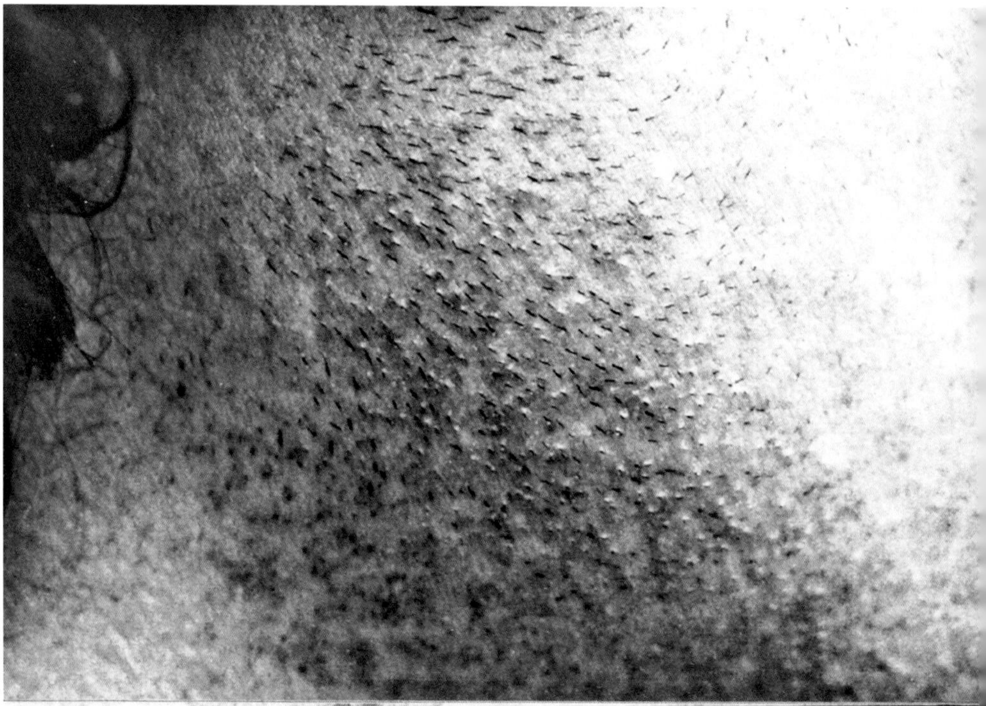

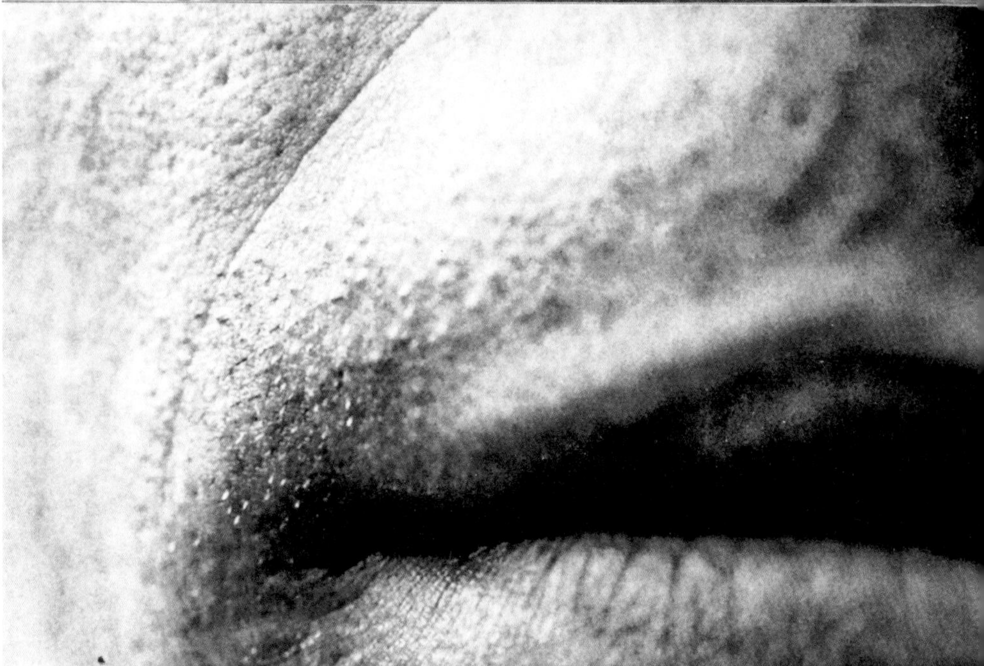

Ryszard Waśko
Portret pocięty / *Cut up Portrait*, 1974
4 Fotografien | 4 photographs, Serie 16-teilig | series of 16 pieces
je | each 27,5 × 40,5 cm
Staatliche Kunstsammlungen Dresden,
Archiv der Avantgarden – Egidio Marzona

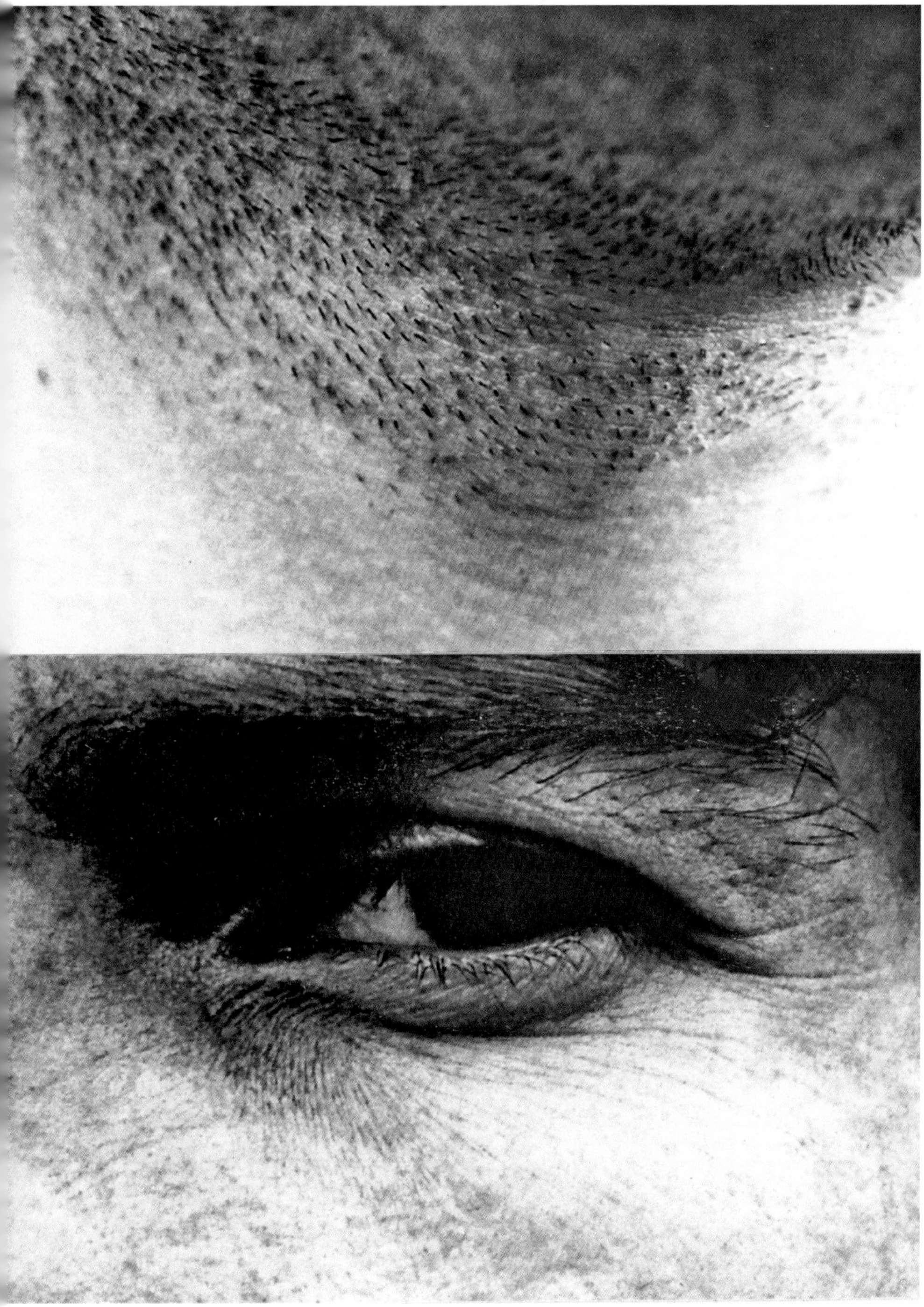

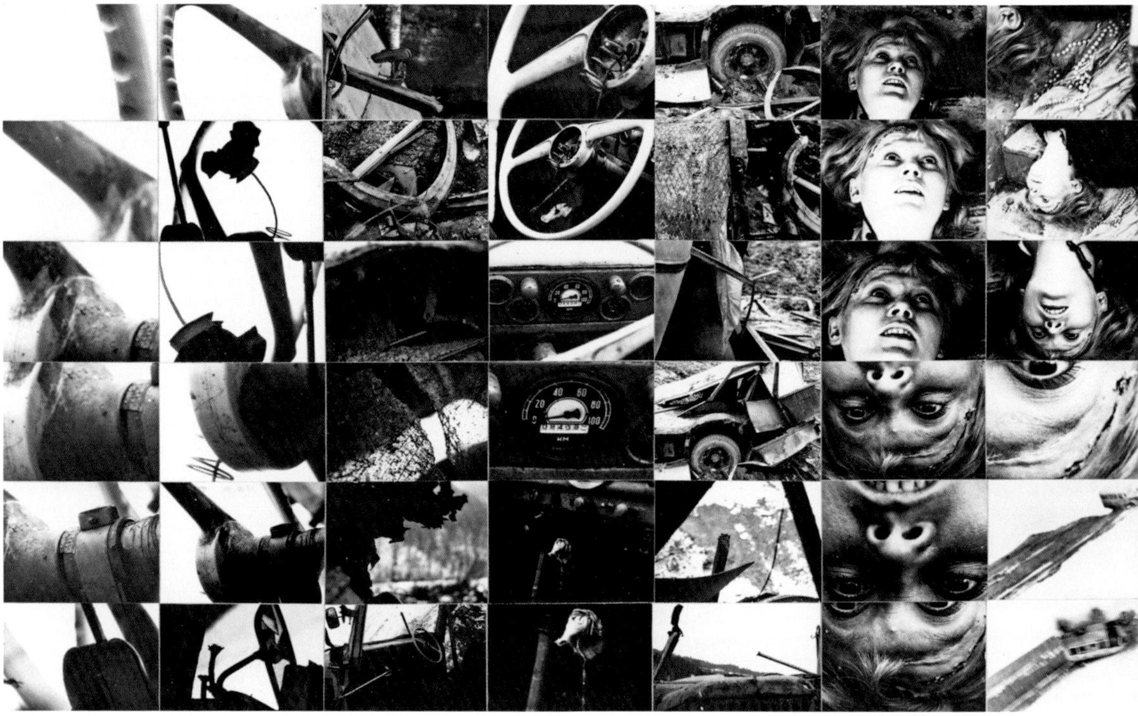

Ryszard Waśko

Ryszard Waśko
Wypadek (zapis policyjny) /
The Accident (a Police Record), 1971
Fotocollage | photo collage
109 × 167 cm
Courtesy ŻAK | BRANICKA, Berlin

Ryszard Waśko
Róg / A Corner, 1976
2 Fotografien | 2 photographs
je | each 27 × 18 cm
Courtesy ŻAK | BRANICKA, Berlin

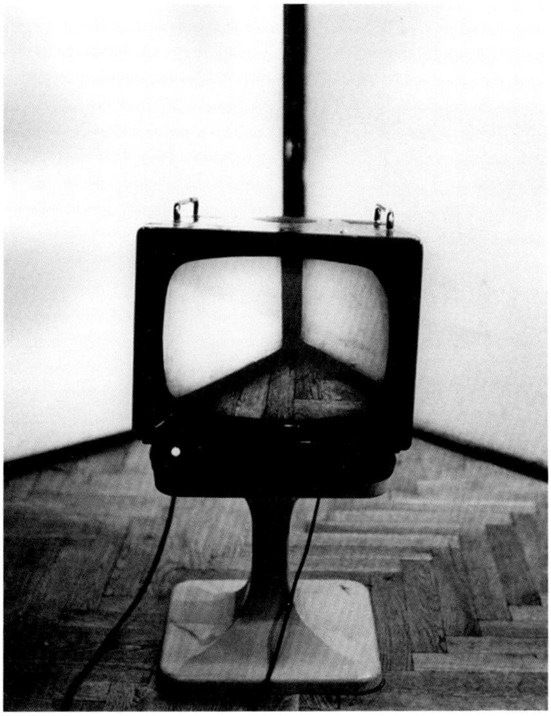

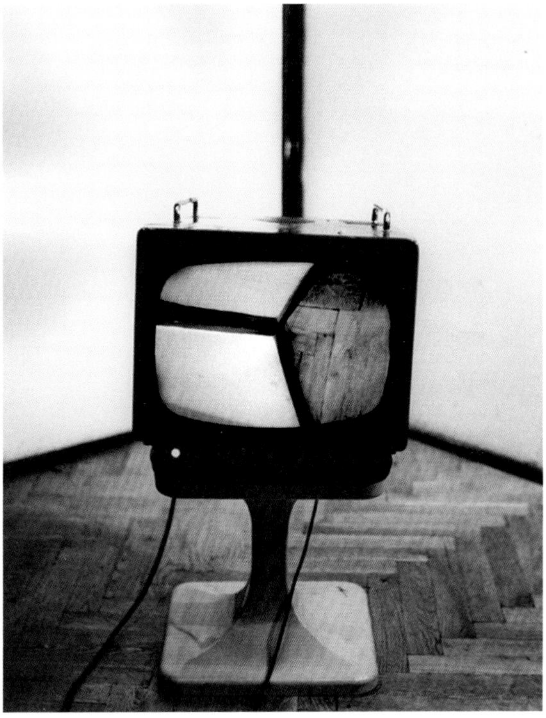

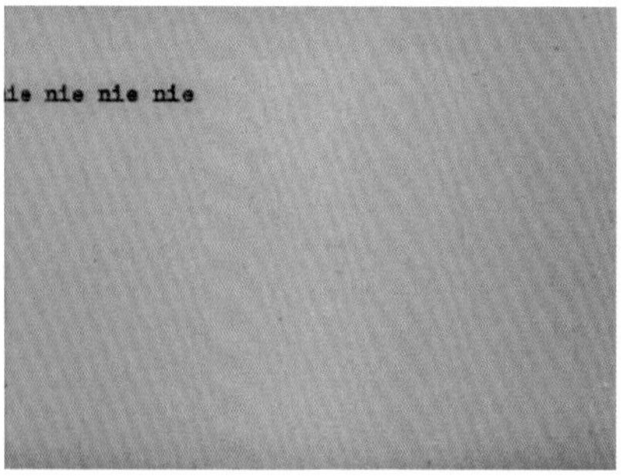

Ryszard Waśko
Negation, 1973
Video, 4:10 min.
Courtesy ŻAK | BRANICKA, Berlin

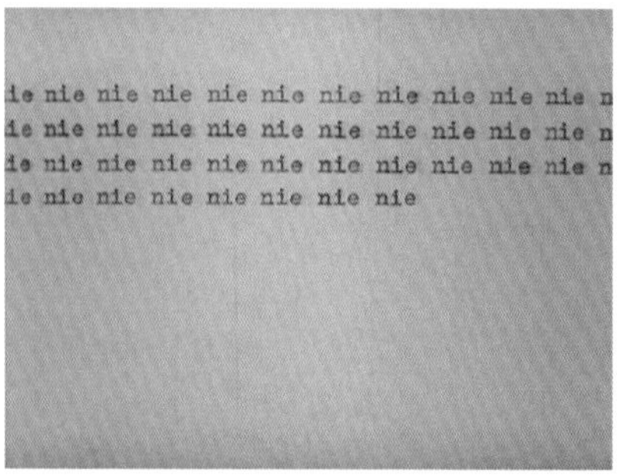

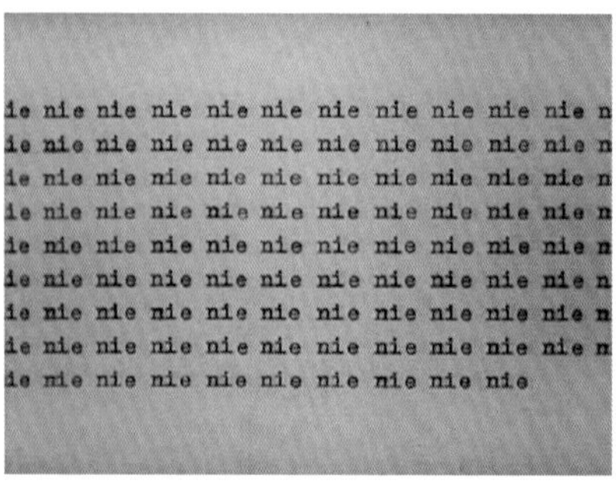

Ryszard Waśko

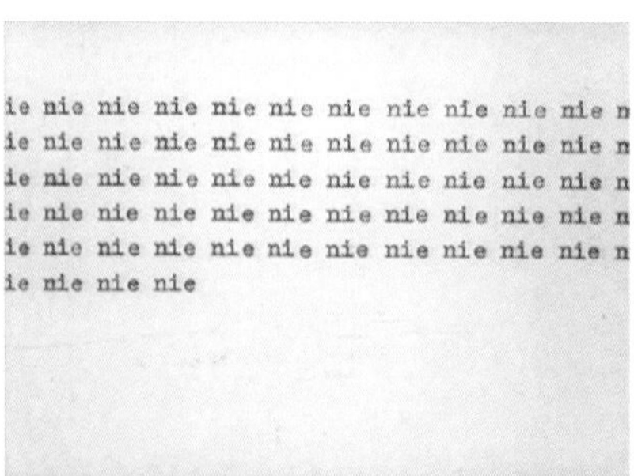

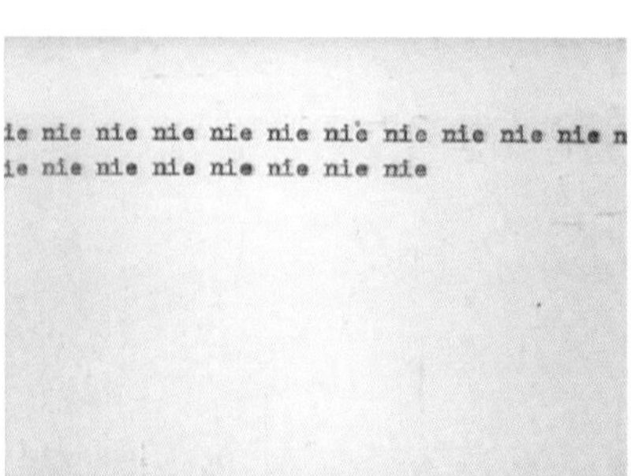

Ryszard Waśko
Record, 1972
Video, 2:47 min.
Courtesy ŻAK | BRANICKA, Berlin

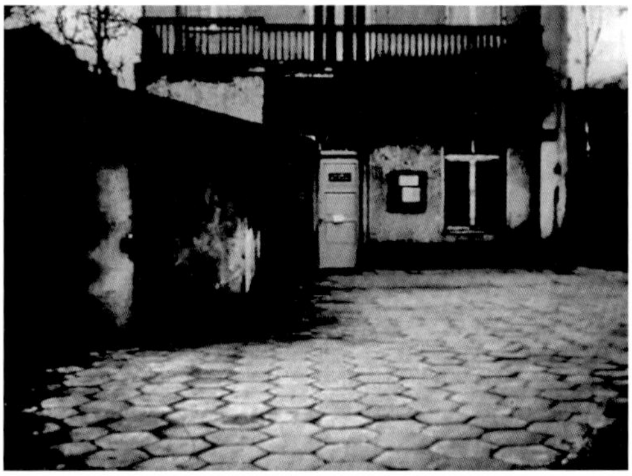
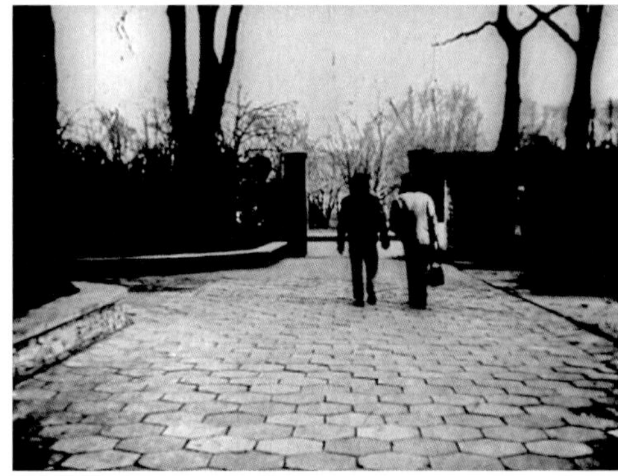
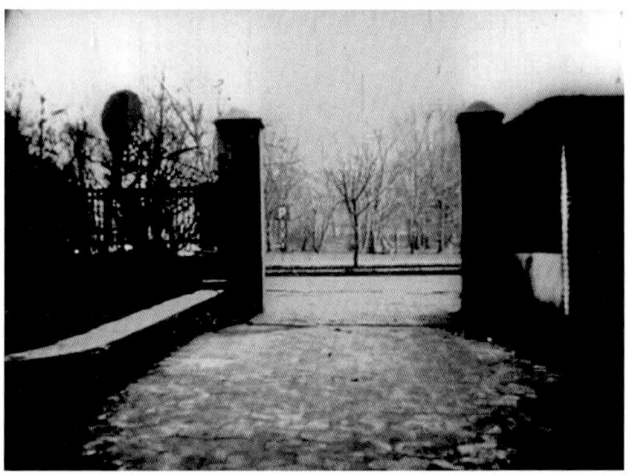
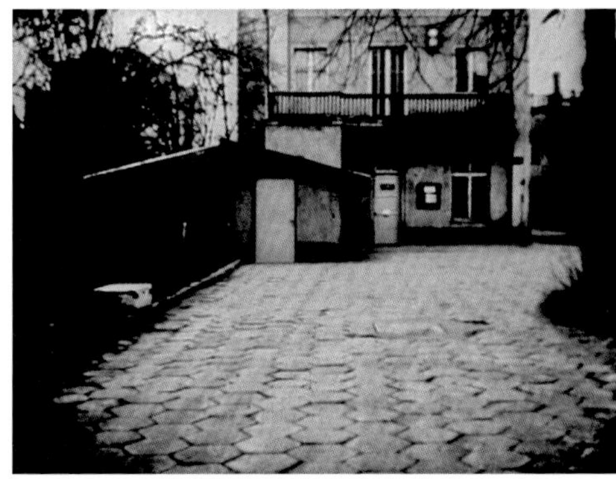
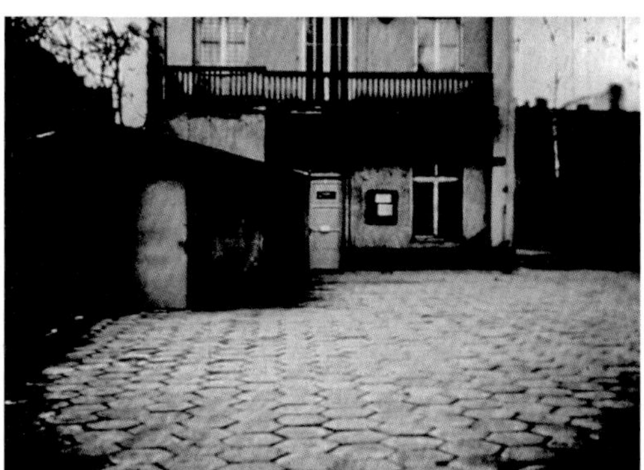
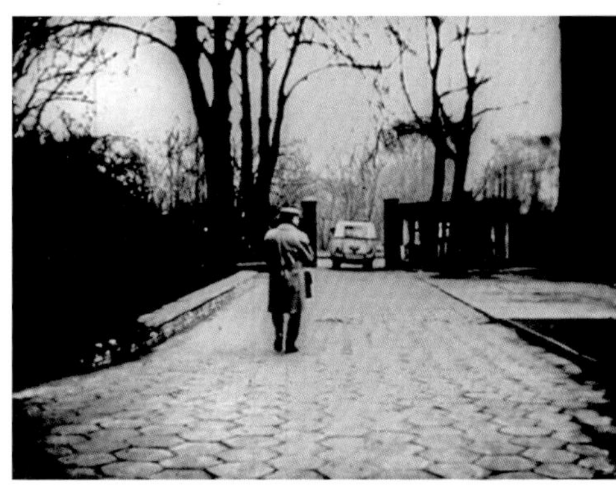
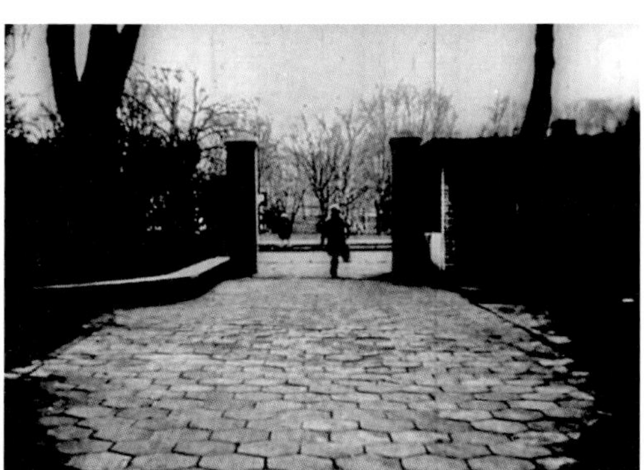
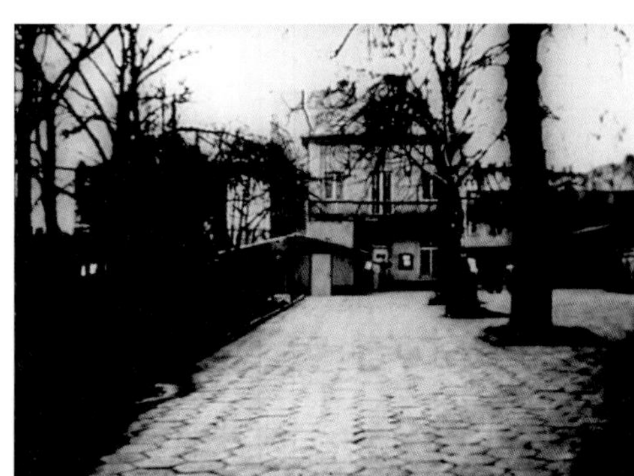

SPRACH- UND BILDANALYSE 2

LANGUAGE AND IMAGE ANALYSIS 2

Struktur und Logik bei Jarosław Kozłowski

Structure and Logic with Jarosław Kozłowski

Jarosław Kozłowski
Ćwiczenie z estetyki / Exercise of Aesthetics, 1976
Künstlerbuch | artist's book
Staatliche Kunstsammlungen Dresden, Archiv der Avantgarden – Egidio Marzona

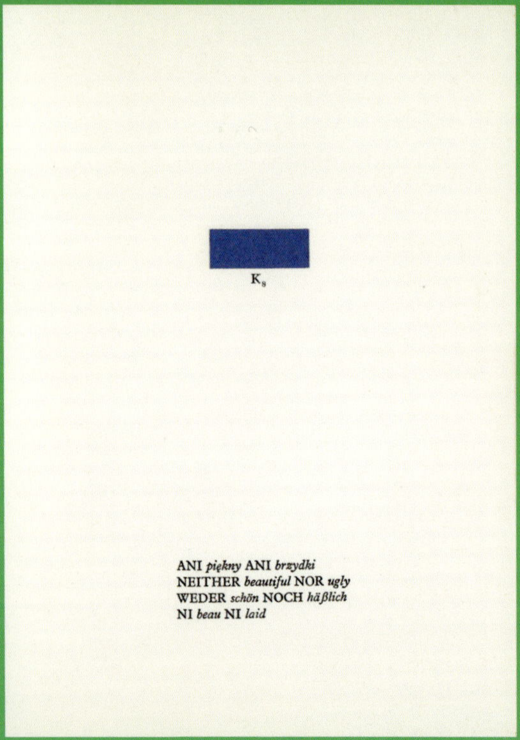

K_8

ANI *piękny* ANI *brzydki*
NEITHER *beautiful* NOR *ugly*
WEDER *schön* NOCH *häßlich*
NI *beau* NI *laid*

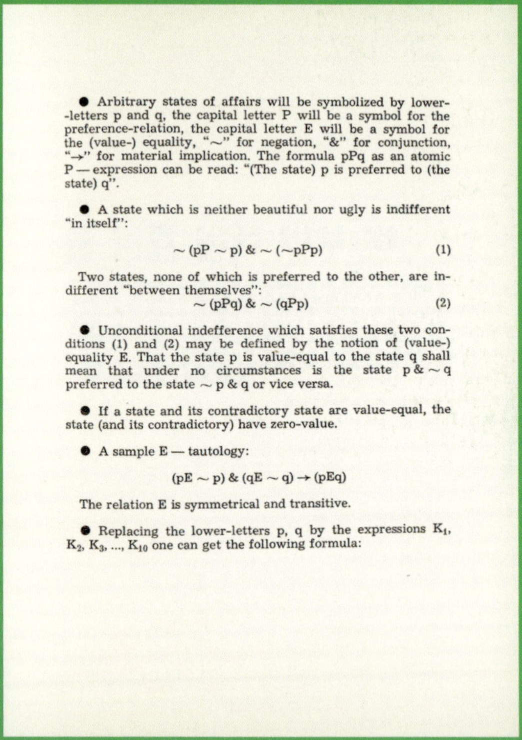

● Arbitrary states of affairs will be symbolized by lower--letters p and q, the capital letter P will be a symbol for the preference-relation, the capital letter E will be a symbol for the (value-) equality, "∼" for negation, "&" for conjunction, "→" for material implication. The formula pPq as an atomic P — expression can be read: "(The state) p is preferred to (the state) q".

● A state which is neither beautiful nor ugly is indifferent "in itself":

$$\sim (pP \sim p) \ \& \sim (\sim pPp) \qquad (1)$$

Two states, none of which is preferred to the other, are indifferent "between themselves":

$$\sim (pPq) \ \& \sim (qPp) \qquad (2)$$

● Unconditional indefference which satisfies these two conditions (1) and (2) may be defined by the notion of (value-) equality E. That the state p is value-equal to the state q shall mean that under no circumstances is the state p & ∼ q preferred to the state ∼ p & q or vice versa.

● If a state and its contradictory state are value-equal, the state (and its contradictory) have zero-value.

● A sample E — tautology:

$$(pE \sim p) \ \& \ (qE \sim q) \rightarrow (pEq)$$

The relation E is symmetrical and transitive.

● Replacing the lower-letters p, q by the expressions K_1, K_2, K_3, ..., K_{10} one can get the following formula:

Jarosław Kozłowski's work *Color* (1978) consists of a horizontal row of eight solid colored cardboards. The artist asked friends to name the color of the paper. The answers range from "czerwonawy" (reddish) to "fioletowy" (purple) and "różowz" (rosy) to associative comparisons: "Jak niebo przed burzą" (like the sky before a storm) or "Jak niedojrzała śliwka" (like an unripe plum). Although all the panels are the same color, the descriptions differ from each other, allowing the artist to make two things clear: that the relationship between an object and its linguistic description is arbitrary, and that therefore even a monochrome surface can be perceived in completely different ways. In his artist's book *Exercise in Aesthetics* (*Ćwiczenia z estetyki*, 1976) Kozłowski approaches the relationship between image and word in the opposite way: all ten of the color patterns are judged as "neither beautiful nor ugly." Marcel Duchamp had used the same formula when explaining that he had chosen his readymades according to the criteria of indifference. Kozłowski, who explored the philosophy of language and logic during his studies at the art academy in Poznań and participated in the VIII. Syncretic Performance by Włodzimierz Borowski as Andrzej Matuszewski's assistant in his gallery odNOWA in Poznań, rejects the idea of the creative artist and refuses to accept a visual representation of reality. Instead, he considers the logical structure of language to be the basis of perception and knowledge and examines in his work how the linguistic system of symbols determines our mental images.

B. E.

Jarosław Kozłowskis Arbeit *Colour* aus dem Jahr 1978 besteht aus einer horizontalen Reihung von acht einfarbigen Kartons. Der Künstler hatte Freunde gebeten, den Farbton des Papiers zu benennen. Die Antworten reichen von „czerwonawy" (rötlich) über „fioletowy" (lila) und „różowz" (rosig) bis hin zu assoziativen Vergleichen: „Jak niebo przed burzą" (wie der Himmel vor dem Sturm) oder „Jak niedojrzała śliwka" (wie eine unreife Pflaume). Obwohl alle Tafeln die identische Farbe haben, unterscheiden sich sämtliche Bezeichnungen voneinander, womit der Künstler zweierlei deutlich macht: dass die Beziehung zwischen einem Objekt und seiner sprachlichen Bezeichnung willkürlich ist und dass folglich selbst eine monochrome Farbfläche auf völlig unterschiedliche Weise wahrgenommen werden kann. In seinem Künstlerbuch *Exercise in Aesthetics* (*Ćwiczenia z estetyki*) von 1976 nähert sich Kozłowski dem Zusammenhang von Bild und Wort auf entgegengesetzte Weise: Alle zehn eingeklebten Farbmuster werden als „weder schön noch hässlich" beurteilt. Diese Formulierung hatte schon Marcel Duchamp benutzt, als er beschrieb, dass er seine Readymades nach dem Kriterium der ästhetischen Indifferenz ausgewählt hatte. Kozłowski, der sich während seines Studiums an der Kunsthochschule in Poznań mit Sprachphilosophie und Logik beschäftigt hatte und als Assistent von Andrzej Matuszewski in dessen Galerie odNOWA in Poznań an der VIII. Synkretistischen Schau von Włodzimierz Borowski beteiligt war, lehnt die Idee vom schöpferischen Künstler ab und verweigert die bildliche Darstellung der Wirklichkeit. Stattdessen betrachtet er die logische Struktur von Sprache als Grundlage von Wahrnehmung und Erkenntnis und untersucht in seinen Werken, wie das sprachliche Zeichensystem unsere Vorstellungsbilder bestimmt.

B. E.

Jarosław Kozłowski

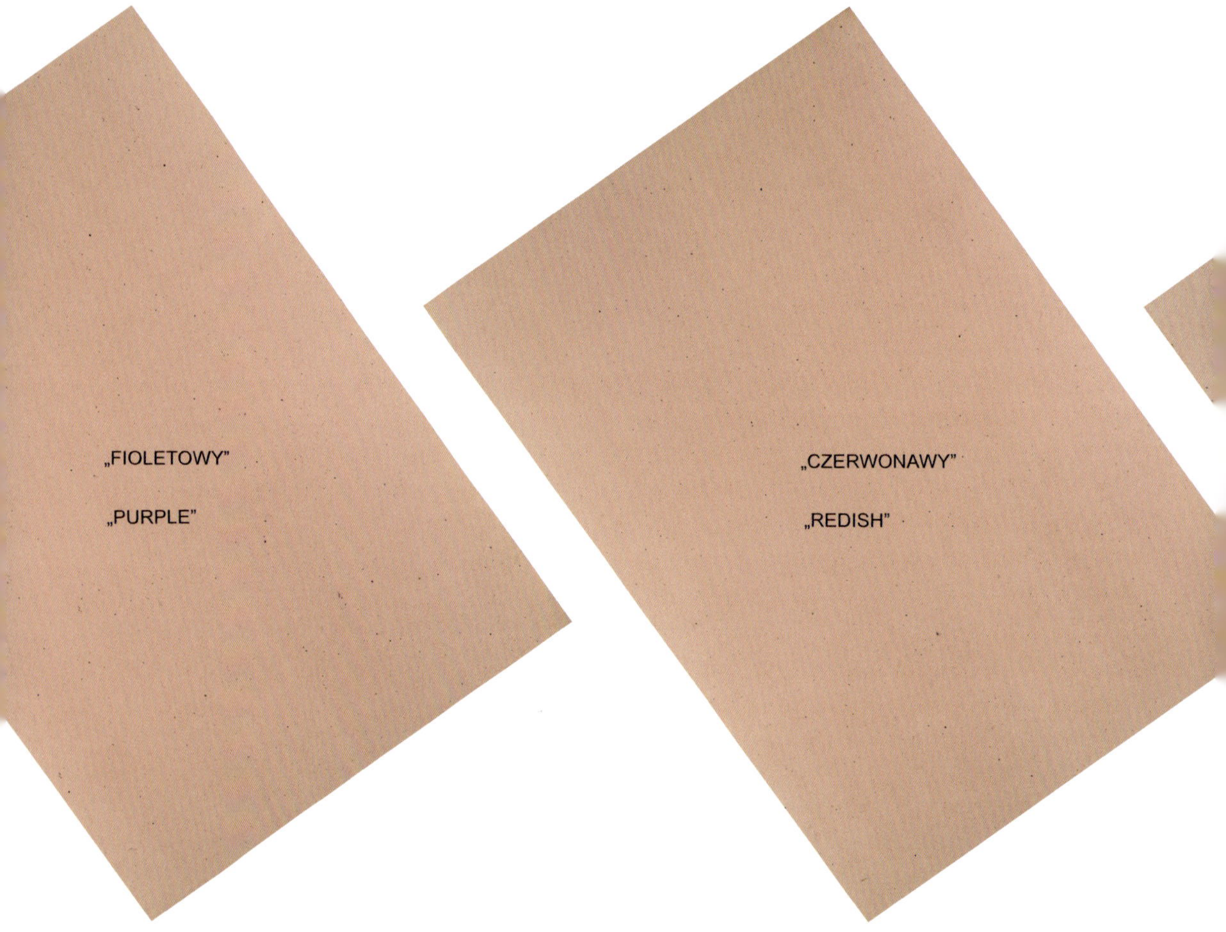

Jarosław Kozłowski
Kolor / Color, 1978
Klebebuchstaben auf Papier |
adhesive letters on paper
8-teilig | 8 pieces, je | each 97 × 67 cm
Courtesy ŻAK | BRANICKA, Berlin,
Profile Foundation, Warschau

„JAK HELIOTROP"

„LIKE A HELIOTROPE"

„JAK NIEBO PRZED BURZĄ"

„LIKE THE SKY BEFORE STORM"

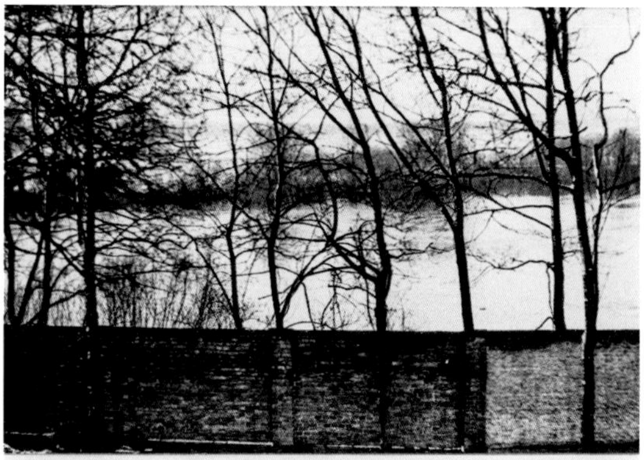

31 stycznia 1977 roku Jan idzie nad Tamizę.

Am 31. Januar 1977 geht Jan an die Themse.
On 31 January 1977, Jan goes to the Thames.

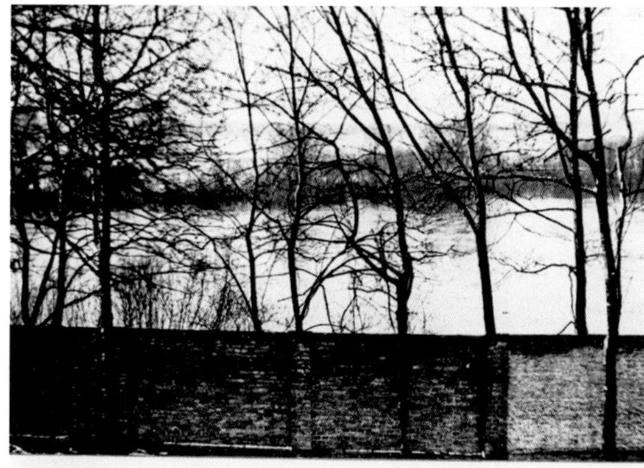

1 lipca 1977 roku Jan idzie nad Wartę.

Am 1. Juli 1977 geht Jan an die Warthe.
On 1 July 1977, Jan goes to the Warta.

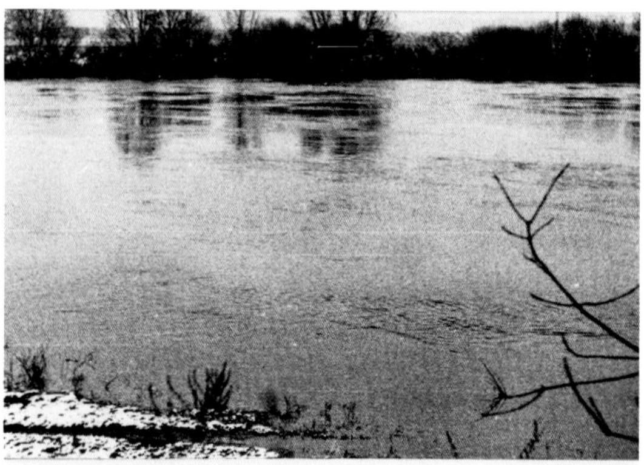

Pewnego dnia Jan idzie nad Wartę.

Eines Tages geht Jan an die Warthe.
One day Jan goes to the Warta.

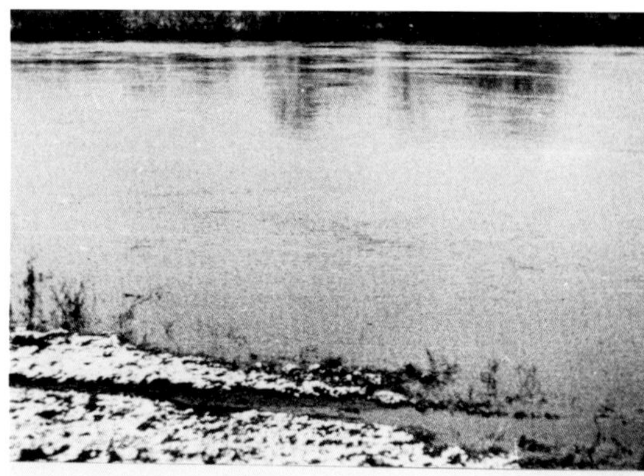

Pewnego dnia jakiś człowiek idzie nad Wartę.

Eines Tages geht ein Mensch an die Warthe.
One day a person goes to the Warta.

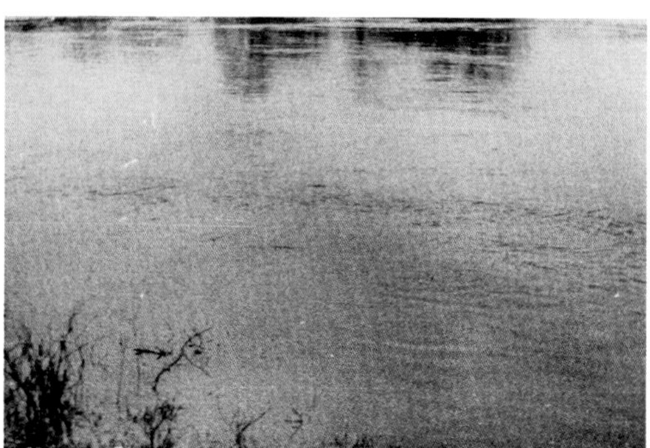

Pewnego dnia jakiś człowiek idzie nad jakąś rzekę.

Eines Tages geht ein Mensch an einen Fluss.
One day a person goes to a river.

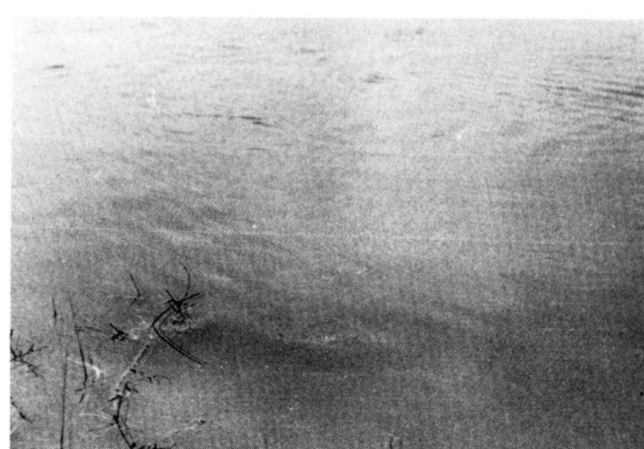

Pewnego dnia ktoś idzie nad jakąś rzekę.

Eines Tages geht irgendjemand an einen Fluss.
One day someone goes to a river.

Jarosław Kozłowski

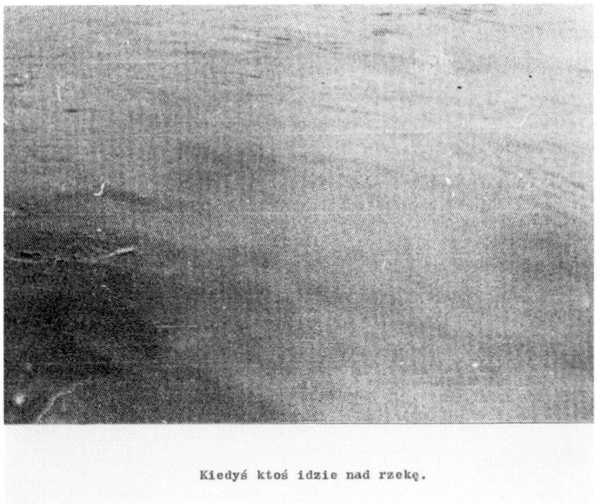

Einmal geht irgendjemand an einen Fluss.
Sometime someone goes to a river.

Jarosław Kozłowski
Ćwiczenia z semiotyki III /
Exercises in Semiotics III, 1977
7 Fotografien | 7 photographs
je | each 19,5 × 17 cm
ŻAK | BRANICKA, Berlin,
Profile Foundation, Warschau

Jarosław Kozłowski

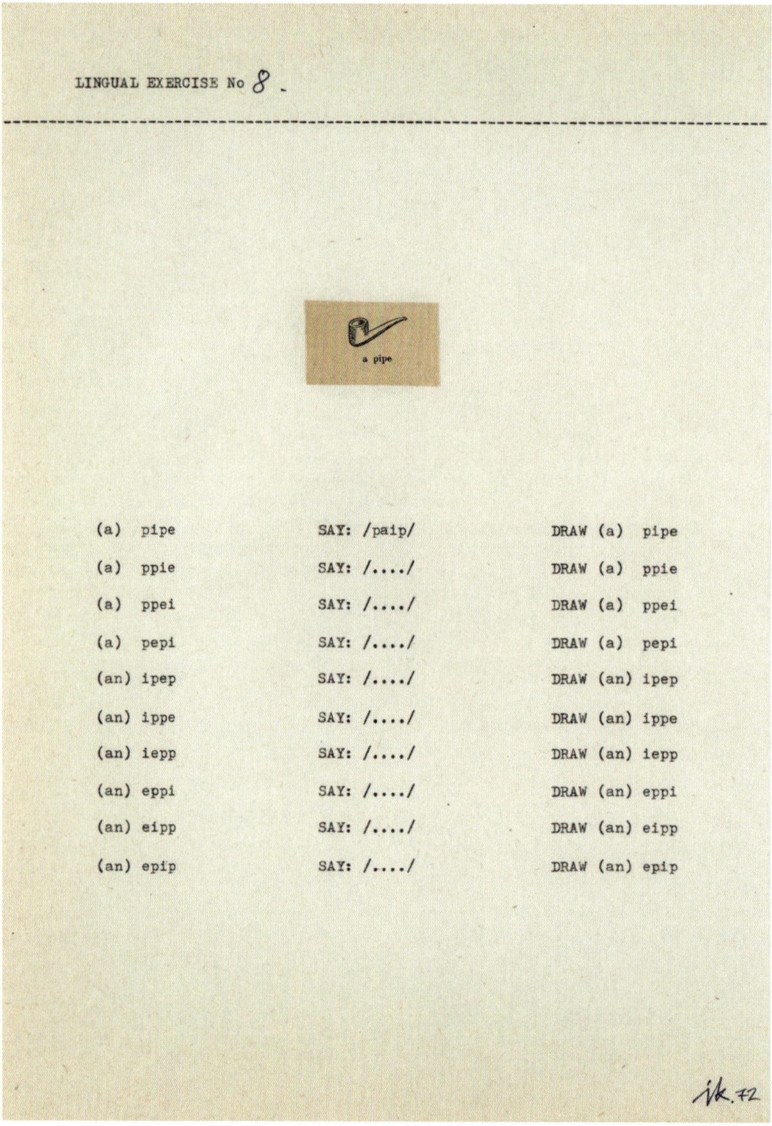
LINGUAL EXERCISE No 8.

a pipe

(a) pipe	SAY: /paip/	DRAW (a) pipe
(a) ppie	SAY: /..../	DRAW (a) ppie
(a) ppei	SAY: /..../	DRAW (a) ppei
(a) pepi	SAY: /..../	DRAW (a) pepi
(an) ipep	SAY: /..../	DRAW (an) ipep
(an) ippe	SAY: /..../	DRAW (an) ippe
(an) iepp	SAY: /..../	DRAW (an) iepp
(an) eppi	SAY: /..../	DRAW (an) eppi
(an) eipp	SAY: /..../	DRAW (an) eipp
(an) epip	SAY: /..../	DRAW (an) epip

jk.72

Jarosław Kozłowski
Ćwiczenia lingwistyczne / Lingual Exercises, 1972
Schreibmaschine, Druck, Kuli auf Papier |
typescript, print, pen on paper
Serie 44-teilig | series of 44 pieces
je | each 32 × 22 cm
Staatliche Kunstsammlungen Dresden,
Archiv der Avantgarden – Egidio Marzona

Jarosław Kozłowski
Ćwiczenia ze swobody /
Exercises in Freedom, 1979
9 farbige Papiere | 9 colored papers
je | each 23 × 24 cm
Sammlung | Collection Block, Berlin

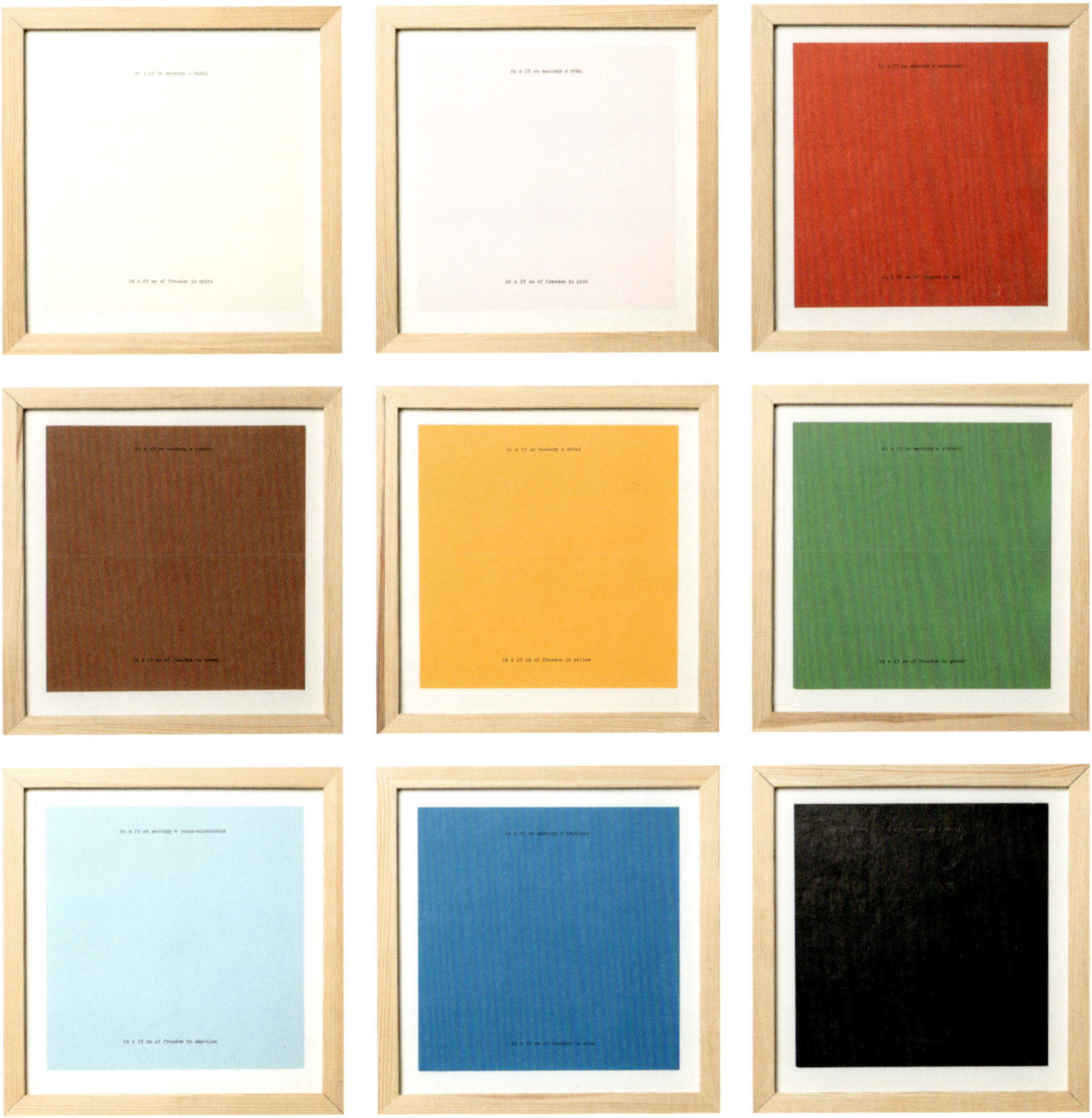

NET

NET

- a NET is open and uncommercial
- points of the NET are: private homes, studios an[d] any other places, where art propositions are arti[cu]lated
- these propositions are presented to persons inte[re]sted in them
- propositions may be accompanied by editions in fo[rm] of prints, tapes, slides, photographs, books, films, handbills, letters, manuscripts etc.
- NET has no centtral point and any coordination
- points of the NET can be anywhere
- all points of the NET are in contact among themse[l]ves and exchange concepts, propositions, projects a[nd] other forms of articulation
- the idea of NET is not new and in this moment it stops to be an authorized idea
- NET can be arbitrarily developed and copied

Jarosław Kozłowski
Andrzej Kostołowski

Jarosław Kozłowski
Andrzej Kostołowski

INTERNATIONALE NETZWERKE 1
INTERNATIONAL NETWORKS 1

NET

A distinguishing feature of the Polish art scene was the close interconnectedness of its members. In addition to numerous independent galleries, festivals and symposia, there were multifaceted initiatives by Polish artists designed to connect with the international scene. Among them, the NET project, founded in 1971 by Jarosław Kozłowski and the art theorist Andrzej Kostołowski, was one of the most comprehensive and successful. Its exhortation proclaiming the open exchange of ideas and material and claiming no control or direction on the part of the initiators, was sent to more than 350 artists in over 30 countries. The response was enormous, in part because many of the international addressees had similar artistic ideas about alternative forms of communication, distribution and institutions. Although NET was first and foremost intended to provide artistic freedom, the initiative was also understood as an appeal for political disobedience. As a result, the Polish security forces disbanded NET's first presentation in 1972 in Kozłowski's apartment after only 45 minutes and did not return the confiscated works of art for another year. The artist himself lost his position at the Poznań art academy and was demoted to a job in the library. Kozłowski responded by founding his private gallery, Akumulatory 2, in Poznań under the auspices of the Polish student organization and, until its closing in 1990, organized nearly 200 exhibitions, lectures and campaigns, among them a large Fluxus-Festival in 1977.

B. E.

Jarosław Kozłowski, Andrzej Kostołowski
NET Manifest / NET manifesto, 1971
Schreibmaschine | typescript
29,7 × 21 cm
Sammlung | Collection Kozłowski, Poznań

Ein Kennzeichen der polnischen Kunstszene war die starke Vernetzung der Akteure. Neben der Vielzahl von unabhängig vom Staat agierenden Autorengalerien, Festivals und Tagungen gab es vielfältige Initiativen polnischer Künstler*innen, mit der internationalen Szene in Verbindung zu treten. Hiervon war das 1971 gemeinsam von Jarosław Kozłowski und dem Kunsttheoretiker Andrzej Kostołowski gestartete Projekt NET eines der umfänglichsten und erfolgreichsten. Der Aufruf, der den offenen Austausch von Ideen und Material proklamierte und keinerlei Regie oder Kontrolle für die Initiatoren reklamierte, wurde an mehr als 350 Künstler*innen aus über 30 Ländern verschickt. Die Resonanz war gewaltig, was auch daran lag, dass viele der internationalen Adressaten ähnliche künstlerische Vorstellungen von alternativen Kommunikations-, Distributions- und Institutionsformen hatten. Obwohl NET in erster Linie für künstlerische Freiräume sorgen sollte, wurde die Initiative auch als Aufruf zum politischen Ungehorsam verstanden. Folglich löste der polnische Sicherheitsdienst die erste Präsentation von NET 1972 in Kozłowskis Wohnung nach 45 Minuten auf und gab die konfiszierten Werke erst nach einem Jahr zurück. Der Künstler selbst verlor seine Assistenzstelle an der Kunsthochschule in Poznań und wurde in die Bibliothek strafversetzt. Daraufhin gründete Kozłowski in Poznań seine private Galerie Akumulatory 2 unter dem Dach der polnischen Studentenorganisation und veranstaltete bis zur Schließung 1990 knapp 200 Ausstellungen, Vorträge und Aktionen, darunter 1977 ein großes Fluxus-Festival.

B. E.

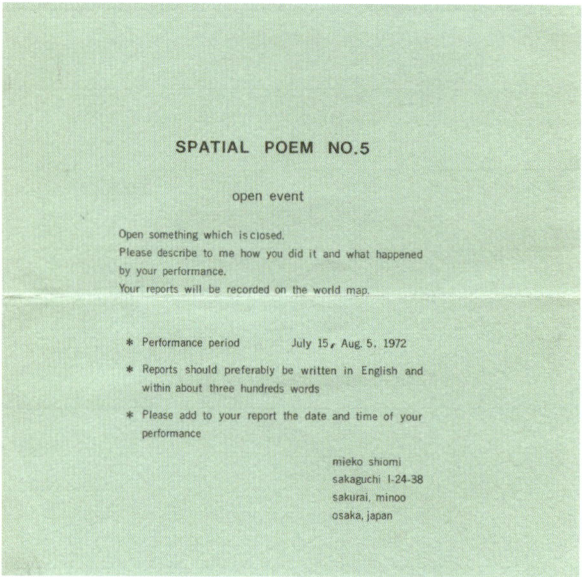

SPATIAL POEM NO.5

open event

Open something which is closed.
Please describe to me how you did it and what happened by your performance.
Your reports will be recorded on the world map.

* Performance period July 15, Aug. 5. 1972
* Reports should preferably be written in English and within about three hundreds words
* Please add to your report the date and time of your performance

mieko shiomi
sakaguchi 1-24-38
sakurai, minoo
osaka, japan

Mieko Shiomi
Spatial Poem No. 5 (Open Event), 1974
Drucksache | printed matter
18 × 18 cm
Sammlung | Collection Kozłowski, Poznań

On Kawara
I Am Still Alive, 1973
Telegramm | telegram
13,8 × 19 cm
Sammlung | Collection Kozłowski, Poznań

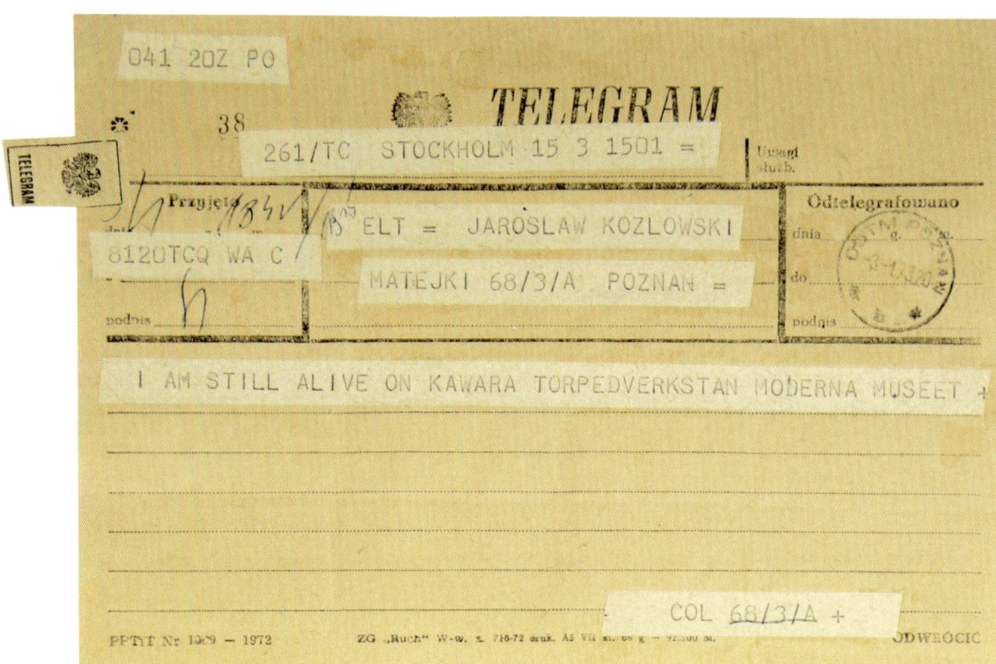

041 20Z PO

TELEGRAM

38

261/TC STOCKHOLM 15 3 1501 =

Uwagi służb.

Przyjęto

8120TCQ WA C

podpis

ELT = JAROSLAW KOZLOWSKI

MATEJKI 68/3/A POZNAN =

Odtelegrafowano

dnia

do

podpis

I AM STILL ALIVE ON KAWARA TORPEDVERKSTAN MODERNA MUSEET +

COL 68/3/A +

PPTiT Nr 1009 – 1972

ODWRÓCIĆ

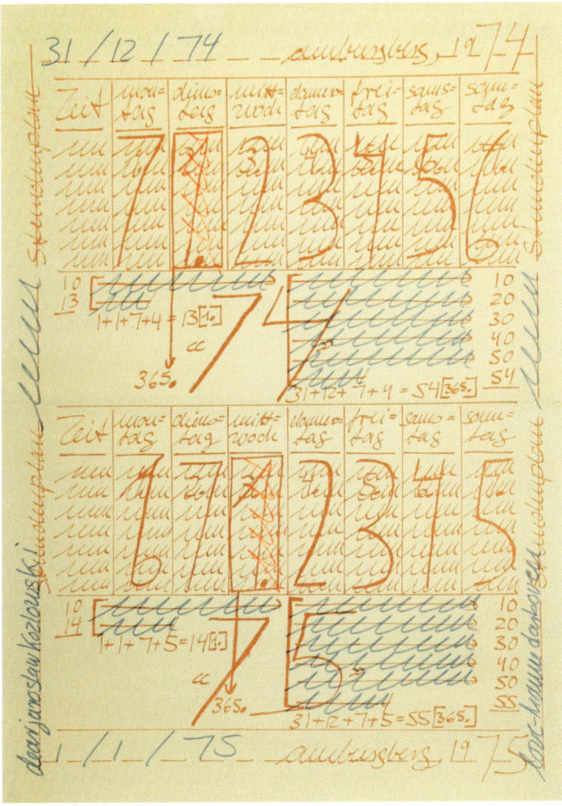

Hanne Darboven
Stundenplan / Timetable, 1975
Zeichnung | drawing
40 × 30 cm
Sammlung | Collection Kozłowski, Poznań

Ben Vautier
Fluxpost Card, 1965
Postkarte | postcard
15,2 × 21 cm
Sammlung | Collection Kozłowski, Poznań

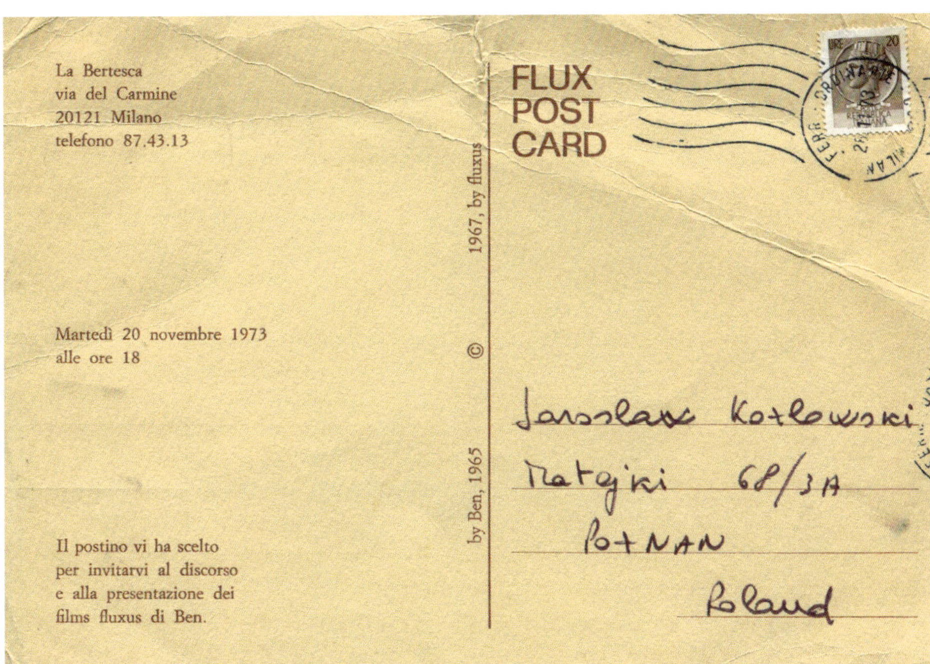

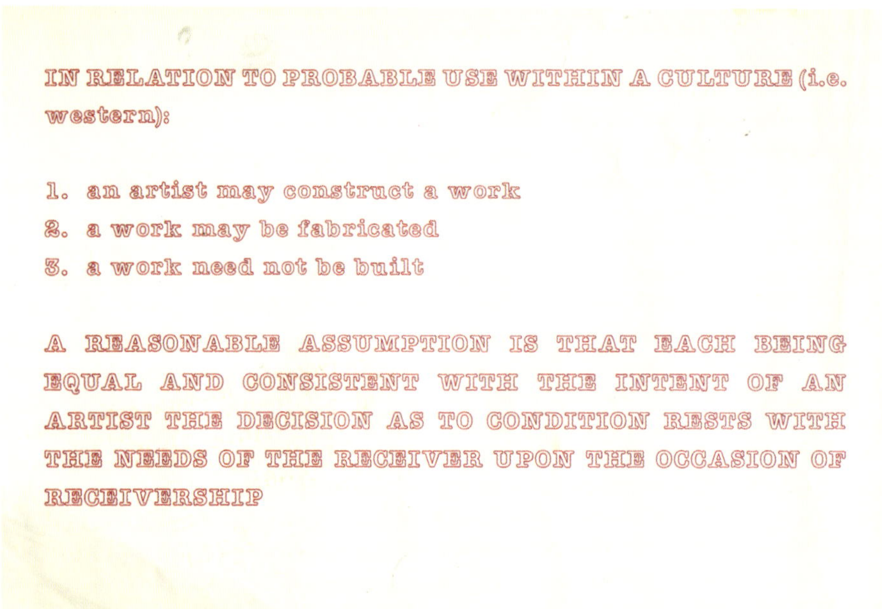
IN RELATION TO PROBABLE USE WITHIN A CULTURE (i.e. western):

1. an artist may construct a work
2. a work may be fabricated
3. a work need not be built

A REASONABLE ASSUMPTION IS THAT EACH BEING EQUAL AND CONSISTENT WITH THE INTENT OF AN ARTIST THE DECISION AS TO CONDITION RESTS WITH THE NEEDS OF THE RECEIVER UPON THE OCCASION OF RECEIVERSHIP

Lawrence Weiner
In Relation to Probable Use Within a Culture, 1973
Drucksache | print matter
14,3 × 20,4 cm
Sammlung | Collection Kozłowski, Poznań

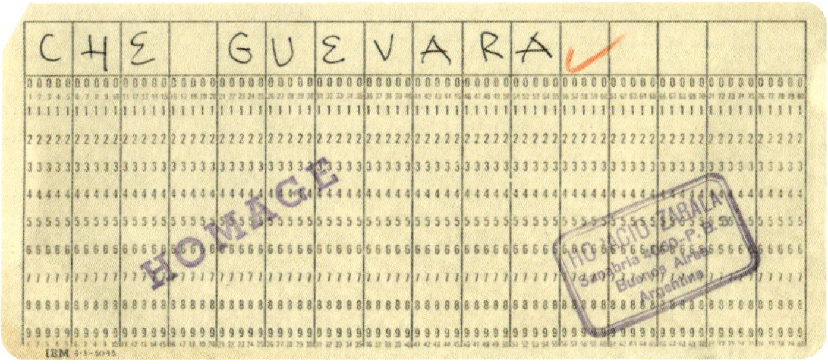

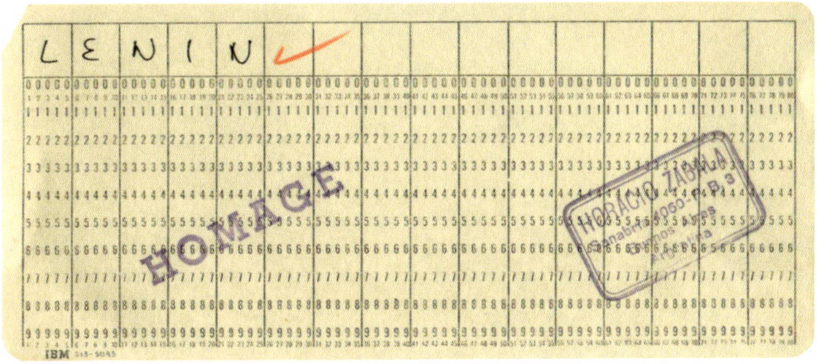

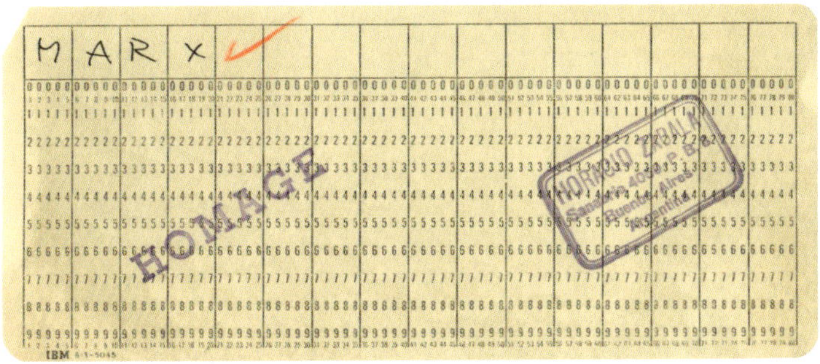

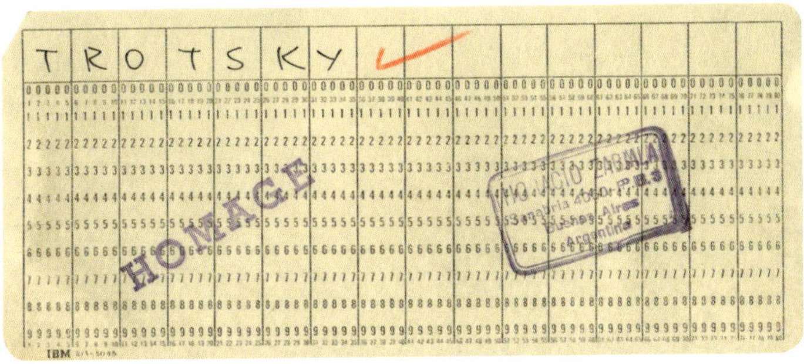

Horacio Zabala
Homage..., 1970er-Jahre | 1970s
Schreibmaschine, Manuskript |
typescript, manuscript,
4-teilig | 4 pieces, je | each 8,3 × 18,7 cm
Sammlung | Collection Kozłowski, Poznań

INTERNATIONALE NETZWERKE 2
INTERNATIONAL NETWORKS 2

CONSTRUCTION IN PROCESS

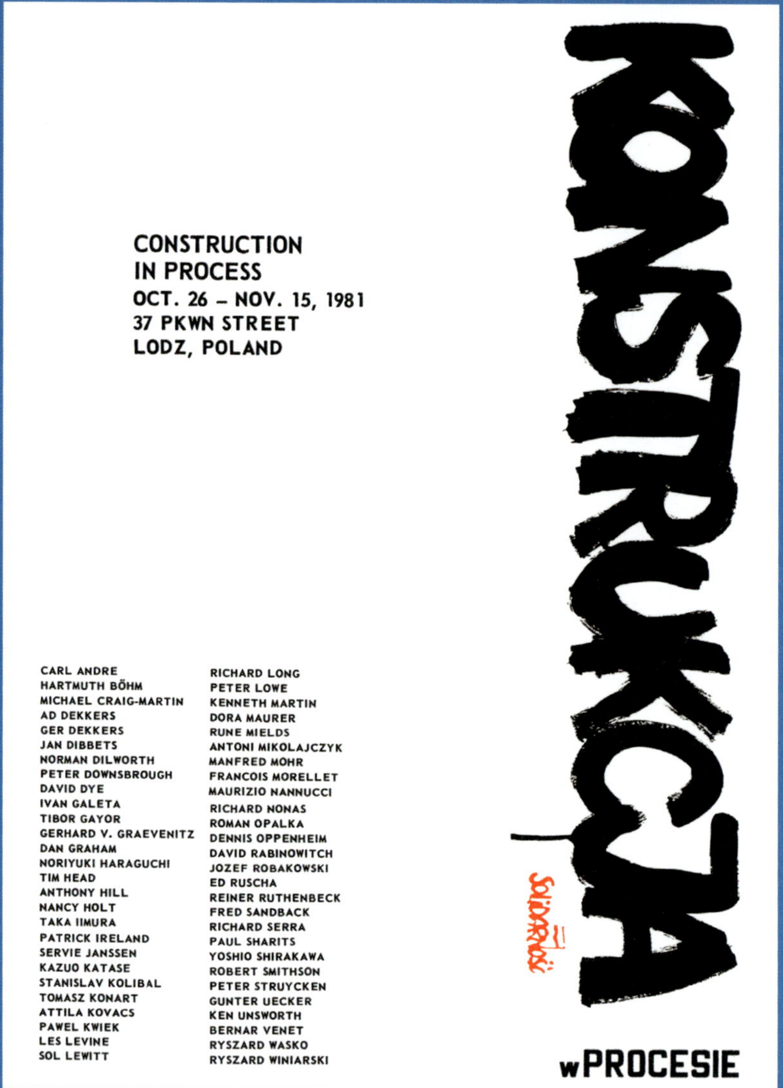

Konstrukcja w Procesie / Construction in Process, Łódź, 1981
Kuratiert von | curated by Ryszard Waśko,
Plakat, Fotodokumentation | poster, photo documentation
Archives of Contemporary Thought

The exhibition *Construction in Process* took place from October 26 to November 15, 1981, in an abandoned factory building in Łódź. It was conceived by Ryszard Waśko and is considered the largest international exhibition of contemporary art not organized by the state in the People's Republic of Poland. It featured works by more than 50 conceptual artists, among them Carl Andre, Jan Dibbets, Sol LeWitt, Rune Mields, and Günther Uecker. The project was modeled on the exhibition *Pier+Ocean.* Construction in the 1970s which appeared in the spring of 1980 at the Hayward Gallery in London, and which included Waśko's work. In contrast to London, the goal for Łódź was to make visible both the artistic process and artistic activities in a social context, which lent the exhibition a political edge given the strained situation in Poland following the strike movements of 1980. To manage the organizational facets of this large project, the organizational committee of *Construction in Process*, comprised of Waśko, Józef Robakowski and other members of the Filmform Workshop (Warsztat Formy Filmowej), contacted the Solidarność union, which supported the project. The social function of art expressed here had its role models, for Waśko and his organizational team, in the Polish constructivism of the 1920s, which is why Henryk Stażewski was asked to join the honorary committee and attended the opening. When martial law was imposed a few weeks after the end of the exhibition, the works remaining in Poland were illegally kept in storage at the Sztuki Museum in Łódź, until being officially integrated into the collection in 2005. Ryszard Waśko continued *Construction in Process* in the following years as a worldwide network of exhibitions, including one in Munich in 1985, in Israel in 1995, in Melbourne in 1998 and at the Venice Biennale in 2001.

B. E.

Die Ausstellung *Construction in Process* fand vom 26. Oktober bis 15. November 1981 in einem leer stehenden Fabrikgebäude in Łódź statt. Sie wurde von Ryszard Waśko konzipiert und gilt als größte nicht staatlich organisierte internationale Ausstellung zeitgenössischer Kunst in der Volksrepublik Polen. Gezeigt wurden Arbeiten von mehr als 50 konzeptuell arbeitenden Künstler*innen, u. a. von Carl Andre, Jan Dibbets, Sol LeWitt, Rune Mields und Günther Uecker. Vorbild für das Projekt war die Ausstellung *Pier+Ocean. Construction in the 1970s* vom Frühjahr 1980 in der Hayward Gallery in London, auf der Waśko vertreten war. Ziel für Łódź war im Unterschied zu London die stärkere Sichtbarmachung des künstlerischen Prozesses und der Aktivitäten im sozialen Kontext, was der Ausstellung angesichts der angespannten Situation in Polen nach den Streikbewegungen von 1980 eine politische Brisanz gab. Um die organisatorischen Aufgaben des großen Projektes zu bewältigen, knüpfte das Organisationskomitee von *Construction in Process*, dem neben Waśko und Józef Robakowski noch weitere Akteure der Werkstatt der Filmform (Warsztat Formy Filmowej) angehörten, auch Kontakte zur Gewerkschaft Solidarność, die das Projekt stark unterstützte. Die soziale Funktion der Kunst, die hier zum Ausdruck kam, hatte für Waśko und sein Organisationsteam ihre Vorbilder im polnischen Konstruktivismus der 1920er-Jahre, weshalb Henryk Stażewski ins Ehrenkomittee aufgenommen wurde und der Eröffnung beiwohnte. Nach Ausrufung des Kriegsrechts wenige Wochen nach Ende der Ausstellung wurden die in Polen verbliebenen Werke illegal im Depot des Muzeum Sztuki in Łódź verwahrt, bis sie 2005 offiziell in die Sammlung gelangten. Ryszard Waśko setzte *Construction in Process* in den folgenden Jahren als weltweites Netzwerk von Ausstellungen fort, u. a. 1985 in München, 1995 in Israel, 1998 in Melbourne und 2001 auf der Biennale in Venedig.

B. E.

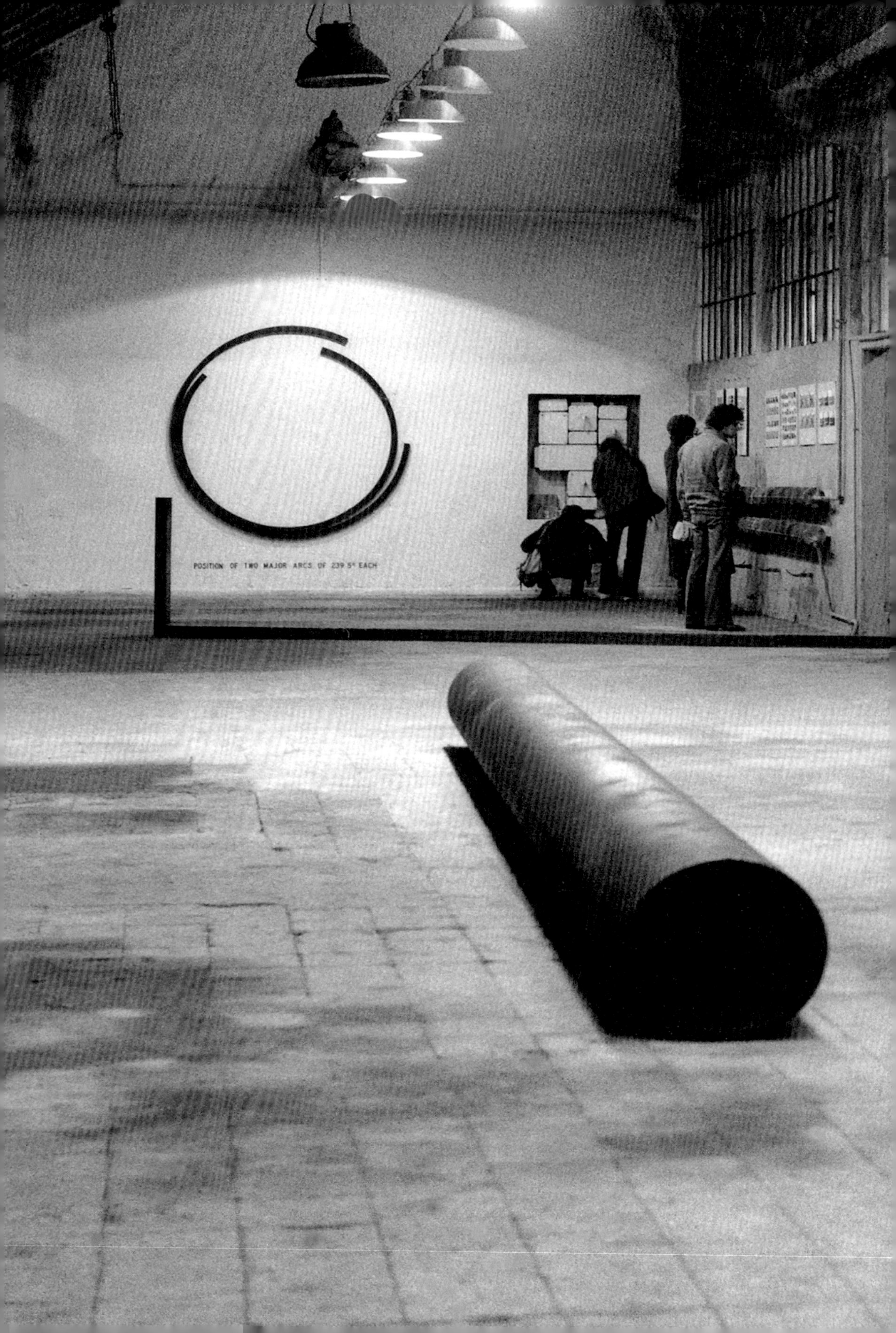
POSITION OF TWO MAJOR ARCS OF 239.5° EACH

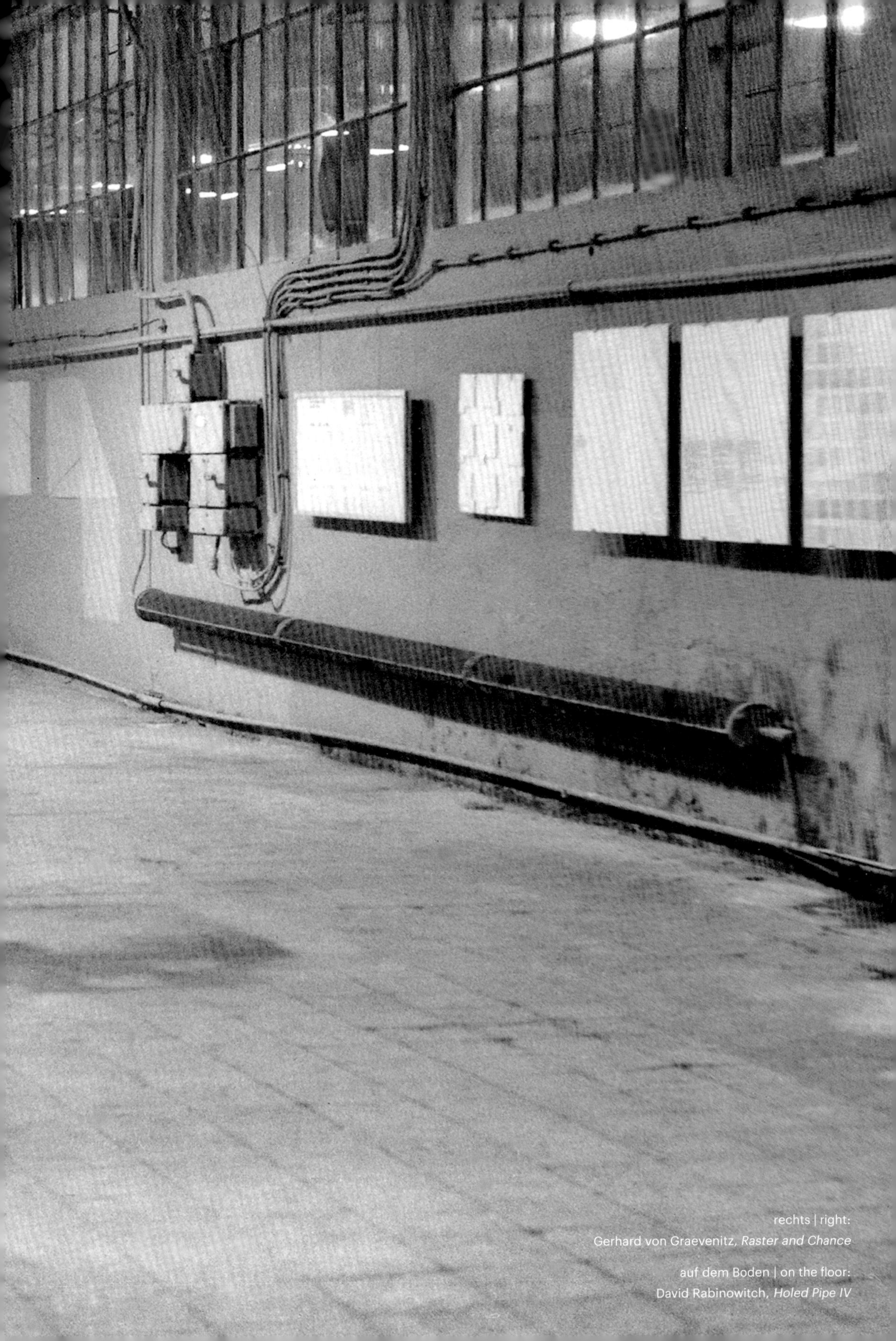

rechts | right:
Gerhard von Graevenitz, *Raster and Chance*

auf dem Boden | on the floor:
David Rabinowitch, *Holed Pipe IV*

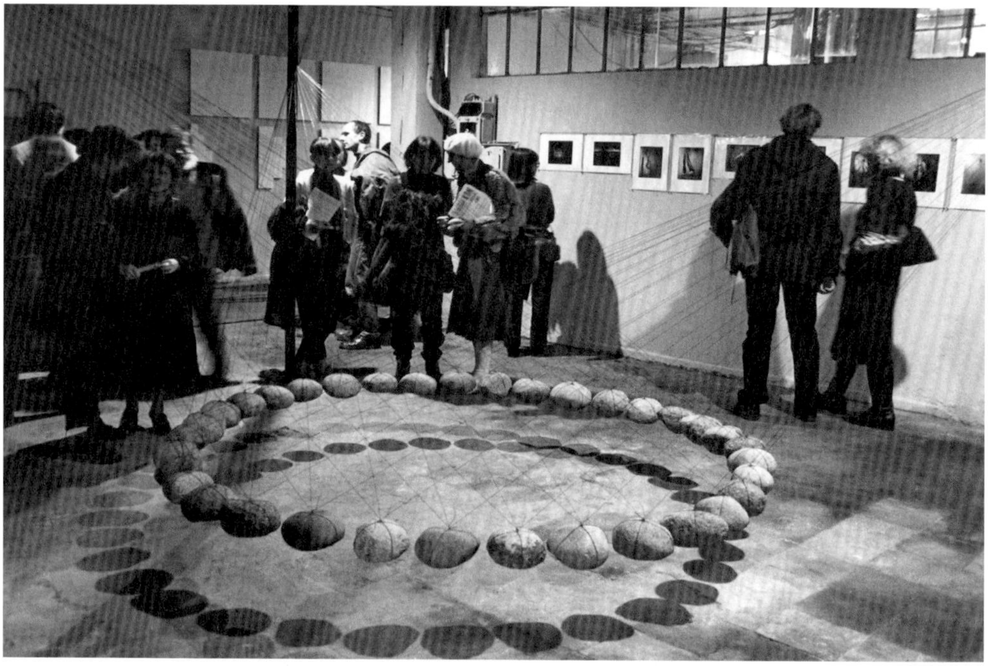

Ken Unsworth
Suspended Stone Circle

von links nach rechts | from left to right:
Richard Nonas, Rune Mields, Patrick Ireland

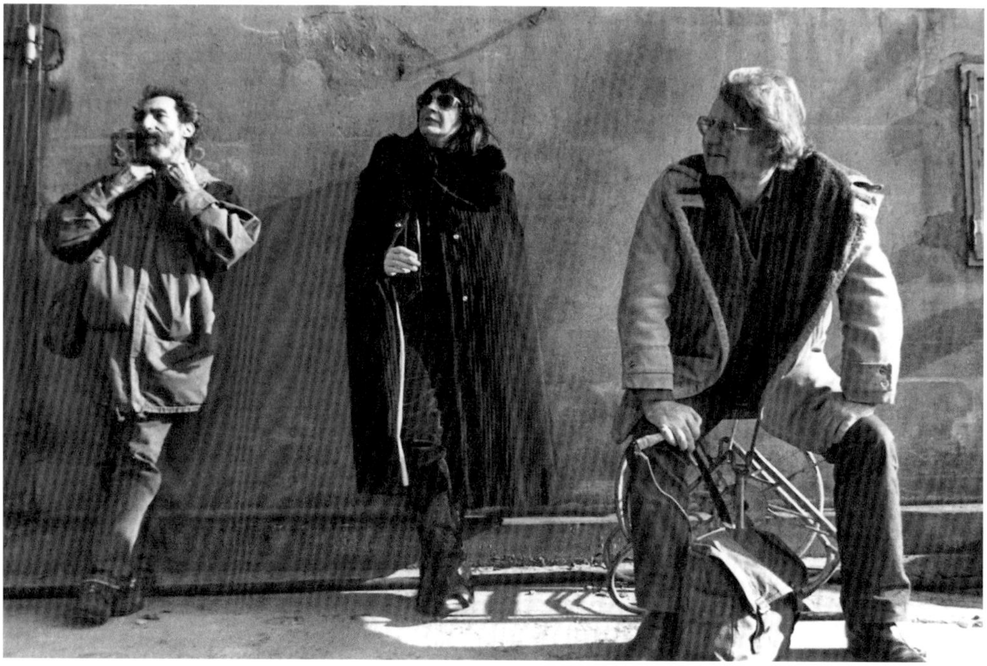

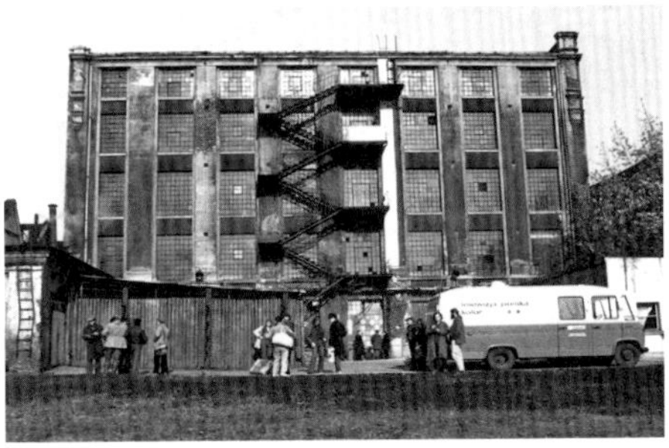

Ausstellungsgelände | exhibition site

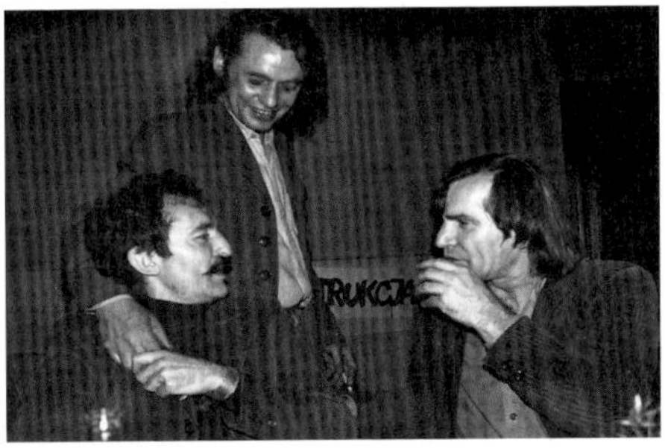

Von links nach rechts | from left to right:
Paul Sharits, Ryszard Waśko, Józef Robakowski

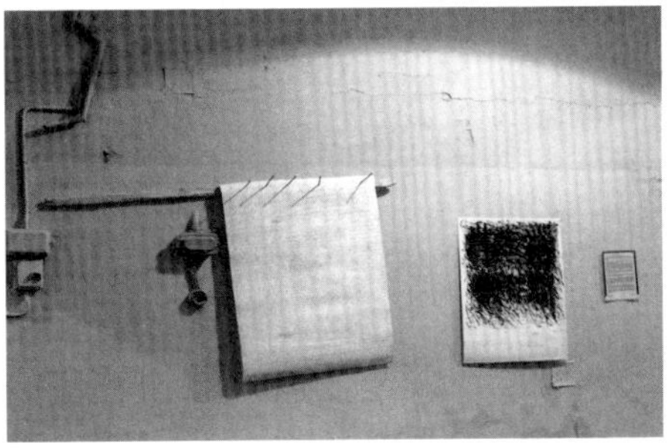

Günther Uecker, links: *Ohne Titel*, rechts: *Reisen in den Tod* | left: *Untitled*, right: *Journeys towards Death*

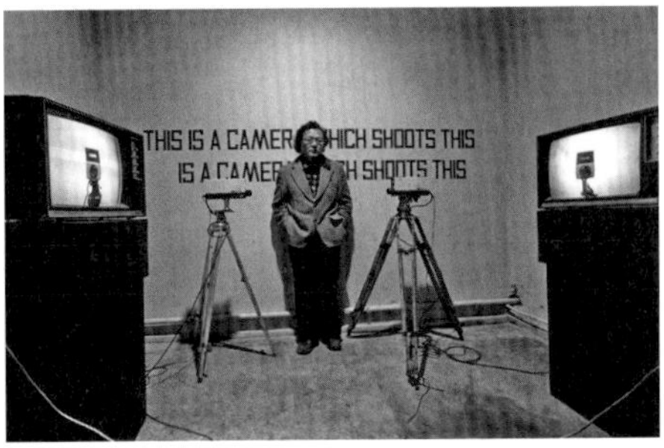

Takahiko Iimura

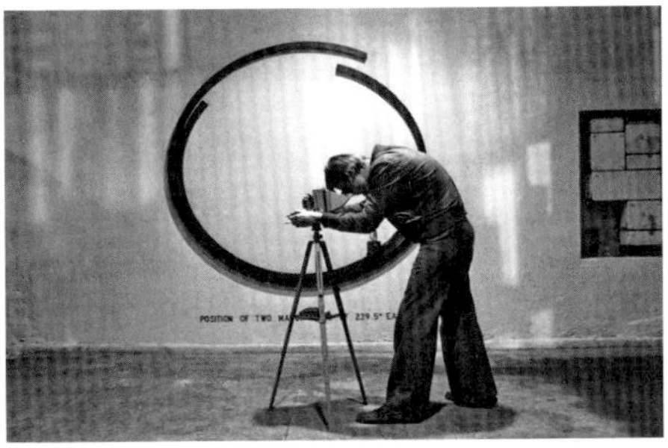

Bernar Venet, *Position of two major arcs of 239,5°*

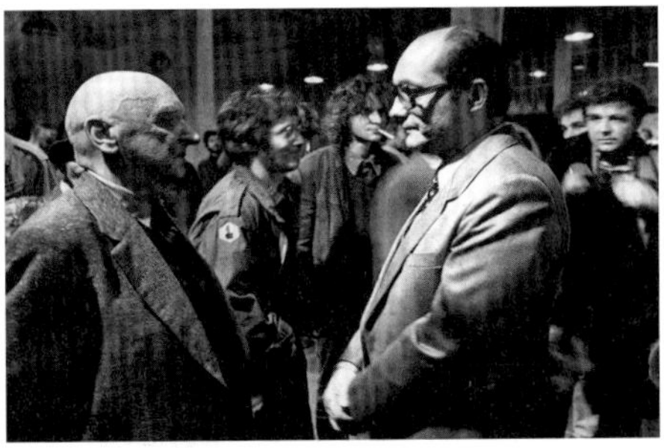

Henryk Stażewski (links | left) während der Eröffnung | during the opening

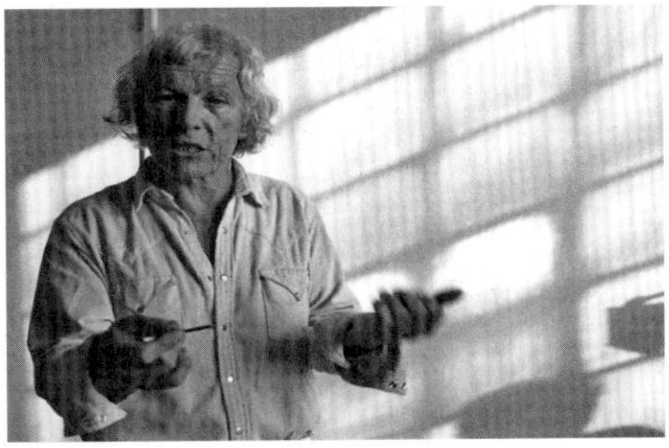

Roman Opałka

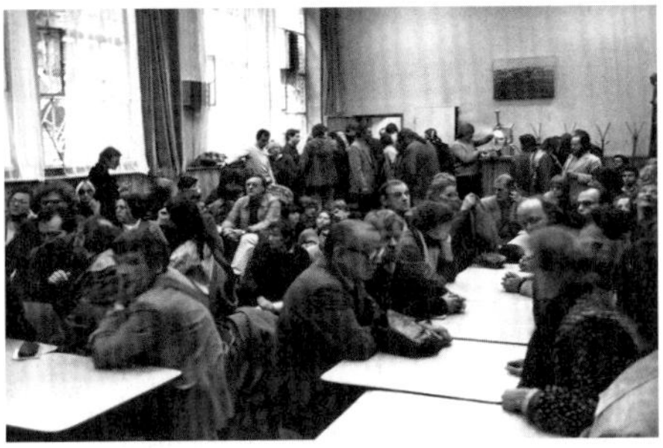

Aufführung von Filmen von Józef Robakowski in der Kantine der Baumwollspinnerei J. Marchlewski in Łódź 1981 | screening of Józef Robakowski's films in the canteen of the J. Marchlewski Cotton Mill in Łódź 1981

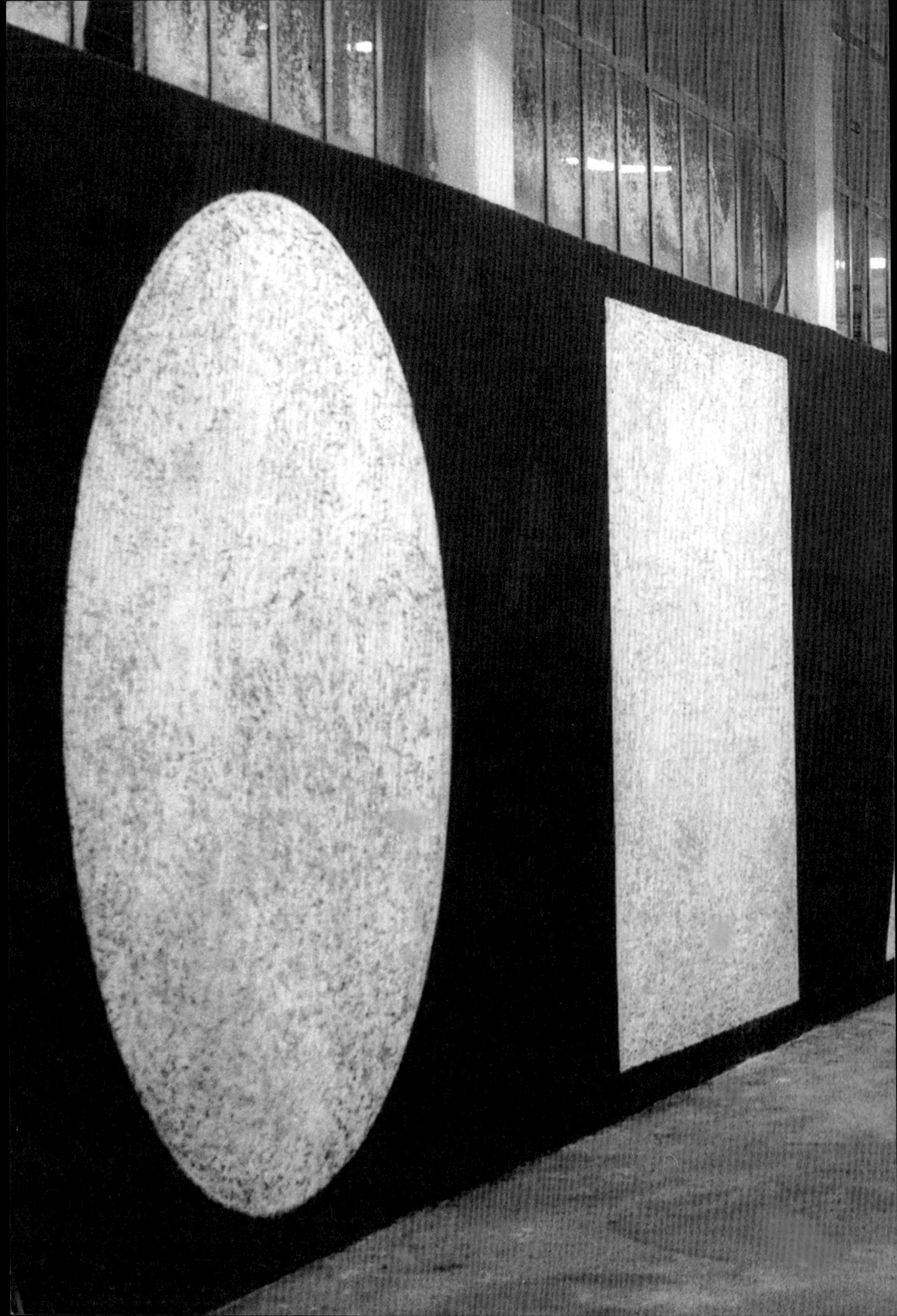

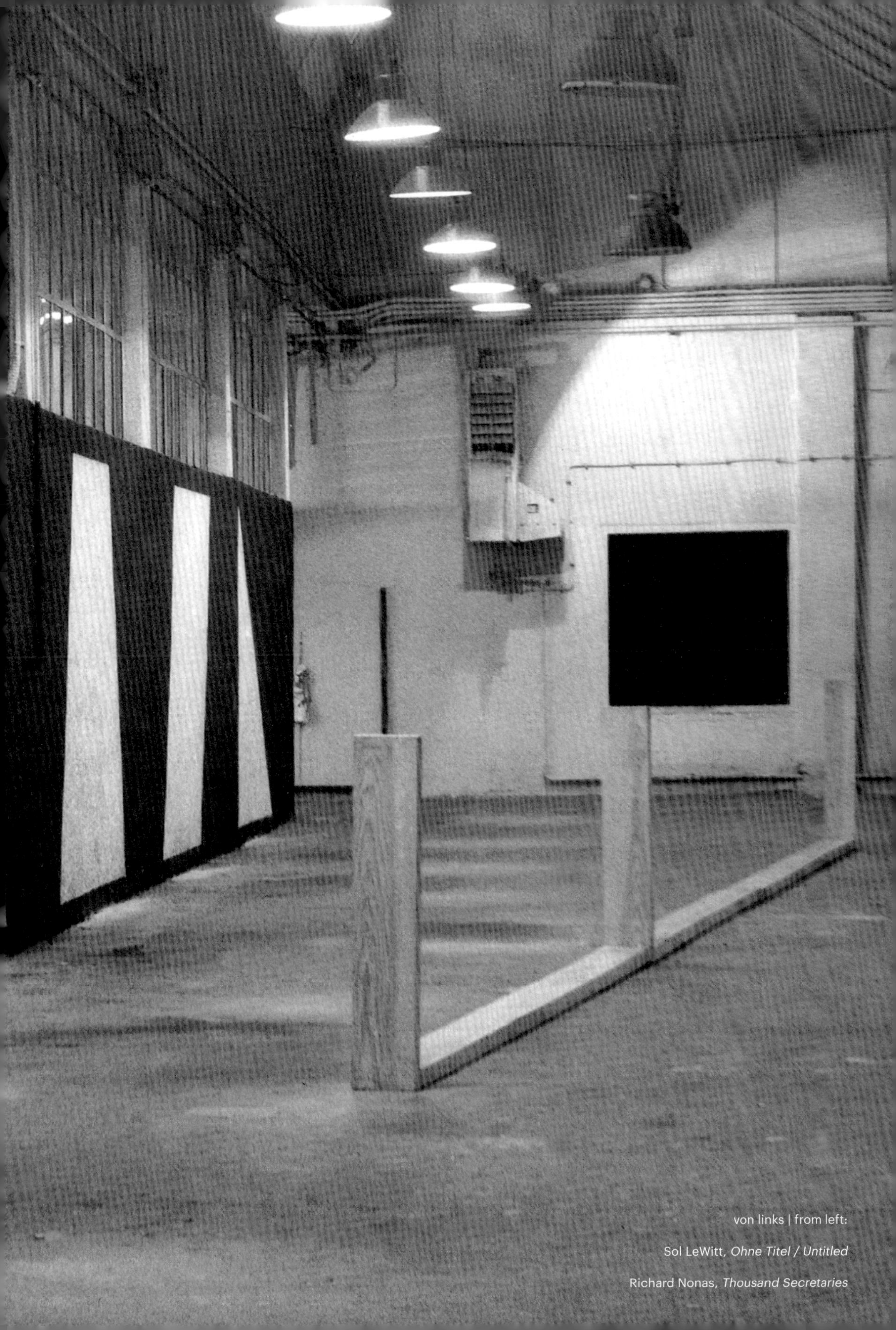

von links | from left:

Sol LeWitt, *Ohne Titel / Untitled*

Richard Nonas, *Thousand Secretaries*

INTERNATIONALE NETZWERKE 3
INTERNATIONAL NETWORKS 3

ARCHIV DER AVANTGARDEN

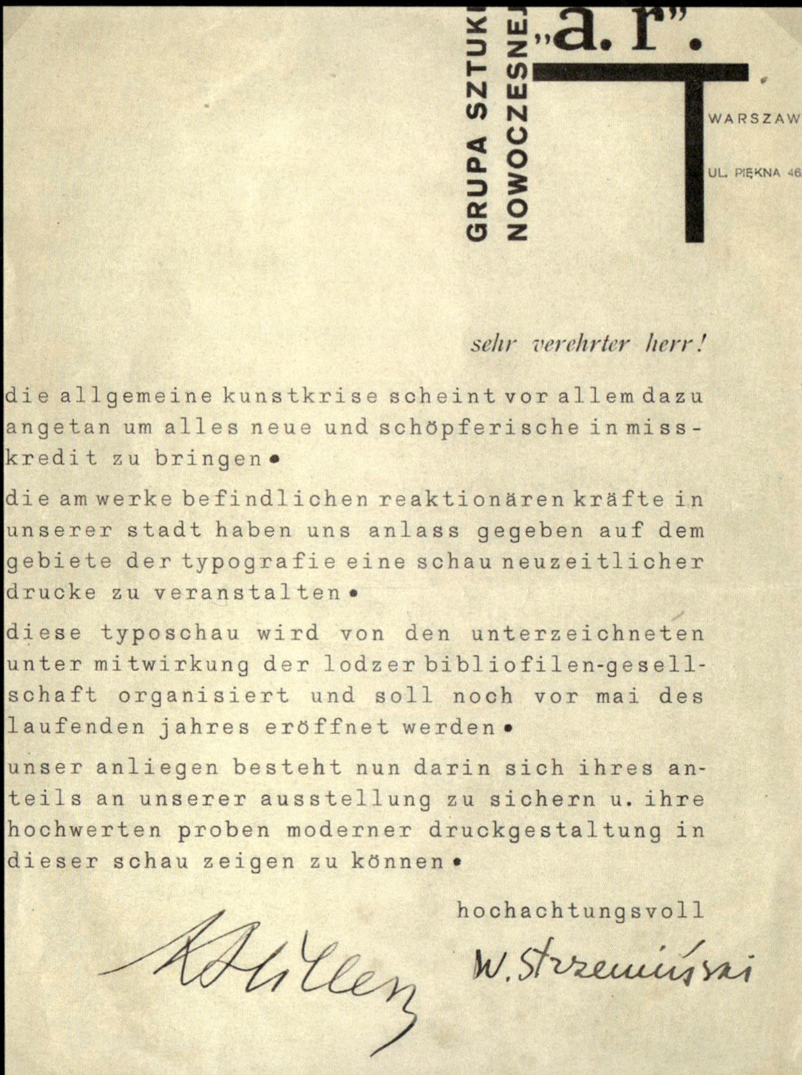

GRUPA SZTUKI NOWOCZESNEJ „a. r".
WARSZAW
UL. PIĘKNA 46

sehr verehrter herr!

die allgemeine kunstkrise scheint vor allem dazu angetan um alles neue und schöpferische in miss-kredit zu bringen•

die am werke befindlichen reaktionären kräfte in unserer stadt haben uns anlass gegeben auf dem gebiete der typografie eine schau neuzeitlicher drucke zu veranstalten•

diese typoschau wird von den unterzeichneten unter mitwirkung der lodzer bibliofilen-gesell-schaft organisiert und soll noch vor mai des laufenden jahres eröffnet werden•

unser anliegen besteht nun darin sich ihres an-teils an unserer ausstellung zu sichern u. ihre hochwerten proben moderner druckgestaltung in dieser schau zeigen zu können•

hochachtungsvoll

K. Hiller W. Strzemiński

Brief von | letter by Władysław Strzemiński und | and Karol Hiller an | to Jan Tschichold, 1932 Staatliche Kunstsammlungen Dresden, Archiv der Avantgarden – Egidio Marzona

Mehr Mut

More Courage

If we want to properly understand the Polish neo avant-garde movement in its full complexity as it developed in the 1960s through the 1970s and 1980s, we have to subject ourselves to "an exercise in time." It is necessary to return to a more distant past, where a museum came out of a collection, and the museum itself became an agent of a radical transformation. The Muzeum Sztuki in Łódź was officially established in 1930, but its story began earlier. As one of the first institutions dedicated to contemporary art, the museum has in its origins in international artistic cooperation, from which sprang the desire to develop art as a tool for social change, with the artists in the forefront of such processes.

The a. r. Group (for "artyści rewolucyjni"—revolutionary artists, and "awangarda rzeczywista"—the true avantgarde), led by Władysław Strzemiński, Katarzyna Kobro, and Henryk Stażewski, not only put together the collection that gave the museum its identity, it also gave an institutional mission its particular spirit. Then came the Second World War, followed by heavy challenges for any kind of utopia. In 1966, the art historian and curator Ryszard Stanisławski became the director of the Muzeum Sztuki in Łódź and he decided to implement Strzemiński's original idea: the museum should be a critical instrument, an agora open to everyone, a supranational structure, as he had experienced in Latin America and elsewhere. In doing so, Stanisławski created a place where the historical Polish avant-garde and Conceptualism could meet, with no respect for a fixed chronology.

This is the story that the Archiv der Avantgarden would like to tell: a tale of more courage in the museum, narrated by art, artists, and exhibitions in Poland.

M. R.

Die polnische Neo-Avantgarde, die sich von den 1960er- bis in die 1980er-Jahre entwickelte, erfordert – wenn man sie in ihrer außerordentlichen Komplexität richtig verstehen will – eine „Übung in Zeit". Wir müssen zurück zu dem Punkt in der Vergangenheit, als aus einer Sammlung ein Museum wurde und das Museum zum Ort einer radikalen Transformation. Das Muzeum Sztuki in Łódź wurde 1931 eröffnet, seine Geschichte aber begann früher: Als eine der ersten Institutionen für zeitgenössische Kunst hat das Museum seine Ursprünge in der länderübergreifenden künstlerischen Zusammenarbeit, die dem Wunsch entsprang, die Kunst zum Werkzeug für den sozialen Wandel zu entwickeln, mit den Künstler*innen an vorderster Front dieses Prozesses.

Die Gruppe a. r. (für „artyści rewolucyjni" – revolutionäre Künstler, und „awangarda rzeczywista" – wirkliche Avantgarde), angeführt von Władysław Strzemiński, Katarzyna Kobro und Henryk Stażewski, trug die Sammlung zusammen, die dem Museum seine Identität verlieh, tat aber noch weit mehr: Sie verlieh dem institutionellen Auftrag seinen besonderen Geist. Dann kam der Zweite Weltkrieg, danach die schweren Herausforderungen für jegliche Utopie. 1966 wurde der Kunsthistoriker und Kurator Ryszard Stanisławski Direktor des Muzeum Sztuki in Łódź und beschloss, Strzemińskis ursprüngliche Idee umzusetzen: Das Museum sollte ein kritisches Instrument sein, eine für alle Menschen offene Agora, eine supranationale Struktur, wie Stanisławski sie in Lateinamerika und darüber hinaus erfahren hatte. Dadurch schuf Stanisławski den Ort, wo sich die historische Avantgarde und die Konzeptkunst ohne Rücksicht auf die zeitliche Ordnung begegnen konnten.

Das ist die Geschichte, die das Archiv der Avantgarden erzählen möchte: Eine Geschichte von mehr Mut im Museum, erzählt von der Kunst, den Künstler*innen und den Ausstellungen in Polen.

M. R.

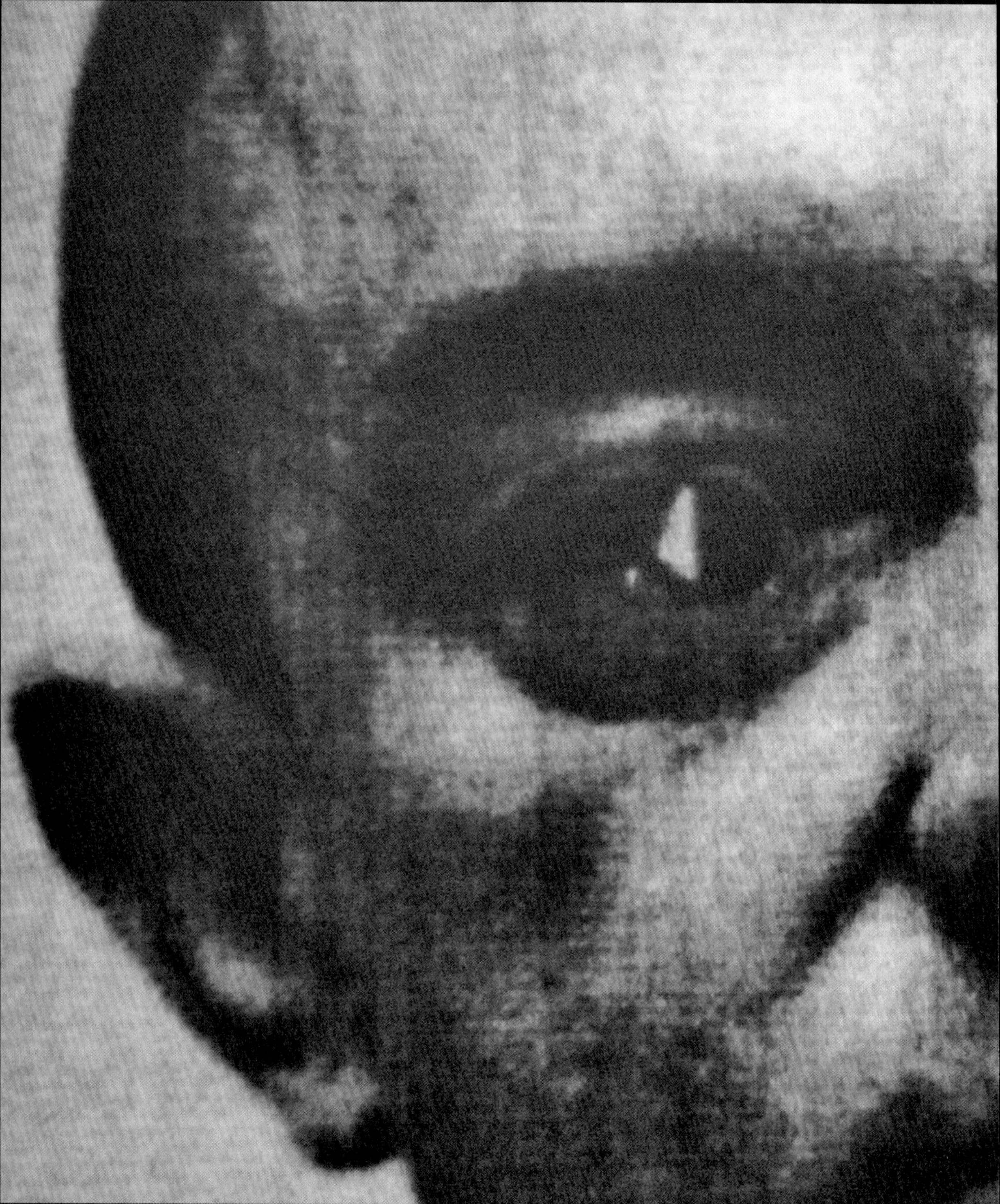

Agnieszka Polska, *Sensitization to Colour*, 2009, Film HD, 5:02 min.
Courtesy ŻAK | BRANICKA, Berlin

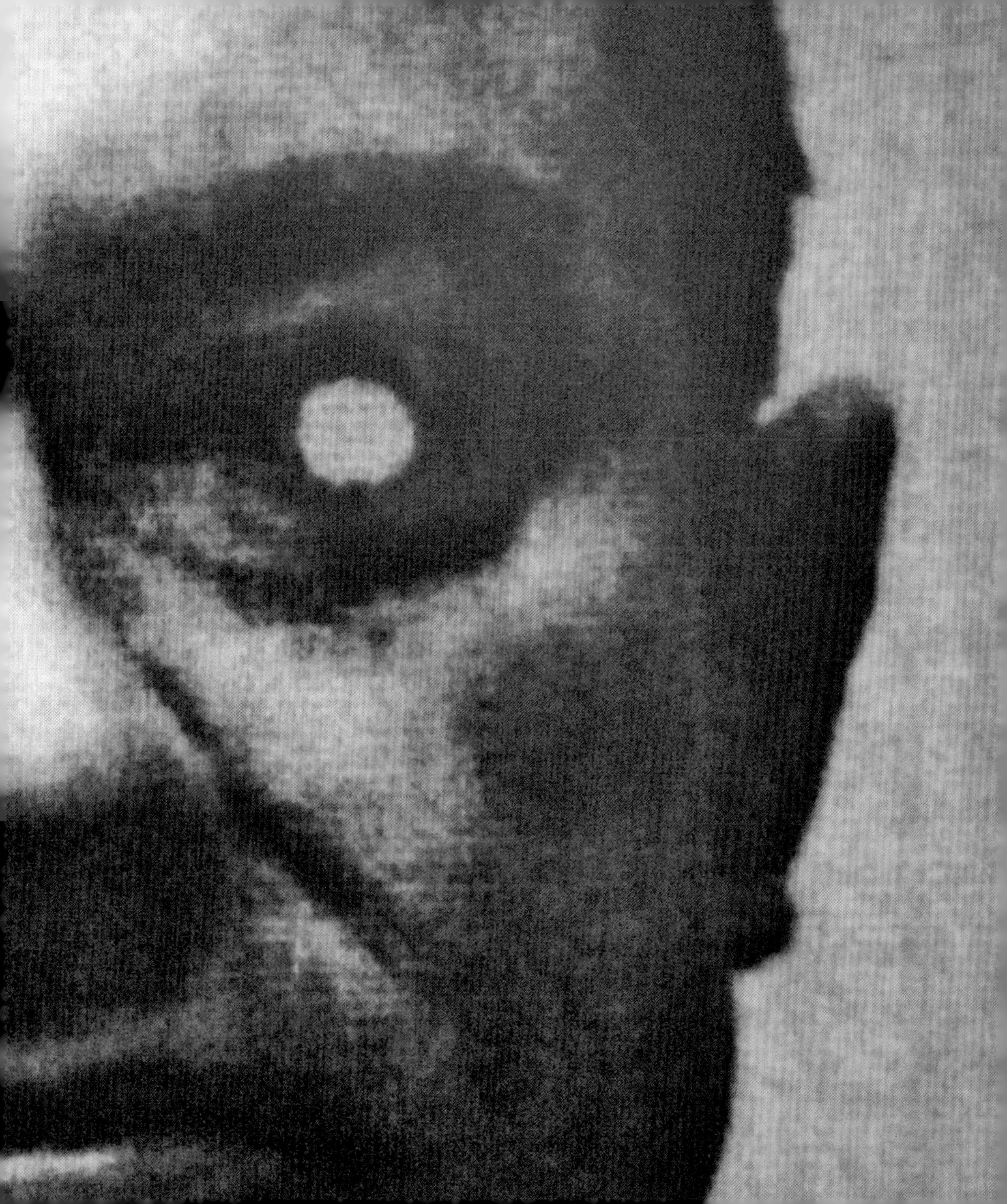

Ausstellung | Exhibition

Exercises in Freedom.
Polnische Konzeptkunst 1968–1981
Staatliche Kunstsammlungen Dresden,
Kupferstich-Kabinett
in Kooperation mit dem Archiv der Avantgarden
29. Juni bis 23. September 2018

Exercises in Freedom.
Polish Conceptualism 1968–1981
Staatliche Kunstsammlungen Dresden,
Kupferstich-Kabinett
in cooperation with the Archiv der Avantgarden
June 29 – September 23, 2018

Generaldirektorin | Director General
Staatliche Kunstsammlungen Dresden
Marion Ackermann

Kaufmännischer Direktor | Director of Finance
Dirk Burghardt

Direktorin des Kupferstich-Kabinetts |
Director of the Kupferstich-Kabinett
Stephanie Buck

Leiter des Archivs der Avantgarden |
Heads of Archiv der Avantgarden
Marcelo Rezende, Rudolf Fischer

Kurator | Curator
Björn Egging

Kuratorische Assistenz | Assistant Curator
Katrin Kruppa

Projektassistenz | Project Assistant
Antonella B. Meloni

Archivarin des Archivs der Avantgarden |
Archivist of Archiv der Avantgarden
Lisa-Marie Schrewe

Ausstellungsarchitektur und -gestaltung |
Exhibition and Graphic Design
Karen Weinert, Dresden
desarteur, Halle

Restauratorische Betreuung | Conservation
Wiebke Schneider, Olaf Simon, Johanna Ziegler, Ines Beyer

Fotobearbeitung | Photo Editing
Angela Rietschel, Andreas Diesend

Ausstellungseinrichtung | On-site Technicians
Matthias Herbst, Juan Miguel Restrepo Valdes

Sekretariat | Office
Kristina Schüffny

Ausstellungsmanagement | Exhibition Management
Barbara Rühl, Lisa Seltmann, Antonella B. Meloni, Thomas Lantzsch

Marketing
Martina Miesler, Andrea Vogt, Anne Böttger, Wenke Ladewig

Presse und Kommunikation | Press and Communication
Stephan Adam, Valerie Eckl, Carolin Bär

Bildung und Vermittlung | Education
Claudia Schmidt, Marion Martin, Liliane Scheunemann

Rechnungswesen und Controlling | Accounting and Controlling
Elke Schmieder, Andrea Feistl

Personalverwaltung | Human Resources
Ingolf Epp

Interaktive Medien | Interactive Media
Martin Zavesky

Technischer Dienst | Technical Service
Michael John, Peter Handrick, Gunter Knehler, Kai-Uwe Metzler

Praktikant*innen | Trainees
Elisa Elß, Martha Greszta, Sara Magdzicka

Katalog | Catalogue

Konzept | Concept
Björn Egging

Redaktion | Editing
Katrin Kruppa

Grafische Gestaltung | Graphic Design
Polina Bazir, Kerber Verlag, Bielefeld

Projektmanagement | Project Management
Verena Simon, Kerber Verlag, Bielefeld

Korrektorat Deutsch | Copy Editing German
Susann Harring

Korrektorat Englisch | Copy Editing English
Sarah Quigley

Übersetzung Deutsch–Englisch | Translation German–English
Jessica Buskirk, Jennifer Heber-Brown

Übersetzung Englisch–Deutsch | Translation English–German
Leo Unglaub

Übersetzung Polnisch–Deutsch | Translation Polish–German
Marcin Zastrożny

Kapiteltexte | Chapter Texts
Björn Egging (B. E.), Katrin Kruppa (K. K.),
Marcelo Rezende (M. R.)

Umschlag | Cover
Jarosław Kozłowski, *Exercises in Freedom* (Ausschnitt | detail), 1979
Sammlung | Collection Block, Berlin

Studentenprotest in Warschau, 1968
Foto | photo: Tadeusz Zagodzinksi

Members of the Solidarność, 1981
Foto | Photo: Gabriel Duval

Leihgeber | Lending Institutions and Collectors
Sammlung | Collection Block, Berlin
Galerie M+R Fricke, Berlin
Privatsammlung | Private collection, Berlin
Courtesy ŻAK | BRANICKA, Berlin
Sammlung | Collection Kozłowski, Poznań
Muzeum Sztuki w Łodzi
Profile Foundation, Warschau
Leihgeber, die nicht genannt werden möchten |
lenders who wish to remain anonymous

Impressum | Colophon

Exercises in Freedom.
Polnische Konzeptkunst 1968–1981
Staatliche Kunstsammlungen Dresden,
Kupferstich-Kabinett
in Kooperation mit dem Archiv der Avantgarden
29. Juni bis 23. September 2018

Exercises in Freedom.
Polish Conceptualism 1968–1981
Staatliche Kunstsammlungen Dresden,
Kupferstich-Kabinett
in cooperation with the Archiv der Avantgarden
June 29 – September 23, 2018

Herausgeber | Edited by
Staatliche Kunstsammlungen Dresden,
Kupferstich-Kabinett, Björn Egging

Staatliche Kunstsammlungen Dresden
Residenzschloss
Taschenberg 2
01067 Dresden
Telefon: +49(0)351 / 49 14 2000
besucherservice@skd.museum
www.skd.museum

Gesamtherstellung und Vertrieb | Printed and published by
Kerber Verlag, Bielefeld
Windelsbleicher Str. 166–170
33659 Bielefeld
Germany
Tel. +49(0)521 / 950 08–10
Fax +49(0)521 / 950 08–88
info@kerberverlag.com

Kerber, US Distribution
ARTBOOK | D. A. P.
75 Broad Street, Suite 630
New York, NY 10004
Tel. +1(212)627–1999
Fax +1(212)627–9484

Die Deutsche Nationalbibliothek verzeichnet diese Publikation in der Deutschen Nationalbibliografie; detaillierte bibliografische Daten sind im Internet über http://dnb.dnb.de abrufbar.

The Deutsche Nationalbibliothek lists this publication in the Deutsche Nationalbibliografie; detailed bibliographic data are available on the Internet at http://dnb.dnb.de.

Kerber-Publikationen werden weltweit in führenden Buchhandlungen und Museumsshops angeboten (Vertrieb in Europa, Asien, Nord- und Südamerika).

Kerber publications are available in selected bookstores and museum shops worldwide (distributed in Europe, Asia, South and North America).

Fotonachweis | Photo Credits
Archives of Contemporary Thought: S. 114–121 / Gabriel Duval: Umschlag (innen vorne) | cover (inside front) / Muzeum Sztuki w Łodzi: S. 29–30, 33–35, 38, 40, 46–47, 50, 62, 87 / Muzeum Współczesne, Wrocław: S. 49 / Natalia LL and lokal_30 gallery, Warschau: S. 71 / Andrzej Polakowski: S. 72 / Profile Foundation, Warschau: S. 84–86, 92–93 / Sammlung | Collection Kozlowski, Poznań: S. 31–33, 108, 110–113 / Staatliche Kunstsammlungen Dresden, Andreas Diesend: S. 16, 22–28, 58, 60–61, 63–67, 76–79, 83, 88–89, 94–96, 100, 102–107, 122 / Staatliche Kunstsammlung Dresden, Schenkung Sammlung Hoffmann: S. 68–69 / Courtesy ŻAK | BRANICKA, Berlin: S. 97 / Tadeusz Zagodzinksi: Umschlag (innen hinten) | cover (inside back)

ISBN 978-3-7356-0494-1
www.kerberverlag.com

Printed in Germany

Powered by

Freistaat SACHSEN

IN DER SAMMLUNGSTRADITION DES HAUSES WETTIN A.L.